PLANNING FOR POPULATION CHANGE

Planning for Population Change

Edited by
W.T.S. Gould and
R. Lawton

CROOM HELM
London & Sydney

© 1986 W.T.S. Gould and R. Lawton
Croom Helm Ltd, Provident House, Burrell Row,
Beckenham, Kent BR3 1AT

Croom Helm Australia Pty Ltd, Suite 4, 6th Floor,
64-76 Kippax Street, Surry Hills, NSW 2010, Australia

British Library Cataloguing in Publication Data

Planning for population change.
   1. Population – Economic aspects
   I. Gould, W.T.S.   II. Lawton, Richard
   304.6'2   HB871

   ISBN 0-7099-1679-5

Printed and bound in Great Britain by
Biddles Ltd, Guildford and King's Lynn

CONTENTS

FIGURES

TABLES

CONTRIBUTORS

Eric Briault is Visiting Professor in the University of Sussex. He was formerly Chief Education Officer, Inner London Education Authority.

Bill Gould is Senior Lecturer in Geography, University of Liverpool. As a Consultant to the World Bank, UNESCO and to Governments directly, he has been actively involved in planning in several countries in Africa, Asia and the Pacific.

Paul Knox was Senior Lecturer in Geography, University of Dundee, when his contribution was written, and is currently Professor in the Urban Affairs Program, Virginia Polytechnic Institute, U.S.A. He has written extensively on social planning issues in Britain and Europe.

Richard Lawton is Emeritus Professor of Geography and Director of the Institute for European Population Studies in the University of Liverpool. He has researched and written on historical and contemporary population problems in Britain.

Maggie Pearson is Lecturer in Medical Sociology in the Department of General Practice in the Faculty of Medicine, University of Liverpool. When her contribution was written she was Director of the Centre for Ethnic Minority Health Studies, Bradford.

John Salt is Lecturer in Geography, University College, London University. His research interests focus on labour markets in Britain and Western Europe, and in particular in internal and international labour migration.

John Whitelegg is Lecturer in Geography, University of Lancaster. He has been actively involved in research and community action over a wide range of planning issues in North-West England.

ACKNOWLEDGMENTS

In a collaborative venture such as this the Editors and individual authors are indebted to colleagues too numerous to mention individually, in several Universities. In Liverpool most of the words were processed by Joan Bell; the maps were drawn by Sandra Mather and Paul Smith in the Drawing Office of the Department of Geography; and Ian Qualtrough and Suzanne Yee of the Photographic Service of the Faculties of Arts and Social and Environmental Sciences provided much of the finished material for camera-ready copy. We are grateful to all of them for coping with our expectations of miracles by yesterday!

W.T.S. Gould
Richard Lawton
August, 1985.

INTRODUCTION

The Editors

The causes and consequences of population growth and its relationship to available resources have been a matter for continuous debate since the onset of modern mortality control in the eighteenth century. The debate has been pursued with renewed intensity over the past thirty years, particularly in the context of a feared depletion of resources in the face of accelerating population growth which, in the view of many pessimists, threatens the very future of mankind. At successive world population conferences, from Rome in 1954 but particularly in Bucharest in 1974 and Mexico City in 1984, governments have debated these problems and sought to identify objectives and propose policies for the better management of population and resources in the interests both of existing populations and for future generations.

Reacting to a growing concern for and understanding of demographic questions, international opinion over the past decade has begun to seek a more balanced approach to population policy. The 1960's and 1970's were dominated by the neo-Malthusian fear of the consequences of sheer growth in numbers, especially in the countries of the Third World, which largely accounted for the doubling of the world's population in forty years to over 4,700 million in 1984, and in consumption, particularly in more developed countries. However, in the 1980's it is now being more strongly argued that the productive capacity of people as creators of wealth has been underestimated (Simon, 1981); indeed that population pressure may, in certain cases, promote economic growth and social change (Boserup, 1981).

It is clear that the factors underlying population behaviour are complex and require detailed investigation at various scales and from different perspectives if underlying causes and interrelationships are to be adequately explored and understood. Alternative explanations of population trends such as those succinctly, if rather flippantly, reported in the following news item can usually be found:

"The fact that Poland's population for the first time exceeds 37 million has brought widely differing explanations. The Government says it confirms the

1

country's stability and popular confidence in official policies. The Church sees it as a sign of success in its crusade against free abortion. Sociologists explain it as the result of a retreat into family life after the stormy years of Solidarity. But people in the street are saying it's the result of shoddy production in the contraceptives industry" (The Observer, 7th October, 1984).

Different kinds of explanations clearly offer different expectations of the course of further change, and will normally elicit different policy reactions. Successful and appropriate planning for change must therefore depend on careful diagnosis of the causes of change which will rely on systematic studies by population analysts. Advances in the frequency, consistency and accuracy of censuses and other population data and in the techniques of their analysis are yielding more precise information on the dynamics, structure and impact of population trends. These, together with improved mathematical techniques of modelling population behaviour, have greatly assisted better methods of population forecasting and helped the identification of key relationships between the complex factors - biological, cultural, social and economic -which influence population trends. Yet these models alone cannot offer a holistic view which encompasses the range of experience and motivations between and within peoples and from individual to individual which are necessary for the understanding of population behaviour and therefore for the development of realistic population policy. The search for explanation must incorporate the behavioural as well as the economic and environmental approaches to population analysis.

Success or failure in responding to population change, however well understood at any point of time or at any one scale of analysis, depends not only upon being able to tap immediately available resources, but also on the ability of society to allocate these wisely. To do so requires well-founded policies which take account of both general trends in population and their effects on its structure and distribution at all levels (Berelson, 1971). There must be a willingness and flexibility which can provide for shifting demand and can take account of differential growth and changing mobility patterns at regional and local level. Hence, population is a key factor in all forms of planning - economic, social, physical and environmental - and at all scales: internationally, for example, in relation to the regulation of trade or the provision of aid; nationally, in developing and allocating public or private investment and consumption between different areas and sectors of public provision; regionally and locally, according to the structure and needs of people between and within town and country.

There are thus two major dimensions to planning for population change. On the one hand it involves the attempt to identify the causes and shape the course of population behaviour in desired directions: to control fertility as a means of reducing over-large increments or to promote growth in declining and ageing populations; to encourage in-movement to areas of labour shortage but discourage it where resources are already stretched; to extend economic along with social services as a means of promoting both better material and physical well-being and an increasing awareness of the role of individual and family in population questions. On the other hand, population planners must identify the consequences of demographic, economic and social trends for existing populations and their descendants: to seek to provide for the needs of mothers-to-be and then for their babies; for their children's education from school to university; in promoting jobs to harness the physical and mental capacities of people through productive work; and in support for the incapable and elderly. This requires approaches which are both wide-ranging - extending from improved population data and techniques of population analysis to appropriate planning and administrative structures - and which can implement policy at the point of need, right down to the individual.

It is with the second of these major aspects of population planning that this book is principally concerned. It developed out of a symposium focused on 'Planning for People', the theme of Professor Lawton's Presidential Address to Section E (Geography) at the British Association's Annual Conference in 1983 (see Chapter 1). The themes around which the following chapters are grouped underline the fact that recent population trends in both the developed and developing world have had different effects on population structure which are reflected in changing patterns of need. This was borne out in many of the discussion documents put before the 1984 International Conference on Population and the Consensus Declaration which emerged from it (see below). Both editors have long-standing research interests in population studies, Professor Lawton through his work on population trends and structures in nineteenth- and twentieth-century Britain (for example, Lawton, 1982), and Mr. Gould through interests in African population problems in general and in particular as a consultant to the World Bank and UNESCO (Gould, 1978) in educational planning in several developing countries. All the contributors are geographers who have worked in a wide range of countries on population and related socio-economic problems at international, national or regional level. They are primarily analysts rather than planners, although several have actively participated in public policy making, while their essays all proceed on the premise that appropriate and successful planning must be rooted in thorough analysis of the causes and consequences of population change.

The book neither attempts to provide a compendium of demographic forecasting techniques nor to evaluate policy formulation procedures. It is concerned, rather, with the consequences of population change for present and future social and economic policy towards such questions as employment, educational provision and health care, as well as the spatial and temporal variations in demand which arise from both demographic and geographical differences between and within different cultural and socio-economic groups, whether at the global scale - such as between core and peripheral areas of Europe - or in different localities such as town and country or within different districts of cities.

The themes explored in the following chapters reflect the major switch in emphasis between the debates on 'the population problem' in the 1960's and 1970's as compared with those of the 1980's. The publication in 1972 of the Club of Rome's report 'The limits to growth', marked, in Huw Jones's phrase, 'the high water mark of modern Malthusianism' (Jones, 1981, p 170), but more generally the decade leading up to the World Population Year and the Bucharest Conference of 1974 was dominated by the fear of population crisis induced by the pressure of over-rapid growth on limited resources. The policy statements and draft Plan of Action prepared for Bucharest were dominated by the neo-Malthusian concern to reduce birth rates in the developing world, though these were generally set in the context of their importance in development planning (Johnson, 1973), while Philip Hauser (1963) saw 'the population dilemma' as essentially focused on "the basic question before the developing world [of] family size". In 1972, 53 per cent of the budget of the United Nations Fund for Population Activity (UNFPA) went to birth control programmes as opposed to only 2.8 per cent for other aspects of population policy. Meanwhile the International Planned Parenthood Federation (IPPF) budget had grown from $30.000 in 1961 to $20 million by 1971.

The 1974 Population Conference was predictably dominated by a fierce debate between the incrementalist western view that population growth was an impediment to development which must be curbed by birth control and the view of most Third World countries that redistribution of the world's economic resources was an essential pre-requisite to population control (Finkle and Crane, 1975). The extensively redrafted World Population Plan of Action (WPPA) bowed to the view that underdevelopment was a cause not a consequence of population growth and its recommendations focused upon economic as well as population factors and stressed the importance of social factors, in particular the status of women, in family planning. Moreover, it took a wider view of problems of population growth than that in the draft plan, stressing problems of mobility in redistribution and urbanization, the need to link family planning to health and educational programmes, and emphasizing that there needs to be a broader training for population planners (Berelson, 1975).

The redrafted Plan of Action carried three main messages: that population problems are only one part of a complex of factors associated with development; secondly, that population policies cannot be solely focused on demographic objectives; thirdly, that effective family planning must persuade individuals through education in the advantages and means of control (Tabah, 1984). Those messages were also implicit in the emphasis of the recommendations of the Brandt Report (1980) which, while admitting the association between poverty and over-rapid population growth, stressed the economic and social dimensions of the problems of the South.

By the time of the 1984 International Conference on Population there was a more general acceptance of the belief that population policy could only succeed as part of a package of policies for economic and social change. Moreover, it was clear that the WPPA needed progressively to tackle problems related to changing population structures, such as employment and ageing; to mobility

4

and distribution, such as urbanization, labour problems and regional development; to social and cultural attitudes, such as the status of women (Harrison and Rowley, 1984). Furthermore, the emphasis was shifting from massive national and international programmes, dominated by fertility control to more integrated schemes for community development. On the other hand the hostility towards family planning policies on the part of many African, Asian and Latin American countries had largely disappeared (Table 1.1, below) and the package of 88 recommendations agreed by consensus in Mexico City embraced the need to avoid unwanted births and related these to family health and educational programmes especially aimed at improving the lot of women and young people (Rowley, 1984).

Perhaps the attitudes of developed countries had become more understanding as a result of concern over their own population problems which followed in the wake of fluctuations in economic prosperity and changing social attitudes. Many European countries were faced with the threat of population decline as birth rates plunged below replacement level. The inability to absorb growing working-age populations into productive employment and acute problems of poverty and unrest among migrant workers and minority groups, together with increasing numbers of elderly people, reflected stagnation in their economies. The difficulty of providing for the needs of large cohorts from the post-war and early 1960's birth bulges as they move into retirement and the work force respectively, has provided troublesome problems in the allocation of scarcer resources. These difficulties are a far cry from the fears evident in the 1960's of excessive pressure from growing high-consumption populations, but they equally call for imaginative and integrated economic, social and population policies.

The demands placed upon their populations by such changes in numbers and structure call for adaptability in meeting the changing needs of nations and communities. In addition, regional inequalities and changes in the geographical pattern of demand require constant readjustment in the type and provision of basic services (see Chapters 4 and 5). 90 per cent of the estimated increase of 3,400 million people in the world over the next 40 years will be in the Third World (World Bank, 1984). Although rates of natural increase are falling (see Chapter 1), the numbers of those in the 20-40 age-group are set to increase by 620 million by the year 2000. With 600 million of these in developing countries, even if the recent fall in numbers underemployed is maintained, the actual numbers without full work will rise (see Chapter 3). Similarly, the increase of children of school age in Third World countries who are not receiving primary education has grown by 5 million (to 115 million) despite an increase in those attending school from 61 per cent of the age group in 1960 to 85 per cent in 1980 (see Chapter 9).

Where rapid changes in population trends have been effected such problems are particularly great. In China in the 1960's largely uncontrolled birth rates, combined with rapidly increasing life expectancy, produced annual rates of increase of between 2.6 and 3.4 per cent per annum (Jowett, 1984). But the Marriage Laws and two- and one-child family campaigns of the past decade have reduced the

5

total fertility ratio from a peak 7.5 in 1963 to 2.7 in 1982 (Banister, 1984). Yet the pressures of past population growth will reach out into the future. The very large birth cohorts, which reached a maximum of 29 million in 1963, have already moved through the schools into the workforce. There will be more women of child-bearing age over the next twenty years, reaching a maximum of 136 million in 1990, so that even with stringent policies of birth control the population of China, already over 1,000 million, could reach 1,300 million by the end of the century (Aird, 1982).

In contrast the brief and modest surge in birth rates in most western countries in the 1960's (see Chapter 1) has raised problems in making short-term provision of educational facilities which now exceed demand in many areas (see Chapter 8). These larger cohorts have recently been launched onto a stagnant labour market adding to levels of unemployment which absorb a growing proportion of public funds to the detriment of needed investment in housing, health care and provision for the increasing numbers of elderly people. The switch of emphasis in providing for changing demands has been difficult to accommodate (see Chapter 4).

Contrasts in adjustment to population change are examined in three contexts in the following chapters. Firstly, they are pursued in a series of themes related to the potential of people as producers (Chapters 2 and 3) and as consumers of a wide range of social services (Chapters 4 and 5) including two specific areas of provision, health (Chapters 6 and 7) and education (Chapters 8 and 9). Secondly, the differing needs arising from widely contrasting population trends in the Third World and the developed countries are systematically explored in relation to each of these themes. Thirdly, the authors have shown the varying impacts of general questions in a range of different contexts and at a variety of scales from international to local, underlining the importance of population to planning at all levels.

Since development and population control are interdependent, the productive potential of people must be recognized. In many countries of the developed world larger cohorts of working age, swollen by immigrants brought in to remedy labour shortages in the 1950's and 1960's, are faced by a decline in employment opportunities due to recession, the decline of older industries and rapid technological change. Sharp regional contrasts reflect the varying ability of fortunate and less fortunate areas to cope with these and raise basic questions about the possibility of restructuring or relocating employment and the means of assisting mobility in the labour force (see Chapter 2). The problems of the Third World are much greater in volume and character. The massive increase in working-age population is common to all countries, but the problem is particularly acute in cities to which young migrants are flocking in increasing numbers. The percentage of urban dwellers is expected to have trebled in Africa between 1950 and the end of the century, and doubled in South and East Asia, while the level of urbanization in Latin America is rapidly approaching that in the developed world. The impacts are staggering. Bombay's population increased by 2.3 million (38 per cent) between 1971 and 1981, with a net gain of 1.4

million by migration, while Mexico City, already one of the world's largest cities, is expected to grow from 16.5 million to anything between 25-36 million in the early part of the next century. Such increases place almost impossible pressure on both the labour market (Chapter 3) and on housing and social services (Chapter 5).

Such large-scale changes in the number and distribution of population require both substantial increase in services but also flexibility in their location. It is also necessary to accommodate decline in some places, for example most inner city areas in western countries (see Chapter 4), and growth in others (whether suburbs or shanty towns). In addition to location, the ability to deliver services to where they are most needed also requires close attention. Health care is often over-concentrated in large centres and on more sophisticated hospital services. Yet there is often difficulty of access for such groups as young mothers or the elderly (see Chapter 6) or there are gaps in remoter areas where more widely dispersed, basic provision could bring benefits out of all proportion to their relatively low cost (see Chapter 7). The question of the right type of provision, in the right places, at the right time is of particular importance in education. Patterns of residential mobility, combined with marked changes in population structure arising from changes in birth rate have greatly changed the pattern of demand in many countries of Europe calling for rapid, but often imperfect, adjustment in the type and location of provision (see Chapter 8). In the Third World maximization of benefits from rapidly increasing investment in education requires clear identification of both the nature and location of educational facilities, especially in rural areas (see Chapter 9).

Matching of supply with demand is crucial if the potential of people as producers is to equal the demands placed upon them by people as consumers. This theme is central to planning for population change as it is considered in the following chapters. Moreover, it is a problem with several dimensions. It is a product of changes in population trends over time which set the levels of need over the lifetime of the respective population cohorts. Furthermore, the structure of populations at particular points of time will point to the pattern of allocation of resources, but these, in turn, change and require changes in spatial allocation of the services and activities of communities and nations alike. Each service has a somewhat different threshold of demand and different criteria of accessibility: for example, patterns of travel to work, to school, and to health facilities differ and in turn must be constantly adjusted to changing patterns of settlements, people and activities and facilities.

Planning for population change is essential to most forms of planning at a series of scales, both spatial and temporal. It is from this perspective on the implications of demographic change for present and future patterns and needs of population that this book has been written.

REFERENCES

Aird, J. (1982) 'Population studies and population policy in China', Population and Development Review, 8, 267-97

Banister, J. (1984) 'Analysis of recent data on the population of China', Population and Development Review, 10, 241-72

Berelson, B. (1971) 'Population policy: personal notes, Population Studies, 25, 73-82

Berelson, B. (1975) 'The World Population Plan of Action: where now?' Population and Development Review, 1, 115-46

Boserup, E. (1981) Population and technology, Basil Blackwell, Oxford

Brandt, W., et al. (1980) North-South : a programme for survival. Report of the Independent Commission on International Development Issues, Pan Books, London

Finkle, J.L., and B.B. Crane (1975) 'The politics of Bucharest', Population and Development Review, 1, 87-114

Gould. W T.S. (1978) Guidelines for school location planning, The World Bank, Staff Working Paper, no. 308, Washington, D.C.

Harrison, P , and J. Rowley (1984) Human numbers, human needs, IPPF, London

Hauser, P.M. (1963) The population dilemma, Prentice Hall, Englewood Cliffs, N.J.

Johnson, S. (1973) The population problem, David and Charles, Newton Abbot

Jones, H. (1981) A population geography, Harper and Row, London

Jowett, A J. (1984) 'The growth of China's population, 1944-1982, Geographical Journal, 150, 155-70

Lawton, R. (1982) 'People and work', Chapter 2 of J.W. House (ed.) The U.K. space: resources, environment and the future (3rd Edn), Weidenfeld and Nicolson, London

Rowley, J. (1984) 'A watershed of ideas', People, 11, 4-7 and 10-12

Simon, J.L. (1981) The ultimate resource, Martin Robertson, Oxford

Tabah, L. (1984) 'Spirit for the future', People, 11, 9-11

World Bank (1984) World Development Report, 1984, Washington, D.C

Chapter One

PLANNING FOR PEOPLE

Richard Lawton

APPROACHES TO POPULATION POLICY

From early times, awareness of the need to balance population and resources has led society and its rulers to concern themselves with the numbers and distribution of their people. Encouragement of colonisation; limitations on migration; promotion of growth for military or economic ends; restrictions on families from fear of want or resource depletion: all are to be encountered in the abundant historical and contemporary precedents illustrative of society's concern with population and its control. Although in general the chief control on population growth in past times was high mortality, in many pre-modern societies fertility levels were held well below the biological maximum by constraints imposed by such social norms as regulation of the age of marriage, child spacing and celibacy. Brutally direct action to control population behaviour - such as forced migration, genocide or compulsory sterilization - may achieve their limited objectives, but general policies which are explicitly designed to shape population behaviour seem to have had little permanent effect. While most communities and individuals are willing to adopt measures to improve health and prolong life - albeit after education in new ways and a demonstration of their efficacy - control of mobility and fertility are largely matters for individual choice. Indirect measures seem more likely to persuade people to change their demographic behaviour than direct policies which seek to compel change.
    There are many reasons why this should be so. For example, regulation of births through official policies touches on intensely personal attitudes and relationships: towards the individual partner; within often deeply rooted social and cultural norms, perhaps involving strongly held religious beliefs and ethical values; and, not least, touching on the value of the individual and the very meaning of life. Moreover, reproductive behaviour is highly heterogeneous and varies markedly between different groups even within the same country. Although the causes underlying family and birth patterns are very varied, the approach to policies seeking to change fertility

levels have generally assumed an economic base, including the value that parents and families set on having children against the cost of raising them, though social influences (education, health, the family) and cultural forces (both traditional and new attitudes towards the family) are also seen as significant forces in shaping attitudes to marriage and having children. However, the responses to such influences vary with individual attitudes and behaviour in ways which are not easy to assess and which may fluctuate over time and vary in effectiveness from one group to another. Hence, the framing and successful implementation of policies of fertility control through economic and socio-cultural measures are difficult and uncertain (Miro et al., 1982).

While regulation of conditions affecting mortality - such as food taboos and practices relating to personal hygiene in some traditional societies - would seem likely to command general assent, in contemporary society regulations over health and environment, to include the control of dangerous working conditions and high standards of sanitation, housing and the production and sale of food, have often encountered opposition from the vested interests of those whose profits are likely to be affected. Control of dangerous emissions from motor vehicles and problems of regulating food additives are two obvious examples. There is a long history of difficulties in imposing quarantine regulations, even in the face of such feared killer diseases as bubonic plague and cholera. The prolonged battles and slow and imperfect development of legislation over public health, sanitation and housing in early modern cities; the problems of persuading or compelling individuals to take precautions or prophylactic measures against communicable disease such as smallpox, diphtheria, and poliomyelitis; and the complacency which can lead to a relaxation of awareness after diseases are - in medical terms- 'controlled': all these show that effective policies of mortality control and health provision are difficult to design and implement (Learmonth, 1978). Moreover, preventive medicine is often given too low a priority in the social policies of both the developed world (see Chapter 6, below) and the developing world (see Chapter 7, below) especially at the community level.

Migration policies have also to cope with complex environmental, social and economic contexts both between and within the nation state. Movement in search of food and water, safety and to open up new territories are as old as mankind and are difficult to control or keep track of, even in developed countries with efficient immigrant controls and well regulated population registration systems. In the developing world, traditional movements of nomads and pastoralists are now less significant than seasonal migration of agricultural workers and short-term employment in mine, factory or the servicing trades (see Chapter 3, below). Moreover, they now frequently involve international migration across national boundaries, such as those superimposed on traditional societies of Africa, or which lie between labour-surplus and labour-shortage areas, including both nearby and, in the case of migrants from former colonial

10

dependencies to the 'mother country', at a distance. In prosperous times such migration may be mutually beneficial: but in times of recession high unemployment among migrant workers and a wish on the part of nationals to be rid of them may cause severe social and even political tensions. The regulation of such migration is difficult, as the numerous illegal Mexican migrants in the United States show (900,000 as estimated in 1982). Again, the problems of nationality or appropriate status for 'guestworkers' raise difficult social and population policy issues regarding both short- and longer-term migrants to North-Western Europe from the Mediterranean and former colonial territories (see Chapter 2, below).

Thus, population policies must seek not only to regulate the determinants of trends - fertility, mortality and migration - but should also be responsive to their effects on structure and distribution. Moreover, since population behaviour is influenced by the complex interplay of genetic and biological factors, varied environmental controls and socio-economic, political and cultural influences (Figure 1.1), population planners face formidable problems both in identifying and reaching their goals and in anticipating the response of individuals and the community to policies.

The identification of population trends can only be retrospective and depends on accurate information on vital rates (fertility and mortality) and migration, and on their varying impact on the age and sex structure and distribution of population. None of these are adequately recorded in most countries of the developing world, where population issues are often most pressing, and even in the more developed countries population data fall short of complete knowledge of temporal and spatial variations in population behaviour, an understanding of which is crucial to the work of the wide range of disciplines involved in population studies.

Demographic variables shape population trends and structure, and are crucial for the estimation of the future needs of the existing population and the likely patterns of population development. For example, in the Third World the consequences of rapid population growth due to reduction in mortality - especially among infants and children - and increasing life expectancies bring a need for future provision of schools, jobs, housing and - in due course as successively larger cohorts age - of care for the elderly (see Chapter 5, below). As mortality control progresses there is need for evaluation of implications of past and present population trends and for population policy alongside and as part of economic, social and environmental planning at national, regional and local levels. In the developed countries the emphasis is more on the social and economic consequences of fluctuations in birth rates which are reflected in changing demands for schools, services and jobs, but especially on the gradual prolongation of life which underlies the increase in the proportion of the elderly and, especially, in the growing numbers of very old people (see Chapter 4, below).

The factors underlying demographic change are many-faceted and complex. For example advances in genetics, micro-biology and

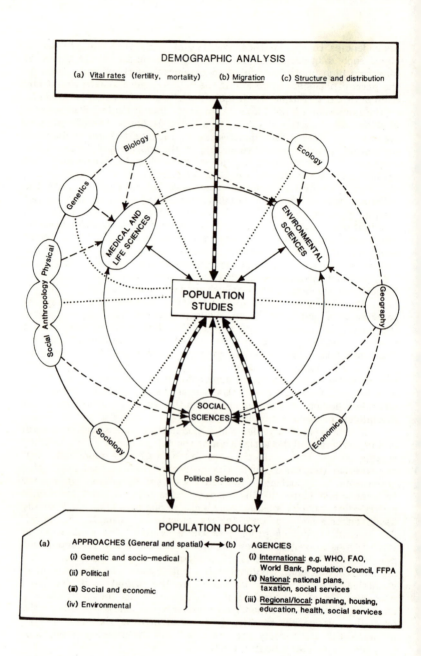

DEMOGRAPHIC ANALYSIS

(a) Vital rates (fertility, mortality)   (b) Migration   (c) Structure and distribution

Biology

Ecology

Genetics

ENVIRONMENTAL SCIENCES

MEDICAL AND LIFE SCIENCES

Physical Anthropology

Social

Geography

POPULATION STUDIES

SOCIAL SCIENCES

Sociology

Economics

Political Science

POPULATION POLICY

(a)   APPROACHES (General and spatial) ◄──► (b)   AGENCIES

(i) Genetic and socio-medical

(ii) Political

(iii) Social and economic

(iv) Environmental

(i) International: e.g. WHO, FAO, World Bank, Population Council, FFPA

(ii) National: national plans, taxation, social services

(iii) Regional/local: planning, housing, education, health, social services

Fig. 1.1   The Area of Population Policy

biochemistry have contributed much to the saving and prolongation of life, and to the ability to promote or inhibit conception. Yet the acceptance of such revolutionary advances in the medical and life sciences reflects the response of society to the possibilities opened up for population control and the social, economic and political implications of the changes induced by new population trends in relationships with our environment and society (Howe and Loraine, 1974). Indeed, human factors are often critical to the success or failure of scientific advances relevant to demographic change: for example control of disease depends on a precise knowledge of environmental and societal conditions among the peoples involved, as problems of malaria control in areas of high population mobility indicate (Prothero, 1965).

It is increasingly recognised that successful identification of the consequences of population trends and the devising and implementation of realistic policies depend not only the will of society at many levels, from local to international, but also on the ability of decision-makers to inform and persuade their populations of the value of such measures. As long ago as the first World Conference on Population in Rome, 1954, it was observed "...how many and varied are the links between demographic phenomena and the rest of social life" which, it was argued, "...has. broken through the narrow circle of pure demography" (Hersch, 1954). The heated debate over development versus population policy as the key to the attack on poverty in the Third World which dominated the Budapest World Population Conference of 1974, and its controversial appearance at the 1984 Conference in Mexico in the American case for social rather than birth control policies - in particular through abortion - in fertility control for the developing world is symptomatic of the wide range of possible approaches to population policies.

The web which connects the demographic behaviour of people to the physical, cultural and ethical nature of mankind is complex and varied. Policies designed to influence that behaviour and, therefore, to shape future population trends are difficult to formulate and implement. Their outcome is all too frequently rather unpredictable, not least because of the difficulty of judging the response to similar policies of people of different cultural, educational and socio-economic backgrounds. As the distinguished demographer Ansley J. Coale has remarked:

> "...our understanding of demographic tendencies and of their causes and consequences is still far from perfect. Demography is linked to economic, political and ethnic questions on which attitudes are often deeply entrenched. This is why we often hear opinions on demography and population policies which, though expressed forcefully, bear no relation at all to scientific reality" (International Union for the Scientific Study of Population, 1984).

However, the development of measures designed to shape the

future numbers and distribution of population is only one aspect of population policy. Many population problems are implicit in actual demographic trends, both past and present, and in the structure of existing populations. By examining the numbers in each cohort, or successive age group, of a population, it is possible to estimate their future needs and, either by deduction from existing vital and migration rates or from alternative assumptions, to form some judgement of the policy implications of the demographic circumstances. With that knowledge it is possible to make practical and flexible provision for successive cohorts of varying size, as they move through school, into the job market and through successive stages of family life into retirement. In many cases, it may be argued, the most realistic policies are those which look to the future needs of existing populations rather than seek to control generations as yet unborn.

In discussing the general implications of the character and objectives of population policy, two themes are, therefore, chosen for discussion: first, the nature and effectiveness of policies of fertility control in underdeveloped countries of the Third World and their relationship to programmes of economic and social development; secondly, the contrasting problems associated with the fertility decline in the European World and, the problems it poses for changes in the population structure of such countries as the United Kingdom, now and in the future.

PLANNING FOR POPULATION GROWTH: THE THIRD WORLD

Much of the concern over the danger of over rapid population growth in the world focuses on the under-developed areas of the Third World. Dramatic reductions in mortality, particularly since the Second World War, have been much more rapid than those experienced in Europe's mortality transition. Whereas, typically, crude death rates in England fell from an average of 33 to 30 per 1.000 in the 1720's and 1730's to 22 4 in the 1860's, and to 13 and 12 per 1,000 respectively after the First and Second World Wars, mortality in the developing world fell rapidly in the mid-twentieth century from these eighteenth century European levels to 12 per 1,000 in 1980 (ranging from 25 to as little as 5 per 1,000). Even in Latin America where the mortality transition was spread over a longer period, crude death rates were frequently halved between the 1930's and the 1960's : for example in Mexico mortality fell from 25.6 per 1,000 in 1930-34 to 11.5 in 1960 and is now only 6 per 1,000. In a high mortality country such as India the estimated death rate of 43 per 1,000 in the 1900's was down to 31 in the 1930's, to 23 in the 1950's and is now only 15 per 1,000.

Such massive and rapid change is, indeed, the basic cause of a fundamental demographic revolution which reflects the general improvements in the economy and in public health of the twentieth century but, even more so, the medical revolution which in only a few decades has virtually wiped out such killer diseases as smallpox, controlled cholera and typhoid, and substantially ameliorated morbidity and mortality from such endemic diseases as malaria. Malaria eradication after the Second World War accounted for much of the dramatic halving of mortality in Ceylon (Sri Lanka) between 1940 and 1956 when, at 10 per 1,000, crude death rate was among the lowest in the developing world. While this reflects post-war economic prosperity and increased provision of health services, malaria control has been credited with 42 per cent of the decline in Ceylon's crude death rate between 1930-45 and 1946-60, and an even a more cautious estimate puts its contribution at 23 per cent of the fall in mortality between 1945 and the early 1970's (Jones, 1981). Despite the resurgence of malaria carried by DDT-resistant strains of mosquito, Sri Lanka's crude death rate remains, at 8 per 1,000, among the lowest in the world.

Rapid reduction in mortality is reflected in much enhanced life expectancy in many developing countries, but the gap between them and the developed world is still wide - 57 years at birth as against 72. Moreover, the range is considerable; between 41 and 56 in Tropical Africa, 43 and 72 in Asia and 47 and 73 in Latin America (see Figure 7.2). Most of this gap between and within countries reflects wide variations in levels of nutrition, in health and social services, and in knowledge and possibility of maintaining good personal hygiene. These account for considerable differences in infant mortality between lower and higher income countries in the developing world with respective rates ranging from 110 to 20 per 1,000 (see Figure 7.3).

The current WHO 'Health for All' campaign for primary health care, better sanitation, water supplies and personal hygiene by the year 2000 in low- and middle-income countries of Latin America, Tropical Africa and Asia could save the lives of many children and substantially reduce infant mortality (see Chapter 7, below). Indeed in 47 developing countries of the 70 pledged to this campaign, infant mortality ranged from 56 to 250 per 1,000 and 51 had life expectancies of only 40-59 years. Given a major breakthrough such as that achieved in Ceylon in the 1940's and 1950's this situation could change rapidly. Historically, expectation of life at birth in most parts of the world ranged from 20 to 30 years as between 'normal' and 'healthy' periods. In Ceylon a life expectancy of around 30 in 1921 more than doubled in 40 years (Notestein, 1964). Moreover, as more children survive into adult life the potential for growth accelerates, given the persistence of high birth rates associated with the early marriage and large families which, until recently, characterized most parts of the Third World. The large increase in the number of women of reproductive age is witness to both the rapidity of recent mortality decline and the potential for accelerating future growth if there were no corresponding reduction in fertility levels.

Herein lies a dilemma: unless mortality control is matched by economic growth and/or fertility control, doomwatch forecasts of the consequences of the population explosion may yet be realized. Views on the relationship between population and resources have oscillated over the past forty years. In the post-war years a growing awareness of pressure on natural resources due to man's abuse of the environment was reflected in a number of influential books by such authors as William Vogt (1949), Fairfield Osborn (1948 and 1954), and Karl Sax (1955), which stressed the potential danger of overpopulation and irreversible environmental damage. The economic boom of the 1960's, reflecting the power of science and technology to increase yields of food grains - the so-called Green Revolution - and to devise more effective means of processing cheaper sources of industrial raw materials, led some to optimistic views of the ability of the world to sustain its growing population (Clark, 1967). But as the implications of the medical revolution for accelerating population growth in the developing world became clearer, a swelling tide of criticism of the 'affluent society' gathered (Galbraith, 1958) and anxiety over growing population pressure was expressed by economists, environmentalists and neo Malthusian population analysts (Ehrlich, 1968). Concern for the growing threat to the attempts of developing countries to break the barriers of poverty which were posed by seemingly uncontrolled population growth alerted international agencies to the importance of population policy.

Computer predictions based on dynamic multi-variate economic models (Forrester, 1971) and using linear projections of current high levels of population growth and consumption of raw materials produced doomwatch forecasts of world shortages (Meadows et al, 1972) and widespread food shortages in many developing areas. These added powerfully to growing criticism of over-exploitation of resources from the environmentalist lobby (Ehrlich and Ehrlich, 1970). As economic optimism waned in the 1970's, the international population planning movement became increasingly dominated by the birth-control lobby, as epitomized in the International Federation for Planned Parenthood and its magazine, People, and as reflected from 1974 in the pages of Population and Development Review, the journal of the Population Council's Center for Policy Studies.

Despite the economic growth of the 1960's, accelerating world population increases undoubtedly presented graver problems, especially for the developing world. The heated debate at the World Population Conference in 1974 between the governments of countries in the developed world, which argued that population control was a necessary prelude to economic growth, and those of the developing world, which argued that development is the best contraceptive, stressed the necessity for a widely-based population policy. Family planning alone without economic and social development will not reduce the very high birth rates of many developing areas, but it will be difficult to improve living standards without some corresponding reduction in population growth (Brandt, 1980).

That debate must be set within the context of the very high rates of population increase in many countries of the Third World in

16

the 1960's. High fertility combined, in most areas, with low or rapidly falling mortality had produced population growth rates twice to four times those found in Europe during the early phases of modernization, reaching 2 to 2.5 per cent per annum in countries at the early transitional (pre-industrial) stage, and 3 to 3.5 per cent per annum in industrializing countries. World population growth has slowed somewhat from its 1965 peak of 2.5 per cent per annum mainly because of a rapid fall in birth rate in China and, to a lesser extent in many middle-income countries of East Asia and Latin America (Frejka, 1973; World Bank, 1984). Nevertheless, standard projections for 1982-2000 suggest that - apart from China, India and Sri Lanka - no low-income countries are likely to experience growth of under 2 per cent p.a. and many may increase at over 3 per cent, especially in Sub-Saharan Africa. Indeed, while many South-East Asian, North African and Latin American states may reduce population growth to under 2 per cent p.a , middle-income countries as a whole are likely to average that level of growth. With limited opportunities for emigration, most of the poorest and many middle-income countries are likely to double their numbers in the next 20 to 40 years (World Bank, 1984, Appendix, Table 1).

Moreover, since mortality decline gives a better chance of life to the younger ages, the proportion of youth dependency and the numbers to be absorbed into the workforce of the 1970's and 1980's have increased rapidly throughout the developing world since 1960 and, with the exception of China and Cuba, are expected to continue to do so up to the end of this century and beyond; the projected index of change ranges from 116 (India) to 231 (Kenya), as compared with 100 in 1980, in the poorest countries, and from 101 (Jamaica) to 207 (Zimbabwe) in middle income areas (World Bank, 1984, Appendix, Table 2). If the productive potential of these young people can be realized, the Malthusian trap may be avoided. Julian Simon (1981) has argued that, despite rapid population growth, living standards have generally increased and that he sees "no convincing economic reasons why these trends ... should not continue indefinitely" (ibid , p.345). Although he admits that temporary and localized shortages are bound to exist, he rejects the 'closed system' terms of the Malthusians arguing instead that the 'ultimate resource is people'.

Nevertheless it is difficult both to sustain rapid population growth and to invest in modernization (whether in the agricultural or the industrial sector), particularly under conditions of world recession which have hit raw material producers with substantial international debts particularly hard. Changing attitudes to population and development have been reflected in changing approaches to policy at both international and national levels. In the 1950's and '60's the growing pressure for population limitation came mainly from international agencies funded from the Western World, though some larger Asian countries had active - sometimes very strong - birth control programmes. At Bucharest the main opposition to the 'population control' solution as opposed to the provision of a better life for their rapidly growing populations came from Catholic Latin

America and the more sparsely-peopled and largely rural nations of Tropical Africa. Already in many of the more industrialized states of the developing world - notably South Korea, Taiwan and Singapore - growing prosperity was leading to social change and adding voluntary family limitation to the forceful government measures already adopted. Faced by the need for rapid reduction of population growth, direct methods of fertility control seem necessary, but are very difficult to enforce, whether through restrictions on marriage or by compulsory contraception, abortion or sterilization. Yet voluntary programmes of birth control are often less effective in traditional rural societies than long-practised controls on marriage and customary methods of birth spacing. It may be, however, that social and economic changes will produce spontaneous change in fertility behaviour, and as a consequence integrated policies may be more effective than direct approaches to family planning in many societies. Education and the mass media may change attitudes towards children and the family. The enhancement of the status of women through better education and a more active role in society is one of the best ways of achieving this.

Conflict, partly over the need for urgent action, more particularly over the most effective approach to population control, did not prevent the adoption in Bucharest of a World Population Plan of Action by 136 governments. Biennial reviews of progress by the U.N. Population Commission have shown that nearly all governments understand the need for an understanding of population trends in national development plans and that many countries now support family planning for other than purely demographic reasons. Leon Tabah (1979) reported that, by the late 1970's, there was no doubt that Third World countries, especially those with large populations, wished to reduce their growth rate and saw population issues as important in development. Nevertheless at that time economic and social factors were thought to have contributed more to reducing population growth than family planning programmes. However, it was the view of Bernard Berelson (1978), the veteran population planner, that to achieve the benefits of modernization, better education, health and nutrition, greater prosperity and social status, very positive policies of population control were needed: strong family planning programmes (including abortion and sterilization); sanctions on marriage and children; restructured development programmes. A target crude birth rate of 20 per 1,000 (around 2.5 children per family) by AD 2000 was, in his view, certain of achievement in only 3 of 29 states analysed, probable in 10, possible in 4 and unlikely in 12. The progression is marked by descending levels of demographic, social and, in general, economic indicators.

Nevertheless, many Third World countries introduced powerful policies of fertility control in the 1970's, at the same time as international agencies were increasingly regarding birth control as part of a package of policies relating to health, nutrition, social and educational improvements. In short, though birth control may well be a necessary part of population policy, it is not, in itself, sufficient to

Table 1.1 : Government attitudes to fertility and family planning by major world regions, 1984

Attitudes Towards

	Fertility Level			Population Policy			Contraceptive Services		
	Too high	Too low	Satis-factory	to Reduce	to Raise	None or maintain	Active support	Restrictive	None or Little
N. Africa	4	-	2	4		2	4	1	1
S. Africa	1	-	-	1			1		-
Inter-tropical Africa	19	5	18	11	5	26	23	1	18
East Asia	3		4	3		4	5		2
S.E. Asia	3	3	2	3	3	2	5	2	1
South Asia	5	-	2	5		2	6		1
S.W Asia	3	2	11	2	2	12	10	1	5
Australasia		-	2			2	2		
Pacific	4	-		2		2	4		
Latin America	3	3	10	3	2	11	13		3
Caribbean	5	-	4	5		4	9		
North America	-		2	-		2	2		
Southern Europe	-	2	4		1	5	5		1
Western Europe	-	4	9		2	11	12		1
Eastern Europe	-	4	4		4	4	6	2	
USSR		-	1	-		1	1		-
TOTALS (No. of States)	50	23 (148)	75	39	19 (148)	90	108	7 (148)	33

Source: People. vol.11 (1984)

bring about a reduction in fertility. In the past decade there has been a growing perception of the need for population planning as part of national economic and social policies leading to easier access to family planning. The U.N. Population Division reported in 1981 that 17 of 40 Asian states thought their rates of increase too high and only six actively opposed contraceptive policies, while 10 of the 25 Latin American states wished to reduce growth and none was opposed to family planning. Even in tropical Africa, the fastest growing area on the world population map, governments are now more sympathetic to family planning (Table 1.1).

Changing attitudes in the Third World are reflected in the reversal of their accelerating population increase over the past 10-15 years, an historical turning point in world population growth according to Tomas Frejka (1981). His 1980-based population projections, which use alternative assumptions on the time over which a stationary population may be achieved, paint a more optimistic picture of estimated growth in the developing world over the next century: a range of 7,100 to 12,500 million people as compared with the then 3,300 million in contrast to his earlier estimates of 6,760 to 13,860 million (Frejka, 1973). By comparison, the World Bank (1984) 1982-based estimates suggest increases of 3,396 million to 8,236 million on standard growth assumptions and a minimum of 6,342 million in the Third World, assuming rapid fertility decline.

It is ironic that after two decades of domination of the international planning agencies by the birth control lobby, especially in Washington, the U.S.A. has shifted its ground from the Global 2000 Report to the President (1980), which called for rapid reduction in population growth to counter the fears of food crises in the developing world and global pressures on natural resources. Advised by Julian Simon and Hermann Kahn (1984), the U.S. delegation to the 1984 U.N. Conference on Population in Mexico City argued that population growth has been an essential element in economic growth which, as standards of living rise, may be expected to moderate.

Hence, the U.S. is now taking a more restrained attitude on birth control and positive opposition to permissive legislation on abortion. While this may reflect a growing confidence in the ability of Third World countries to develop balanced policies of economic and social development which include, but do not mainly rely on, fertility control, this is in sharp contrast to the view of The World Development Report (World Bank, 1984) which sees population limitation as an essential prerequisite of economic and social progress, but it is in line with the view in many parts of the developing world, not least in Marxist countries (Pearce, 1984).

Moreover, the fall in total fertility rate in the developing world in the 1970's from 5.7 to 4.8 children per woman may justify this new-found optimism as do the preliminary findings of the World Fertility Survey of 1972-82, based on sample studies in 41 developing and 19 developed countries, which suggest a general fall in mean family size. Social change is contributing much to fertility control: increases in the age of marriage, especially among educated town-dwellers; more women in jobs; changing attitudes towards the role of women in society. Thus although in Kenya mean completed family size is 8 children as compared with 7 twenty years ago, despite government supported family planning services, lower fertility is evident among educated or skilled townspeople and westernized Kikuyu. Tanzanian surveys also link lower levels of fertility to education: 87 per cent of the national level for women with 5-8 years schooling and only 43 per cent for those with over nine years education.

The most dramatic fall in birth rate has occurred in countries of East Asia - South Korea, Hong Kong, Taiwan and China - where rapid economic growth and social change have been accompanied by some of the most stringent policies of family limitation. In China, under the 1980 Marriage Law and 1981 Constitution, a strict policy of deferral of marriage and restriction of families to one child has been

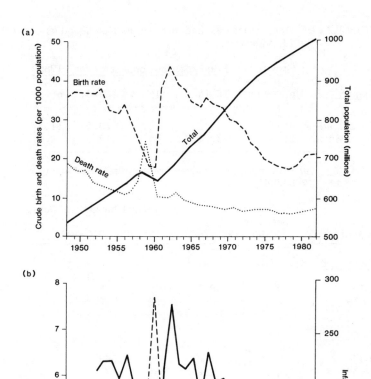

Fig. 1.2   (a) Population trends in China, 1949–82
            (b) Total fertility rate and infant mortality rates in China, 1953–82

Source: (a) Jowett, 1984
         (b) Banister, 1984

Table 1.2 : (a) Age structures and growth in Developed and Third World regions

(a) Region	Growth (per cent) p.a.	Age distribution (per cent) 1980			
		0-14	15-44	45-64	65+
Developed	0.6	23.1	44.8	20.8	11.3
Third World	2.1	39.1	44.3	12.6	4.0

(b) Total and percentage increase in selected age groups, 1960-2000

Age group	Change (per cent p.a.)		Total Change (millions)	
	1960-80	1980-2000	1960-80	1980-2000
Developed				
0-19	0.3	-0.1	19	-5
20-39	1.0	0.3	60	20
Third World				
0-19	2.3	1.0	623	380
20-39	2.4	2.6	355	635

Source: McNicoll (1984)

adopted: benefits in child allowances, schooling and pensions go to parents who conform, but there are penalties (as well as great social and political pressures) for those who do not. The fall in birth rate by over 50 per cent from 1963 to 20.9 per thousand in 1981 has been dramatic (Figure 1.2). Even so, the number of women of marriageable age will rise steeply to a peak in 1986 and remain high until the mid-1990's, so that population will grow relatively rapidly for another generation. If zero growth is to be achieved within the next 25 years, as the government hopes, such dramatic restrictions are necessary, though the personal and social costs must be painful (see Chapter 5, below).

The consequences of such rapid changes in mortality and fertility for the population structures of developing countries are considerable. They involve not only direct, proximate factors such as age structure and family/kinship structure, but also must take account of their economic, social and political consequences, including the consequences of differential growth for the changing resource demands between regions with different patterns of

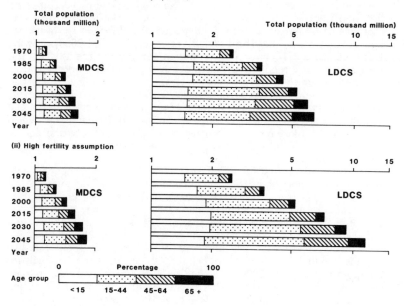

Fig. 1.3 Estimates of population structure (1970 base), 1985–2045

population change, between town and country, and within individual communities (McNicoll, 1984). In the early 1960's the proportion under 15 years in major regions of the Third World ranged from 40 to 45 per cent; in contrast, fewer than 5 per cent survived beyond 65 in most LDCs. This is still basically true (Table 1.2).

Improved life expectancy has meant more people surviving into old age: but since all age groups, particularly young children, have benefited from improved disease control, the proportions of children, adults and elderly has changed little. Where family size has been reduced by longer birth intervals, the loss is partly made up by better chances of survival. Nevertheless, in areas of rapid fertility decline a growing proportion of people will be found in older age-groups from the end of this century. At present only 4 per cent of the population of the developing world is over 64 (as compared with 14 per cent in North-West Europe) but in areas of recent rapid fertility control, such as China, it is already 6 per cent. This will become more typical of Third World countries in the next 30 years and with moderate total growth the proportion could be over one-eighth by the mid-21st century (Figure 1.3).

A more pressing issue for these countries is the increasing number of adults from the large post-war birth cohorts. In many countries the workforce increased 50 per cent more rapidly than jobs in the 1960's (see Chapter 3, below). This is reflected in rural

23

underemployment, but massive movements to seek work in the towns have also created great social and housing problems, despite the 'informal sector' employment generated there. The ILO estimates an increase of 69 per cent (from 1,130 to 1,910 million) in the working-age population in the Third World between 1975 and 2000, growing from the present 22 million to 50 million per year by the 1990's. The capital increase required to sustain these potential workers and to improve incomes is considerable: Brazil, for example, faces an increase of working-age population 1980-2000 of 65 per cent; Egypt, Ethiopia and Kenya of 68, 76 and 134 per cent respectively; and Thailand, Bangladesh and Nepal, of 73, 74 and 78 per cent (World Bank, 1984). Moreover, the proportion of people of working age in the developing world will not reach its peak until the third decade of the next century.

More education for increasing numbers is also needed, even though the proportion of the school age population is beginning to fall in many areas (see Chapter 9, below). The costs are considerable. For example, even assuming standard fertility decline, 1980 primary school costs in Malawi could increase by 130 per cent by 2000 and 260 per cent by 2015 at present enrolment rates and by 253 and 546 per cent respectively with 100 per cent enrolment. If rapid fertility decline could be achieved, savings of 22 per cent on expenditure could be achieved by 2000 A.D. and of 57 per cent by 2015. In most countries of Sub-Saharan Africa rapid fertility decline could bring similar savings (World Bank, 1984, pp.84-86). Moreover, many see education, especially of women, as the best hope for family planning and education in the home.

There is a pressing need for jobs and homes for young adults, especially in the cities to which they now migrate in such large numbers and where the problems of work and housing present some of the biggest social problems of the day (see Chapters 3 and 5, below). An effective workforce and decent life depend on good health. There is need for close links between population planning and health and welfare services. The success of local clinics and para-medical services in a number of parts of the developing world point to their effectiveness for education in personal hygiene and in family care (see chapter 7, below).

The policy implications for Third World countries of such population trends are enormous. Already hard-pressed to develop limited resources in a harsh economic situation, they must seek to provide for many more people at all life stages. Much of the available public and personal capital will be absorbed by population growth. Increased economic, technical and human skill resources are needed to improve the quality of life. Unenviable public and private choices of action must be made in the attempt to balance the population:resources budget. Planning for people is much wider than the sometimes myopic and insensitive equating of population policy solely with contraceptive control. It can and should be a focus for social, even economic development in which individuals, the community and the state, and voluntary services as well as national and international agencies, can collaborate.

PLANNING FOR POPULATION DECLINE : THE WESTERN WORLD

The West's population problems are very different. By the inter-war years mortality was controlled, though modern medicine and better child care have substantially reduced disease and mortality in all classes of society since then. Similarly, birth rates fell rapidly in all classes of society from the late nineteenth century. The average completed British family size, over 6 in mid-Victorian times, was below replacement level in many countries by the 1930's, partly a consequence of World War I, partly of the slump. The completion of families earlier in marriage pointed to the changing role of women and, in many areas, their greater involvement in the workforce.

The transition to low mortality and low to moderate fertility has continued and spread throughout the European world in the post-war era in capitalist and socialist states alike. Fluctuations in population are now the product of short-term changes in birth rate and differential migration mainly reflecting differential labour demands. Much of the population increase in Europe (24 per cent between 1950 and 1981), the U.S.S.R. (49 per cent) and North America (53 per cent) was due to increasing life expectancy - now around 72 to 73 years -which has improved since 1950 (from between 1 year to around 10 in some countries of Southern Europe) and which has been more marked among women than men, especially so in North America. Hence the population of the West is progressively ageing: the present 11 per cent over 64 years will increase to 16 to 17 per cent over the next 50 to 60 years, and more rapidly if births remain around their recent low level.

Recent estimates for the U.K., taking account of alternative 'moderate' trends in both fertility and mortality, suggest an increase in the proportion of over-65's from 15.1 per cent in 1981 to between 17.0-17.3 per cent by 2021, though the most optimistic mortality assumption could increase the proportion to 22.4 per cent (Benjamin, 1984). In West Germany if population continues to shrink slowly, the present 15 per cent over 64 years of age could be as high as 23 per cent by 2030 (Wander, 1978). In Japan, the rapid fall in fertility, which led to a halving in birth-rate between 1947 and 1960 and a further decline in the 1970's to a total fertility rate of 1.74 in 1980, has led to a substantial change in its previously youthful age structure. Combined with a substantial fall in mortality there has been a sharp increase in the proportion of over-65's from 4.9 per cent in 1950 to 9.0 per cent in 1980; estimates suggest that this could rise to 21.3 per cent by the year 2025 (Ogawa, 1982).

One of the dominant characteristics of demographic trends in the developed world since the 1920's has been the relatively wide fluctuations in births. After the post-war baby boom, falling birth rates suggested a return to below-replacement fertility characteristic of the 1930's. Pro-natalist policies, such as family allowances, better ante- and post-natal care, and housing provision were adopted in many countries. Though their effect is questionable,

(a)   (b)

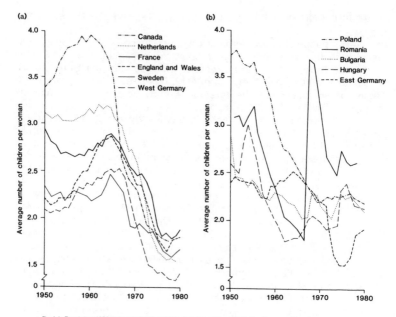

Fig. 1.4 Trend since 1950 in the total fertility rate in selected countries of (a) Western Europe and Canada
(b) Eastern Europe
Source: Bourgeois–Pichat, 1981

by the late 1950's fears of population and economic decline and ageing populations were alleviated - at least in Western Europe - by increasing birth rates. Economic prosperity and changes in social attitudes reflected in younger marriages and earlier pregnancies led to average families of up to 2.5 to 3.0 children in many parts of the Western World, enough to promote steady growth. Indeed by the mid-1960's governments and ecologists in some countries began to worry about the consequences of increased population growth: pressure on land and resources; more housing; additional services for both the young and the elderly; increasing dependency on a relatively smaller workforce (see Chapters 2 and 4, below).

Moreover, adverse age-structures and full employment led to labour shortages in most industrial countries in the late-1950's and 1960's. To fill the gap, migrant labour was imported in considerable numbers from former dependencies and from rural areas of Southern Europe (White, 1984; Chapter 2). These mainly youthful migrants continue to add to the birth rates, especially in the large cities, of the host countries. Had the difficulties of the 1970's and '80's been foreseen more cautious migration policies might have followed. In West Germany, despite the banning of recruitment from 1973, gastarbeiter (guest workers) now number 4.5 million, 7.5 per cent of the population, special provision for whom under Common Market law

26

places extra demands on educational facilities as well as housing and social services. France's 1.8 foreign million workers are largely semi-and unskilled: they and their dependants (8 per cent of the population) are very vulnerable to unemployment and exploitation, for example over housing. The U.K.'s immigrants, numbering some 3.4 million (6 per cent of the total) of which 1.5 million are of New Commonwealth and Pakistani origin, all too often experience discrimination in the competition for jobs and housing and even over citizenship.

From the late 1960's falling fertility and a partial reversal of migration has led to a sharp reduction in population growth throughout Europe. In the West, even in traditionally high fertility countries such as Ireland and Spain, marital fertility has fallen by almost one-quarter since the late 1960's (Eversley 1979). With average family size now ranging from 1.5 to 2.2, reproduction in nearly all West European states is below replacement level (Figure 1.4). In parts of Eastern Europe legalized abortion contributed to fertility decline in the 1960's: despite substantial child allowances to encourage second and third children, reproduction rates fell again below replacement level in the late 1970's. Undoubtedly the general fall in European fertility reflects adverse economic conditions and changed social attitudes to the family and children as well as more effective and widespread contraceptive practices. It extends through most cultural groups and all classes of society; indeed the fall is often sharper among semi- and unskilled manual workers, as in Britain. Despite unease in some countries over the prospect of decline, long expressed in France in pro-natalist literature and politics (Ogden and Huss, 1982), it seems unlikely that there will be any substantial increase in fertility in the near future.

In other parts of the Western World similar trends have been experienced. While total fertility rates in North America (1.9) and Australasia (2.1) are still higher than those for the majority of Western European countries - Iceland and Ireland excepted - they have fallen proportionately as much, or more, since the early 1960's. For example, The Commission on Population Growth and the American Future (1972) expressed some concern over the implications of the prolonged baby boom of 1944-69 which led them to recommend the Federal Government to undertake 'population-related programs' and to strengthen research and administrative and legislative action in population and related welfare issues. Yet such has been the rapidity of the fertility decline in the 1970's with crude birth rates falling from over 18 per 1000 in 1969 to 14.9 in 1974 that the high fertility forecasts of 300 million people by the early twenty-first century have given way to expectations of a move towards zero population growth and a population in the year 2000 of around 268 million as compared with the mid-1980 total of 227.7 million. Such trends would inevitably produce an ageing population: at replacement level (a completed family size of 2.1) the median age would rise from 28.1 in 1972 to 34.3 in 2000, but the current total fertility rate of 1.9 is likely to produce a 25 per cent increase in the proportion of over-

65's between 1980 (10.7 per cent) and the year 2000 (13.4 per cent) rising to 19.5 per cent by 2025, from the present 31.8 million to an estimated 58.6 million.

The dramatic fall in fertility in Japan from a peak birth rate of 34.5 per 1000 (TFR, 4.54) in the post-war baby boom to the present, below-replacement, total fertility rate of under 1.8 (and crude birth rate, 14.2). The associated ageing of the population is reflected in a sharp fall in the under-15 dependency ratio from 59.5 in 1950 to 34.9 in 1980 and an increase in elderly dependents from 8.3 per cent to 13.3 per cent in the same period (Okita and Kuroda, 1981). Estimates from the 1975 Census suggest that the proportion aged over-65 in Japan's population could increase from 7.9 in 1975 to 14.3-14.9 per cent in the year 2000 and between 18.1 and 21.3 per cent (according to fertility assumptions) by 2025.

The consequences of relatively large fluctuations over a short time period, set against a gradual increase in life expectancy and larger numbers of elderly people, are highly significant. Governments and society will need to adjust to changing population structures and to anticipate and be willing to shift resources from one section of the community to another. In this new demographic regime there are greater numbers of 'life stages', with three or four generations living simultaneous but largely separate lives; different household and family patterns; changed roles of men and women at work and in the home; different patterns of activity and dependency through life; greater mobility and leisure in retirement for the 'third age' but a longer period of increasing dependence in old age (Girard, 1983). These are only some of the consequences and challenges for demographic and policy studies in the developed world.

The case of Britain

The implications of such demographic changes may be exemplified by recent and anticipated population trends in Britain. Fewer marriages and smaller families reduced fertility to below replacement level in the 1930's and, with an ageing population, forecasts including the projections for the Royal Commission on Population (1949) predicted future decline. Most commentators took a gloomy view: Roy Harrod (1945) spoke of "a major crisis in our affairs"; the Fabian Society (1945) argued "it is...essential in the national interest that the present decline in birthrate should be arrested" to avoid a declining role in world affairs and a less vigorous social and economic life for the nation.

These gloomy fears did not materialize. First, births were above the levels of the 1920's and 1930's, markedly so in the post-war baby boom and in the 1960's, a product of more universal and younger marriage with somewhat bigger families (Figure 1.5). Secondly, from the mid-1950's to the early 1960's considerable immigration from the New Commonwealth to make good labour shortages in London and the major industrial cities was reflected in a net inward movement of 479,000 between 1958 and 1962. As a result Britain's population increased from 49.9 million in 1951 to 54.1 million in 1971. Though

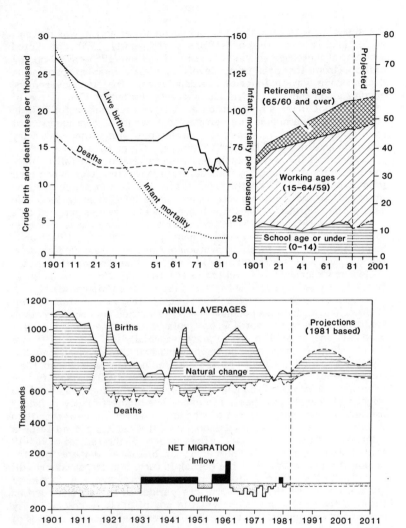

Fig. 1.5   U.K. vital trends, components of population growth, 1901–83; Age structure, 1901–2001; Population changes and projections, 1901–2001

Source : Lawton, 1982

the annual growth rate of 0.5 to 0.6 per cent per annum was modest, all estimates from the mid-1950's to the early 1970's predicted substantial increases varying between 53 million (1955-based) and 67 million (from the peak birth levels of 1964). Fear of population decline gave way to fears of overpopulation. The first government enquiry since the 1949 Royal Commission, the Select Committee of 1971, did not offer an opinion on an optimum population for Britain but did urge government intervention "to prevent the consequences of population growth becoming intolerable for the everyday consequences of life" (House of Commons, 1971, p. x).

Yet in 1977 only 632,000 births were recorded, a fall of one-third from the 1964 peak of 980,000, and for the first time since civil records began in 1837 deaths exceeded births. Moreover, controls on immigration and declining job opportunities have been reflected in substantial migration losses which are expected to continue - if at a more modest rate - into the future. Economic stagnation is reflected in demographic stagnation. If the generation born in the 1960's baby boom were to have families averaging 2.0 or less as suggested by recent trends, Britain's population could decline, though 1979-based projections suggest 56-57 million in the first decade of the twenty-first century as compared with 54.3 million at the 1981 census.

Fluctuations in births are largely responsible for recent fluctuations in Britain's population structure, though improvements in health and living standards - particularly from the 1940's - have gradually increased life expectancy, especially for women. These trends have left their mark on the present structure of population but also have policy implications for succeeding generations and their future needs. The low birth cohorts of the 1930's made for an inevitable shortage of people of working age in the 1950's. This might well have been expected to encourage high efficiency in labour use and greater participation of women in the workforce rather than drawing heavily on immigrant labour to fill what has proved to be a relatively short-term gap. The larger birthrates of 1943-49 contributed to the mid-1960's peak of births as did the greater prosperity and optimism of the period; in turn, that larger cohort will be reflected in more children in the 1990's. Are the fortunate generations those that are born into periods of prosperity, such as those of the 1960's, only to grow up in one of pressure on University places and few job prospects, or those fewer people born in periods of economic difficulty whose opportunities may be correspondingly greater? Society tends to regard dependency of young and old upon a smaller labour force as a problem as compared to situations which produce relatively large numbers in the workforce and fewer dependents. Yet both produce difficulties. Periods of fertility increase produce more juvenile dependents who, on reaching the labour market, may find difficulty in getting jobs. Shrinking populations with a growing workforce and increasing proportions of the retired and very old may find it equally difficult to provide for their dependents.

The difficulties for policy makers raised by such questions

should not be underestimated. For example, the gap of 348,000 between the peak (1964) and trough (1977) of births in post-war Britain, combined with considerable shifts in population (regionally and within cities) creates problems in the provision and long-term viability first of primary and then of secondary schools (see Chapter 8, below). In Liverpool the numbers of children born fell by 63 per cent between 1962 (16,479) and 1977 (6,166). Combined with large-scale dispersal by rehousing this reduced the number of primary school age (4-10) by the late 1970's in almost all areas of the city, but especially in the inner city and on local authority housing estates (Brown and Ferguson, 1982). Perhaps some of the facilities and teachers released by the decline in this sector of education could be reallocated to the growing need for continuing education, not least among mature persons. But in <u>national</u> planning, e.g. for higher education, it defies demographic and economic argument to cut back on University and Polytechnic places when the peak post-war age groups are reaching University age and when, as in the U.S.A., lack of employment opportunities for school leavers could push more towards higher and further education as an alternative to the dole queue. The so-called economies in student grants and cutbacks in University posts (which deny jobs to highly qualified scientists) is surely a short-sighted policy in an economic situation which demands the fullest possible training and use of skills.

A more fundamental problem arises from the sharp increase in the numbers of working age. In marked contrast to stagnation in the 1950's and 1960's, the potential workforce rose by 1.3 million in 1971-81 and is expected to grow by a further 1.4 million by the end of the century. This basic demographic fact is too little discussed in our concern with the economic aspects of the unemployment crisis (see Chapter 2, below). An alarming proportion - around one quarter - of the long-term unemployed are in the 16-24 age group which reached its peak in the early 1980's (Figure 1.6). The palliatives of work-experience, job-creation and new youth-training programmes provided a year's work for perhaps three-quarters of 400,000 school-leavers in 1983; but only one-quarter are expected to find a job. While estimates are more optimistic that the government's 1984 job-creation programmes will lead to more young people finding work, it is doubtful whether sufficient permanent jobs will be created through such schemes to offset the combined effect of demographic pressure on the workforce in a severe recession. It is feared that many will join the million long-term unemployed. // 1994 - 2.7m.

Even in those sectors of the labour force which expanded in the 1970's, particularly in the service sector and public service, recession and deliberate cut-backs have reduced jobs. Ironically, with more people needing care - especially the elderly - cuts in NHS staffing may soon be reflected in fewer jobs and unemployment for nursing and medical staff, the numbers of whom in training are already carefully controlled. Even among married women, the proportion of whom in work has expanded rapidly and accounted for most of the increase in the labour force since 1961, the pinch is being felt as job

31

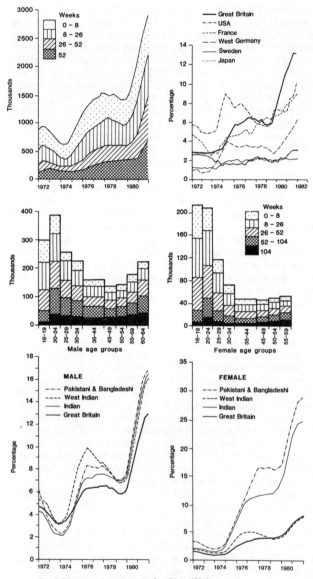

Fig. 1.6 The structure of unemployment in Great Britain, 1972–81

The upper diagrams show the adjusted total annual employment rates for Great Britain and selected countries (right) and duration of unemployment (000's) in Britain (left).

The middle diagrams give duration of unemployment, 1981, for males (left) and females (right).

The lower diagrams give adjusted total annual unemployment rates for males (left) and females (right) of New Commonwealth and Pakistani origin.

prospects decline. This is serious since in many families wives are now the principal wage-earners. Furthermore, recent forecasts of unemployment prospects in the 1980's suggests a 1 per cent increase in the proportion of women in the workforce, while the total workforce is expected to decline and unemployment rise (to perhaps 4 million by 1990) despite a substantial increase in part-time workers (Institute for Employment Research, 1983).

Rising unemployment hits hardest at the less educated and unskilled, especially manual workers. A disproportionate number are young coloured people. The 1981 Labour Force Survey showed that unemployment is much higher among non-whites (16.7 as compared with 9.3 per cent). For 16-29 year olds the difference is over 9 percentage points (15.3 as against 24.9 per cent). The most alarming feature is the staggering one-third of U.K.-born coloured people who are unemployed. A second and growing problem is the growing proportion of long-term unemployed among the over 50's: over one-third in the 50-59 group and 41 per cent of the 60-64 year olds. For many middle-aged people redundancy effectively means an end to their working life. For many disadvantaged and poorly-educated young people working life as we have understood it may never begin.

This new form of dependency is now added to pre-school, school-age and elderly dependents. The ratio between these and working-age married population grew from 53.9 to 70.8 between 1941 and 1971 - a 34 per cent increase of young dependents and 53 per cent growth of retired people as against only 2 per cent increase in working population. Although the plunging birth rate reduced that ratio in the 1970's, the numbers of the elderly will increase into the mid-1980's. This is a generation born in the 1920's or earlier, who grew up through slump and war, and whose efforts have contributed to growing living standards and social services in the post-war years. Yet with the potential workforce greater than ever (as noted above) the Prime Minister has expressed concern, mainly on the grounds of expenditure implications, about the "burden on the working population" of young and old dependents (The Times, July 29th, 1983).

In Britain those of pensionable age increased by 30 per cent from 1951 to 1971, when they numbered 9 million, and they now total $9\frac{1}{2}$ million (17.7 per cent of the total population). Although their rate of growth is past its peak, their numbers are expected to increase by 3.4 per cent to a maximum of 9.8 million in 1986. But the older age groups continue to increase: the over-75's from 2.5 million to 3.2 million, 1971-81, and an estimated 4.1 million in 2001 (1981-based projections); the over 85's by 2.5 per cent in the 1970's and by a probably 34 per cent to over one million by the end of the century (Craig, 1983). An increasing proportion of the elderly live alone: whereas in 1951 there were 917,000 single-person households of pensionable age (13.4 per cent of all retired people) there were 2.2 million (24.8 per cent) in 1961, 2.77 million (28.9 per cent) in 1971 and 2.77 million (28.8 per cent) by 1981, a figure that might be over 3.6 million (37 per cent) by 1991. Since survival rates are much better among women than men, a high proportion of single people living alone are women: indeed the ratio of women to men in Britain, which was 1.057 in 1981 in the population as a whole, is 1.548 among over-65's but 2.077 in the over-75's, though the gap is narrowing as mortality differentials between the sexes decrease.

In spatial terms, differential migration has produced wide variations in the residential patterns of the elderly. There are marked concentrations of older people for example in the South-West and Wales and. in particular at the sub-regional level, in coastal and attractive inland areas where 20-30 per cent of the population may be of retirement age (Warnes and Law, 1984). Conversely immobility of older people, especially those with limited resources, has led to relatively high proportions in some old industrial towns and older suburbs and some inner metropolitan areas. The character and particular needs of such communities (Warnes, 1982) are increasingly attracting the attention of planners and social scientists, including geographers, and should be high on the agenda of both national and local policies (see Chapter 4, below).

Although it would be a mistake to over-emphasize the special needs of the elderly, turning the late-twentieth century into a conservative age in contrast to the over-emphasis on youth in the 1960's, these trends in the geography of the elderly (Warnes, 1981) are important but should surely not be seen simply as 'a burden'. Older people contribute much to their family and communities but do place increasing demands on the medical and social services (see Chapter 6, below). These are too often tackled separately. Local authority services, including appropriate housing, should attempt to better provision of and access to shopping and other services. Community clinics could and should integrate medical, welfare and advisory services. Neither should older people be segregated nor their care increasingly left to 'the government', but should involve and be involved with family and community. A healthy modern society should be a balanced society: "...it should be regarded as intolerable that retirement should ever represent a second-class or second rate or even second-best existence...we must grasp it joyfully as a great and exciting human opportunity" (Midwinter, 1983). We have much to learn from traditional societies about the place of and caring for the elderly in both family and community.

CONCLUSION

Although the problems I have discussed in this introductory chapter are large, wide-ranging and complex, a few broad conclusions may be drawn. A stable population, one in which growth and structure are relatively constant, may be the ideal population system. But varying cultural and individual responses to changing economic, social and political circumstances make demographic stability almost impossible to achieve. We have 'advance notice', however, of the future implications of past and current population trends and can therefore estimate likely need - national, regional and local - often well beforehand. The size and structure of populations is determined by previous demographic events and, in turn, influence the course of future population trends. While forecasting the demographic future is a hazardous business, dependent on the quality of demographic data and the accuracy of the assumptions made about future trends as well as the insights into the processes and forces likely to shape those trends, the outcome of past events is more predictable. Analysis of the changing size of successive cohorts born into a population, their mortality experience and the modifications to the original group brought by migration, make it possible to anticipate their needs at various stages of their life history. Cohort planning parallels demographic cohort analysis and is crucial to any programme of social and economic provision for the future.

In the Third World the full demands of the population explosion of the past two generations have yet to be felt as the pressure on scarce resources for schools, health, jobs and, in all too many areas, for the basic necessities of life, mounts. But the emphasis is beginning to shift from the youngest age groups in many less developed countries to people of working age and, gradually, to the growing numbers of the elderly as the effects of a longer life span begin to be experienced. The demands of three generations require not only more investment in social services and a growing economic base, but the ability to shift resources from one sector to another, from one group of the population to another, and from one region to another often to provide for rapidly growing cities as well as for crowded rural areas. This is a massive task, far more complex and far-reaching even than the attempts to limit the natural growth of population in the Third World which have obsessed most population planners for the past thirty years.

The more developed countries are faced with the complex consequences of fluctuations in birthrate over the past sixty years and - at national and regional level - with shifts in the pattern and structure of mobility. Thus in Britain, following the pressure on services for the young arising from the post-war 'baby bulge' and the increase in birth-rate of the late-1950's and 1960's, we are now faced with the largest cohort of people reaching working age in recent times. Moreover, the proportion of people aged over 65 is greater than at any time in our history and the numbers of those over 75 will continue to grow into the next century, placing heavy demands on hospital and domiciliary services.

While the 1970's and '80's are likely to be seen, in retrospect, as a period of economic, social and demographic pressure, the 1990's may well be a more benign period, given that there is no dramatic upturn in fertility or any very rapid extension of life expectation. The sudden pressure on schools of the late 1960's and '70's, on housing, universities, jobs, some health services, social security and pensions, should be eased in the 1990's, though provision will have to be made for schooling of the children of the current large cohort of young adults and for increasing numbers of the very old (Ermisch, 1983). Changes in society, especially the increase of one-person

35

households and single-parent families, is creating a continuing demand for housing, but the demand for new jobs, running at some 200,000 per year in 1981-86, will probably slacken to around 36,000 per year by 1991-96. The disadvantage will be that there will then be fewer working people to support those on pensions, the cause of recent government concern over and impending review of the looming 'burden' on pension funds as the ratio of working-age population to the retired falls from 2.8-2.9 in the period from mid-1980's into the first decade of next century to possibly as low as 2.0 by 2031 (Ermisch, 1983).

Such changing needs are an inevitable consequence of demographic trends. Moreover, they differ from region to region and locality to locality as the following chapters will show. Yet changing demographic needs are too often looked at separately and regarded as conflicting rather than interlocking. It is surely not beyond the wit of planners and architects to design schools for future use as clinics or community centres; or to provide flexible housing systems, adaptable to smaller families of the four generations for which advanced societies must provide; or to seek to use additional labour - our 'ultimate resource' - productively rather than let it go to waste. We have always had to 'plan for people' in the family and the community. We are able and should be willing to do so nationally and internationally, to have a shared concern for the future of mankind.

REFERENCES

Benjamin, B. (1984) 'Demographic trends in the U.K.: social and economic implications'. Liverpool Papers in Human Geography. Working Paper No. 16, Department of Geography, University of Liverpool, Liverpool

Berelson, B. (1978) 'Prospects and programs for fertility reduction. What? Where?', Population and Development Review, 4, 579-616

Brandt, W. (1980) North-South: a programme for survival , Report of the Independent Commission on international development issues, Pan Books, London

Brown, P., and S.S. Ferguson (1982)'Schools and population changes in Liverpool', in W.T.S. Gould and A.G. Hodgkiss (eds), The resources of Merseyside, Liverpool University Press, Liverpool

Clark, C. (1967) Population growth and land use, Macmillan, London

Craig, J. (1983) 'The growth of the elderly population', Population Trends, 32, 28-33

Ehrlich, P.R. (1968) The population bomb, Ballantine Books, New York

Ehrlich, P.R., and Anne H. Ehrlich (1970) Population, resources, environment: issues in human ecology, W. H. Freeman and Co., San Francisco

Ermish, J. (1983) The political economy of demographic change, Heinemann (for the Policy Studies Institute), London.

Eversley, D. (1979) Population decline in Europe, Arnold, London

Forrester, J.W. (1971) World dynamics, Wright-Allen Press, Cambridge, Mass.

Frejka, T. (1973) The future of population growth. Alternative paths to equilibrium, John Wiley and Sons, New York

Frejka, T. (1981) 'Long-term prospects for world population growth', Population and Development Review, 7, 489-511

Galbraith, J.K. (1958) The affluent society, Houghton-Miflin, Boston

Girard, A. (1983) 'Les ages de la vie', Population, 38, 465-77

Hersch, L. (1954) Quoted in IUSSP statement 'Background document E/CONF76/NGO' to the U.N. Conference on Population, 1984, International Union for the Scientific Study of Population, Liege

House Of Commons (1971) 'Population of the U.K.', First Report of the Select Committee on Science and Technology, HMSO, London

Howe, G.M., and J. A. Loraine (eds.) (1974) Environmental medicine, Heinemann, London

Institute of Employment Research (1983) Review of the Economy and Employment, University of Warwick, Warwick

Jones, H.R. (1981) A Population Geography, Harper and Row, London

Learmonth, A.T.A. (1978) Patterns of disease and hunger, David and Charles, Newton Abbott

McNicoll, G. (1984) 'Consequences of rapid population growth: an overview and assessment', Population and Development Review 10, 177-240

Meadows, Donella H., D.L.Meadows, J. Randers and W. W. Behrens III (1972) The limits to growth. A report for the Club of Rome, Potomac Associates Inc., Earth Island Ltd., London

Midwinter, E. (1983) Ten million people, Centre for Policy on Ageing, London

Miro, Carmen, A., G. Gonzalez, & J. McCarthy, (1982) Social Science research for population policy design, IUSSP Papers No. 21, International Union for the Scientific Study of Population, Liege

Notestein, F. (1964) 'Population growth and economic development' Proceedings of the 20th Annual Session of the Ceylon Association for the Advancement of Science, reproduced in Population and Development Review, 9, 345-60

Ogawa, N. (1982) 'Economic implications of Japan's ageing population: a macro-demographic approach', International Labour Review, 121, 17-33

Ogden, P.E., and Huss, M.M. (1982) 'Demography and pronatalism in France in the nineteenth and twentieth centuries', Journal of Historical Geography, 8, 283-98

Okita, S., and T.Kuroda (1981) 'Japan's three transitions', Populi, 8, 44-54

Osborn, F. (1948) Our plundered planet, Faber and Faber, London

Osborn, F. (1954) The limits of the earth, Faber and Faber, London

Pearce, F. (1984) 'In defence of population growth', New Scientist, 9th August, 1984, 12-16

Prothero, R.M. (1965) Migrants and malaria, Longman, London

Sax, K. (1955) Standing room only, Beacon Press, Boston

Simon, J. (1981) The ultimate resource, Martin Robertson, Oxford

Simon, J.L., and H. Kahn (1984) The resourceful earth, Blackwell Oxford

Tabah, L. (1979) 'A deeper understanding since Bucharest', People, 6, 5-7

The Times, August 12th, 1983, 'Places in society for young and old'.

Vogt, W. (1949) Road to survival, Gollancz, London

Wander, Hilde (1978) Zero population growth now: the lessons from Europe, Academic Press, London

Warnes, A.M. (1981) 'Towards a geographical contribution to gerontology', Progress in Human Geography, 5, 319-41

Warnes, A.M. (ed.) (1982) Geographical perspectives on the elderly, John Wiley and Sons, London

Warnes, A.M., and C.M. Law (1984) 'The elderly population of Great Britain: locational trends and policy implications', Transactions Institute of British Geographers, New Series 2, 37-59

White, P. (1984) 'International migration and the city', Chapter 5 of The West European city: a social geography, Longman, London

World Bank (1984) World Development Report, 1984, Washington D.C.

Chapter Two

LABOUR FORCE AND EMPLOYMENT IN WESTERN EUROPE

John Salt

Many problems face the people of the affluent countries of the developed world, but the problem which puts their apparently privileged position into sharpest focus is the future of work. Unemployment, at a post-war high throughout the developed world, shows considerable national variations: in March, 1984, rates varied from 19.4 per cent in Spain and 16.9 per cent in Eire to 3.2 per cent in Sweden and 2.9 per cent in Japan. Prolonged recession has reduced demand; a new international division of labour favours employment growth in the newly industrialized countries; the full job impact of new technology is awaited with apprehension. Yet demographic trends dictate that the number of people of working age will continue to increase for some time in many countries, including the UK, fuelling demand for work. Meanwhile more women, especially married women, have sought an income-earning activity. However, the link between total population change and labour force change is not entirely clear cut. In this chapter the nature of that link is explored through a discussion of the salient aspects of people as producers in advanced industrial economies.

In terms of total human resources 'production' may be regarded in a narrow sense as participation in some form of gainful employment, or, much more broadly, to include people's productive activities in the home, the voluntary sector, leisure and, through education and training, in future welfare-creating capacity (Ermisch and Joshi, 1984). While there are good grounds for thinking of future human activity in these broader terms, the narrower, traditional role of people as a labour supply for paid work will be the primary focus here. In spatial terms the view presented is largely European, with examples from the EEC and especially the UK, though the last part of the chapter invokes a wider geographical canvas.

THE LABOUR MARKET SYSTEM

The productive role of people may be regarded as part of a labour market system in which supply and demand interact through

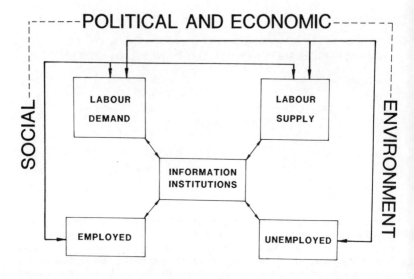

Fig. 2.1 The macro–environment of the labour market

institutions governing information flows resulting in one part of the labour force which is in employment and another which is unemployed, the whole operating in a macro-environment set by social, political and economic conditions (Figure 2.1). The system operates at national, regional and local levels.

The factors affecting labour demand include the range of industries and occupations available, and whether trends are towards concentration or diversification. While some local labour markets are still highly specialised the tendency now is for greater industrial mix. One effect of regional policy in Britain, however, has been a trend towards greater occupational polarisation, with the assisted areas having disproportionately more of the routine, less skilled occupations, while higher level expertise is concentrated elsewhere (Massey, 1979). Demand may also be characterised by the regularity and flexibility of work on offer. Certain sectors of the economy, such as shipbuilding, construction and dock-work, have traditionally been associated with 'hire and fire' methods of work organization in response to 'feast and famine' production needs. Furthermore, the recruitment policies operated by firms may also be critical in shaping demand: some firms are choosy in recruitment, refusing to take on older workers, people of particular ethnic groups, or those from occupations and industries regarded as militant or unstable. Of considerable and growing importance within large organizations are internal labour markets, in which firms recruit at the bottom and fill vacancies by internal promotion and placing. In Britain this practice has assumed major dimensions (Salt, 1984). Trade union attitudes also affect recruitment through restrictive practices, closed shops, and general effects on wages and conditions of work. These may result in uneconomic levels of staffing or control of entry. Local labour demand may also be affected by the location, accessibility of places of work and in the possibilities for increasing jobs on site by some form of building expansion or reorganization. Old and cramped sites might lead to closure and the transfer of jobs elsewhere. In the City of London prime sites now depend not only on location but also on whether the building is wired for modern information technology.

Labour supply has two principal components: one quantitative, the other qualitative. The total quantity of labour available depends upon both the supply of workers and the hours they are willing to work. The determinants of worker supply are natural change of population and migration, each of which can increase or reduce the size of the population of working age. The supply of hours worked by the available workforce depends upon the participation rate, itself a reflection of willingness to enter the workforce, and of leisure preference once entry has occurred, i.e. the actual amount of time spent at work. The participation rate is crucial, for it identifies the proportion of those of working age actually in the labour force: these, the economically active, consist of those actually working or looking for work. An active person may be self-employed, an unpaid family worker (though contributing to overall family income, especially in agriculture), an employee holding a job, or an unemployed person seeking a job. Hence, while the population of working age constitutes the potential workforce, which can only be increased in the short term by migration, the number of active persons is determined by such factors as the structure of labour demand, social standards and individual aspirations.

Labour quality, normally expressed in terms of education and skill, has tended to increase. Matthews et al. (1982) suggested that over the period 1857-1973 improvements in labour quality were six times as important as quantity, expressed in simple growth of man-hours, in increasing total labour input in Britain. Better education also seems to enhance the benefits of industrial training (Psacharopoulos and Layard, 1979). Routh (1980) showed a tendency in the UK, 1911 71, for the numerically less important unskilled to increase relative to skilled and semi-skilled manual workers, though manual workers as a whole fell by 20 percentage points as a proportion of the total labour force. Recent decades have seen more polarisation, and in the 1980's there is a clear trend, for both males and females, for those in younger age groups in any given socio-economic group to be better qualified (Department of Employment, 1983). Females are more likely to move from manual to clerical work, males into professional, managerial, supervisory and administrative occupations.

Supply and demand are brought together by both informal

means -word of mouth, personal recommendation, ad hoc advertising on employers' notice boards - and, more formally, through public and private recruitment agencies, careers departments and specialised journals. Skilled people generally use formal channels of information, often covering wide geographical areas. The geographical migration of labour, therefore, reflects to a considerable degree the information fields used by employers and potential workers. The information institutions of the labour market are complemented by a host of legal or customary practices which affect contracts and conditions of work, but whose effect is generally not geographically variable.

Each part of the labour market system, both those in and those out of work, has its own industrial, occupational and personal composition, varying in scale from place to place. Much attention is given to rates of unemployment, as indicative of local economic vitality, but the scale and nature of employment and unemployment have both positive and negative feedback effects on demand and supply, and can also influence interaction between local labour markets, for example migration and multiplier effects.

Hence, in an advanced industrial economy the labour supply is part of a strongly interacting system, but one in which changes in population size and composition have important consequences for employment.

STRUCTURE AND DEVELOPMENT OF THE WESTERN EUROPEAN POPULATION

Throughout most of Western Europe fluctuations in population growth in the early postwar period have been succeeded in recent years by a marked slowdown which seems likely to persist for some time (Commission of the EEC, 1984). In the EEC, an average annual population growth of 0.8 per cent in the 1960's was halved during the 1970's, and estimates suggest annual growth at a little more than 0.1 per cent during the 1980's; indeed in some years some countries have experienced more deaths than births. In the longer term there is likely to be a fall in entry into the workforce. Not all countries are equally affected: thus in the 1970's Ireland and Greece had increased rates of population growth, while West Germany, Belgium and the UK had only marginal gains. National figures mask regional variations. During the 1960's some two-thirds of the regions of the EEC recorded an annual population growth of between 0.2 and 1.4 per cent, falling to 0 per cent to 0.8 per cent during the 1970's. The underlying deceleration in regional population growth was general, apart from such peripheral areas as Greece, Ireland and North-east and Southern Italy.

The decline in growth rates has been due to lower birth rates and, in most cases, stable or falling immigration. Migration has been the principal component in regional population change (Table 2.1), with net outward movements from large metropolitan regions in the more industrialised countries and growth in some peripheral areas as, for example, in the resurgence of some of the remoter rural areas of the UK (See Chapter 4). From the mid-1970's, however, there has been a reaffirmation of the 'drift south' phenomenon, a return to net in-migration in South-East England, and even some slowing down in the rate of population decline of London (Champion, 1983).

Table 2.1 : Regional developments in total population, natural increase and migration, 1970-79 (annual average change as a percentage of total population) (1)

	Regional maxima			Regional minima			Regional dispersion (2)			National averages		
	Contribution of			Contribution of			Contribution of			Contribution of		
	Total pop.	Natural increase	Migra- tion	Total pop.	Natural increase	Migra- tion	Total pop.	Natural increase	Migra- tion	Total pop.	Natural increase	Migra- tion
EUROPE(3)	1.5	0.4	1.1	-0.5	-0.1	-0.4	0.5	0.4	0.5	0.4	0.3	0.1
Germany	2.5	-0.1	2.6	-1.1	-1.0	-0.1	0.7	0.2	0.7	0.2	-0.1	0.3
France	1.4	0.2	1.2	-0.1	-0.3	0.2	0.3	0.3	0.4	0.6	0.5	0.1
Italy	1.1	0.8	0.4	0.1	-0.2	0.3	0.3	0.4	0.3	0.7	0.6	0.1
Netherlands	1.5	0.8	0.8	0.3	0.4	-0.2	0.5	0.2	0.4	0.8	0.6	0.2
Belgium	1.0	0.8	0.2	0.1	-0.1	-0.0	0.2	0.2	0.1	0.2	0.1	0.1
Luxembourg	-	-	-	-	-	-	-	-	-	0.8	-0.1	0.8
United Kingdom	1.3	0.2	1.0	-0.2	0.1	0.3	0.3	0.1	0.3	0.1	0.2	-0.1
Ireland	-	-	-	-	-	-	-	-	-	1.5	1.1	0.4
Denmark	0.5	0.2	0.4	0.0	0.2	-0.2	0.2	0.1	0.2	0.5	0.4	0.1

(1) Numbers in corresponding columns add up to the growth rate of population, differences are the result of rounding.
(2) Standard deviation weighted by the regional share in total population.
(3) Max. and Min. for the Community = average of 10 regions with highest or lowest rates of population change. Max. and min. for natural increase and migration refer to the same regions as those for total population.

Source : EUROSTAT - Demographic Statistics and Regional Statistics, reproduced in Commission of the EEC (1984)

International migration

One of the major features of the geography of Europe since 1945 has been the tidal flow of international migrants in search of work. These economic migrations reached a climax around 1970, since which date governments have been trying to resolve the consequences of past trends and to devise new policies towards labour migration.

Before World War II migration flows within and from Europe were often of oppressed peoples seeking a more favourable political climate. The war itself involved something like 25 million migrations of one sort or another, with a great sorting out of the ethnic map of Europe at the end of the war. Contemporaneous with this immediate post-war phase was the beginning of the labour migration that was later to draw into the industrial areas vast numbers of less skilled workers from the Mediterranean, producing a pattern of large-scale movement over long distances from a diversity of supply countries: hence, by 1973 France and West Germany each had about $2\frac{1}{2}$ million foreign workers, Switzerland 600,000, Belgium and Sweden each 200,000, The Netherlands 80,000 and Luxembourg 33,000 (Salt 1976).

After 1973 worker immigration rates fell dramatically, for a while producing net outflows. However, although there were general bans on recruitment, not only did some new workers continue to arrive, but there were massive inflows from the families of earlier migrants. Thus, despite eight years of low worker recruitment, stocks of foreign workers have remained remarkably firm. But these represent only a proportion of the total immigrant population resident in the industrial countries, and total immigration has remained high, with wives and children entering in very large numbers to join husbands with residents' permits. The inflow has exceeded departure in most countries of immigration (OECD, 1983). The spread of deep recession has produced inevitable conflict for jobs between native and immigrant populations, while governments face enormous tasks in accommodating and integrating alien populations and their children.

Family reunion has created a time-bomb that is ticking away rapidly. In France there were 963,164 children of foreign extraction under the age of 16 in 1981; in West Germany the figure was 1,165,648, and in Sweden there were 73,000 foreign-born aged 0-17 and a further 81,000 second generation immigrant children of the same age in 1981. Between September, 1974, and September, 1981, the numbers of Turkish children under 16 in West Germany rose by 145 per cent to 555,266 (47.6 per cent of all foreign under 16s); in the Netherlands in 1981, 14,500 children of foreign nationality were born, 8,500 of whom were of Turkish or Moroccan parents (OECD, 1983). Such foreign children are generally less well educated, have higher failure rates and are more likely to need special education than are native-born children. In France the Ministry of Education has set up 'priority education zones' in areas where large numbers of immigrant families have settled (OECD, 1983). In West Germany nearly 50 per cent of foreign children leave school without the post-primary education certificate which is important in getting a place on a formal training scheme. Hence large numbers of young people, many of them less well educated than the host population of the same age groups, are released onto a limited job market, further swelling the high unemployment rates of the immigrants and fuelling the resentment felt by those who are seen as 'second-class citizens'.

Population of working age

In the changing structure of the population of all post-industrial countries there are more elderly, fewer children and, for the moment, an increase in the population of working age (See Chapter 4). In the EEC working-age population rose from 63.25 per cent to 64.5 per cent of the total during the 1970's, and though national and regional figures do not deviate greatly from the community average, some regional variations continue to exist, ranging in 1980 from 60 per cent to 67.5 per cent. The population of working age, which largely determines the potential labour force, grew more slowly during the 1970's than in the 1960's, and also more slowly than the total population, but there was a somewhat wider range of regional trends, reflecting the age-selective nature of migration (Table 2.2). The continuing growth of the working age population - and therefore of the potential labour force, and its associated regional variations - has significant implications for the labour supply in Western Europe.

Table 2.2 : Regional growth of total population and population of working age (annual average percentage change)

| | Total population | | | | | | | | Population of working age (15 to 64) | | | |
| | 1960/1970 | | | | 1970/1980 | | | | 1970/1979 | | | |
	max.	Regional min.	disp. (1)	National average	max.	Regional min.	disp. (1)	National average	max.	Regional min.	disp. (1)	National average
EUROPE(2)	2.1	-0.2	0.6	0.8	1.4	-0.4	0.4	0.4	1.8	-0.2	0.6	0.6
Germany(3)	3.4	-0.4	0.7	0.9	0.9	-1.1	0.4	0.2	1.1	-1.4	0.9	0.5
France	2.3	0.0	0.5	1.1	1.3	-0.0	0.3	0.6	1.5	-0.4	0.4	0.7
Italy	1.8	-1.1	0.6	0.7	1.0	-0.0	0.3	0.6	1.4	-0.2	0.4	0.6
Netherlands	1.9	0.8	0.4	1.3	1.4	2.6	0.5	0.8	2.1	0.7	0.6	1.4
Belgium	1.5	-0.0	0.4	0.6	0.9	-0.1	0.3	0.2	1.9	0.2	0.4	0.6
Luxembourg	-	-	-	0.8	-	-	-	0.7	-	-	-	1.2
United Kingdom	1.2	0.1	0.3	0.6	1.2	-0.2	0.3	0.1	1.6	-0.0	0.4	0.2
Ireland	-	-	-	0.4	-	-	-	1.4	-	-	-	1.8
Denmark	0.9	0.3	0.2	0.7	0.7	-0.1	0.3	0.4	0.7	-0.2	0.5	0.4
Greece(4)	-	-	-	0.5	1.6	0.3	0.6	1.0	-	-	-	0.8

(1) Standard deviation weighted by regional shares in total population or population of working age.
(2) Max. and min = average of 10 regions with highest or lowest rates.
(3) Figures not fully comparable as between 60s and 70s due to changes in regional boundaries.
(4) 1961/1971 and 1971/1981 respectively.

Source : EUROSTAT - Demographic Statistics and Regional Statistics, reproduced in Commission of the EEC (1984)

Labour force change

The population of working age is a direct demographic input into the overall size of the labour force. Between 1970 and 1982 the EEC labour force as a whole grew by 0.5 per cent p.a., with some significant regional variations, ranging during 1970-79 from a 7 per cent decline in the worst ten regions, all in West Germany, to a 17 per cent increase in the ten with the highest growth, widely distributed throughout the community (Figure 2.2) (Commission of the EEC, 1984). Declining male and increasing female participation rates have been generally evident for the 1970's for the EEC as a whole, though individual countries exhibited different trends: West Germany's rate was initially above the EEC average, but fell as the decade progressed, perhaps reflecting the influx of immigrants' dependents; in contrast, Denmark and the UK, already with the highest participation rates in 1970, experienced further increases; Ireland and the Netherlands were below average in 1970, declined for a few years, then levelled off. Other EEC members had moderate

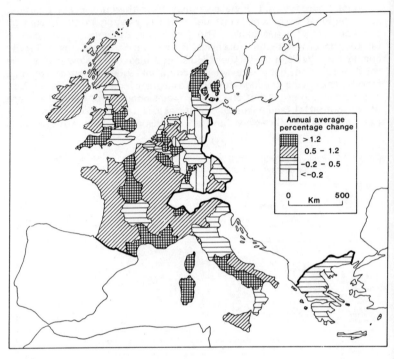

Fig. 2.2   E.E.C. : labour force growth, 1970–79

Table 2.3   Regional participation rates, 1970 and 1979
(Labour force as a percentage of population of working age 15 to 64)

	1970				1979			
	max.	Regional min.	dispersion (1)	National average	max.	Regional min.	dispersion (1)	National average
EUROPE(2)	75.1	53.4	6.9	66.4	76.3	51.8	7.2	66.3
Germany	82.6	61.7	5.1	69.2	84.3	59.6	5.3	65.5
France	75.0	56.6	5.3	66.4	76.5	60.7	5.3	67.8
Italy	65.9	51.6	4.2	59.1	69.8	52.7	4.4	60.9
Netherlands	62.1	51.1	3.4	57.9	58.5	47.6	3.5	53.8
Belgium	69.7	52.4	5.2	62.1	68.4	58.7	3.3	64.5
Luxembourg	-	-	-	63.2	-	-	-	64.5
United Kingdom	76.9	65.0	4.1	72.6	77.1	68.3	2.7	74.2
Ireland	-	-	-	65.4	-	-	-	62.4
Denmark	-	-	-	72.7	-	-	-	78.7
Greece (3)	-	-	-	-	-	-	-	(60.8)

(1) Standard deviation weighted by the regional share in population of working age.
(2) Max. and min. for the Community = average of 10 regions with highest or lowest participation rates.
(3) OECD estimate for labour force.

Source : EUROSTAT - demographic and regional statistics, regional accounts and statistics on registered unemployed, reproduced in Commission of the EEC (1984)

46

increases (Commission of the EEC, 1984).

Regional variations in these total participation rates remained sharp. By 1979 the average for the ten regions with the lowest rates was only 53 per cent, due to low female participation rates, in the Netherlands and parts of Southern Italy, compared with 76 per cent for the ten highest, in parts of Denmark, the UK and West Germany (Table 2.3). There was no noticeable trend towards greater regional convergence in the 1970's as a whole. However, Labour Force Survey data for 1975-81 do indicate some reduction in regional dispersion, suggesting that one effect of the recession has been to encourage greater homogeneity in regional participation rates.

Any assessment of the respective contributions of demographic and participation factors has to take account of geographical scale. The growth of the working-age population in the EEC as a whole has determined labour supply, since overall participation rate during the 1970's remained constant. Nationally the significance of components varied: participation rates added to the labour supply in France, Belgium, Italy, Luxembourg, UK and Denmark, resulting in increased pressure on a labour market already feeling the demographic pinch; in other EEC countries demographic factors were more important. At the regional level there seems to be no clear-cut general relationship between labour supply and participation rate: in parts of the UK and Belgium demographic factors and participation rates moved together to increase labour supply; in France both components worked together to reduce regional differences in labour force growth; while in most regions of West Germany, Italy and the Netherlands there was no common pattern - though the demographic component was stronger in Southern Italy.

Labour market imbalances
To meet the inexorable rise of the labour force of Western Europe new jobs will be needed simply to cater for new entrants if participation rates are not to fall. Yet marked imbalances between supply and demand already exist (Figure 2.3). During the 1970's rising unemployment and declining employment growth in the EEC (Table 2.4) have been accompanied by sectoral shift as agriculture has universally declined and manufacturing has generally done so, countered only by growth in service employment. Hence employment growth has fallen from 0.3 per cent p.a. (1970-73) to 0.1 per cent p.a. (1973-79), and unemployment has risen rapidly from 2.5 per cent in 1973, 8 per cent in 1981, to 10.5 per cent (12 million) in 1983 (Figure 2.4). There have been even greater regional disparities : unemployment in the least affected regions of the Community increased in 1973-82 by 4.5 percentage points compared with 9.5 in the worst affected. Regions with the highest unemployment rates also lagged in per capita GDP and growth in productivity as employment failed to keep pace with growth in the labour force (Table 2.5), especially for young people (Figure 2.5), and should these rates persist could pose severe social and political problems.

How likely is it that these imbalances will continue? Some

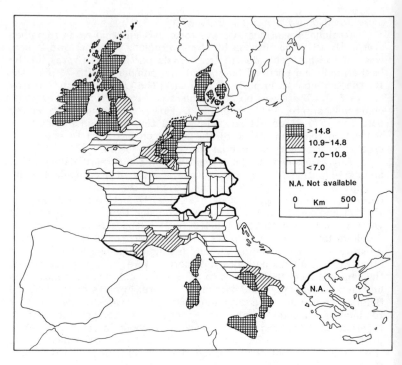

Fig. 2.3   E.E.C. : total unemployment rates, 1983

Table 2.4 : Regional developments in employment
(annual average change)

	1970/1979				1970/1973				1973/1979			
	max.	Regional min.	disp. (1)	National average	max.	Regional min.	disp. (1)	National average	max.	Regional min	disp. (1)	National average
EUROPE(2)	1.4	-1.1	0.7	0.1	2.8	-1.5	1.0	0.3	1.4	-1.4	0.8	0.1
Germany	(1.4)	(-1.8)	(0.8)	-0.5	(6.1)	(-2.9)	(1.6)	0.1	(1.3)	(-2.6)	(0.7)	-0.7
France	1.0	-0.1	0.2	0.4	1.5	-0.2	0.4	0.7	0.9	-0.3	0.3	0.3
Italy	1.4	-0.1	0.3	0.5	1.4	1.5	0.6	-0.1	1.5	-0.1	0.3	0.8
Netherlands	1.2	-0.8	0.6	0.2	1.8	-1.5	1.1	-0.1	0.9	-1.0	0.4	0.3
Belgium	2.6	-0.4	0.8	0.3	3.8	-0.3	1.0	0.7	2.0	-0.7	0.7	0.1
Luxembourg	-	-	-	1.4	-	-	-	2.5	-	-	-	0.8
United Kingdom	1.6	-0.4	0.6	0.2	1.7	-0.1	0.4	0.3	1.8	-0.6	0.7	0.1
Ireland	-	-	-	0.9	-	-	-	0.1	-	-	-	1.3
Denmark	-	-	-	0.8	-	-	-	1.3	-	-	-	0.6
Greece	-	-	-	0.4	-	-	-	0.0	-	-	-	0.7

(1)   Standard deviation weighted by the regional share in total employment.
(2)   Max. and min. for the Community = average of 10 regions with highest or lowest rates of employment change.

Source : EUROSTAT - Regional Accounts, reproduced in Commission of the EEC (1984)

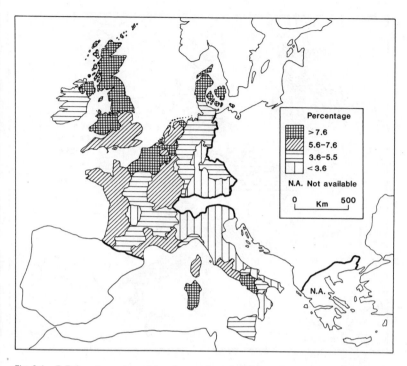

Fig. 2.4   E.E.C. : change in registered unemployment rates, 1971–83

Table 2.5 : Regional developments in registered unemployment, employment and the labour
force, 1970–79
(Total change as a percentage of the labour force) (1)

	Regional maxima			Regional minima			Regional Dispersion (2)			National averages		
	Unempl.	Empl.	Labour Force	Unempl.	Empl.	Labour Force	Unempl.	Empl.	Labour Force	Unempl.	Empl.	Labour Force
EUROPE(3)	8.9	5.5	14.4	1.0	0.6	1.6	2.1	6.0	6.8	3.7	1.3	5.1
Germany	4.6	2.3	2.4	1.3	8.0	-6.8	0.8	6.8	6.9	2.7	3.9	-1.2
France	7.5	4.6	12.1	3.3	0.4	3.7	1.0	2.3	2.5	5.2	3.7	8.9
Italy	12.2	4.7	16.9	0.2	0.7	0.5	3.3	2.9	5.0	3.7	4.1	7.8
Netherlands	7.4	0.3	7.7	2.1	-1.6	0.5	1.4	5.2	5.8	3.4	1.5	4.9
Belgium	13.0	25.2	38.3	5.1	20.3	25.4	1.6	7.6	8.6	7.2	2.7	9.9
Luxembourg	–	–	–	–	–	–	–	–	–	0.7	13.0	13.7
United Kingdom	5.0	5.0	10.0	1.9	-1.7	0.2	1.0	5.4	5.7	3.1	1.6	4.7
Ireland	–	–	–	–	–	–	–	–	–	2.8	8.3	11.0
Denmark	–	–	–	–	–	–	–	–	–	4.9	7.5	12.4

(1) Numbers in corresponding columns add up to the growth in unemployment, differences are the result of rounding
(2) Standard deviation weighted by the regional share in the Labour force.
(3) Max. and min. for the Community = average of 10 regions with highest or lowest rates of unemployment change.
    Employment and Labour force max. and min. refer to the same regions as those for unemployment.

Source : EUROSTAT   Regional Statistics, reproduced in Commission of the EEC (1984)

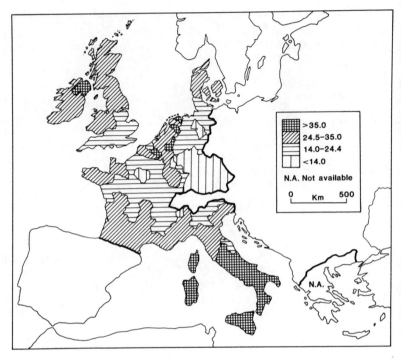

Fig. 2.5 E.E.C. : youth unemployment rates, 1983

answers are provided by the <u>LABEUR</u> study carried out for the Commission of the EEC by the Netherlands Economic Institute which projected regional labour market imbalances for 1985 and 1990 (Commission of the EEC, 1984). The results suggest that given constant (1981) participation rates the EEC labour force will rise by 700,000 per annum, 1980-85, and by 450,000 per annum, 1985-90, the impact varying between member states. Pressure is likely to be strongest in Ireland, Northern Ireland, Southern Italy, most Dutch and some French and West German regions. These have 15 per cent of the EEC's present working population, but account for 30 per cent of the projected total labour force increase in the EEC resulting from demographic trends.

These projections imply increasing job deficits in the EEC as a whole, and regional disparities in them will be substantially higher at the end of the 1980's than they were at the start of the decade: the jobs situation will get worse. Other projections under a range of supply and demand side assumptions all point in the same direction: job deficits well above the Community average in Ireland, Northern

Ireland, Southern Italy, in some parts of Greece and Belgium and in the Netherlands, and improvements in only a few regions of West Germany, Northern Italy and Southern France. If this is to be avoided massive increases in jobs are needed; an estimated 3.5 million in the EEC between 1984 and 1990 (or 600,000 p.a.) merely to prevent unemployment rising above its 1983 level. These figures, a direct consequence of the demographic pressure on labour supply, assume constant (1981) participation rate and zero international migration. Moreover, increases will need to be differentially spread if regional unemployment levels are to be reduced. About a third will be needed in those regions (listed above) which at present contain only 15 per cent of the EEC's working age population. If the assumption on participation rates are changed - for example, that rates for females in those regions where they are currently low will reach the current EEC average - then the additional jobs needed to avoid further labour market imbalances will be 1 million per annum. Unless these jobs are created in the right places regional unemployment disparities related to labour market disequilibria will widen since it is unlikely that migration could offset the differences.

LABOUR FORCE TRENDS IN GREAT BRITAIN

National trends and outlook
During the 1970's the UK labour force grew, on average, by 130,000 p.a. (0.5 per cent), but a surge occurred in 1976-7 with a growth of 401,000 reflecting the change in school leaving age, followed by a check during 1977-9 (Department of Employment, 1984a). In the later 1970's and early 1980's movements in the labour force have been dominated by two opposing tendencies: a rapid increase in the population of working age and a fall particularly in male participation rates, the latter brought about by early retirements and a falling tendency for men to work after retirement age. The rise in the female participation rate has ended and between 1977 and 1981 the female labour force grew more slowly (Table 2.6).

The immigration experience for the postwar UK has been rather different from other Western European countries. During the 30 years, 1946-76, in only one five-year period (1956-61) did the UK show new migration gains. Davis (1982) attributes this to three developments: active recruitment of West Indians during the 1950's; the stabilization of immigration after 1962 due to legislation restricting inflows and a return to net emigration; and the absence of the guest worker phenomenon in the UK. To these might be added a generally worse performance by the UK economy compared with the rest of Western Europe, and Peach (1982) has demonstrated the sensitivity of immigration to rising employment and low economic growth.

The prognosis for British labour force growth gives cause for concern in the planning for jobs. Demographic pressure will continue during the 1980's, with a rise of one million in the population of

Table 2.6 : Great Britain : components of change in the civilian labour force   (000)

	Popul-ation effect	1971-77 Activity rate effect	Change in labour force	Popul-ation effect	1977-81 Activity rate effect	Change in labour force	Popul-ation effect	1981-88 Activity rate effect	Change in labour force	Popul-ation effect	1988-91 Activity rate effect	Change in labour force
Total civilian labour force of which	292.2	694.8	987.0	576.2	-281.2	195.0	857.4	-141.4	716.0	79.3	-65.3	14.0
Male	246.3	-238.3	8.0	317.8	-246.8	71.0	523.9	-283.9	240.0	72.8	-104.8	-32.0
Female	45.9	933.1	979.0	258.4	-34.4	224.0	333.5	142.5	476.0	6.5	39.5	46.0

1. The change in the labour force that would have occurred if the activity rate in each age group had remained over the period at its value in the initial year.
2. The residual change - total change less the change due to the population effect.

Source : Department of Employment (1984a)

working age expected between 1981 and 1988. The extent to which such pressure affects the size of the labour force will depend on participation rates. The most recent projections assume that the level of unemployment will stay around 3.1 million. On the basis of this the British workforce can be expected to grow by 720,000 between 1981 and 1986, males by 240,000, females by 480,000, but a change of 100,000 in the unemployed would lead to a change in the labour force of 35-40,000 in the opposite direction. After 1988 the population of working age will cease to grow and the labour force is projected to be stable into the early 1990's. Since a continuing unemployment level of 3.1 million now looks to be optimistic, participation rates may well be lower because of a 'discouraged worker' effect, and the labour force growth will be below the level forecast.

It is worth looking in more detail at demographic and participation rate trends because their respective influences are important in labour market planning. Low birth rates during World War I meant that fewer men have reached retirement age (65) in recent years, but the baby boom following that war will mean a flurry of men leaving the labour force around 1985, followed by a gradual decline, reflecting 1920's birth rates (there is a similar pattern for women, but five years earlier because of their earlier retirement age). The numbers entering the working age population are affected by the very high birth rates of the 1960's, augmented by the children of immigrants who entered in the late 1950's and early 1960's. Though numbers of school leavers peaked in 1980-1, the numbers of both men and women reaching working age will continue to exceed exits until the late 1980's, when the situation will become fairly stable until the end of the century. Thus in the absence of any change in participation rates, population growth alone will increase the labour force by half a million males and a third of a million females between 1981 and 1988.

Male participation rates, which have generally declined in the past decade, have been nibbled at from both ends as a result of prolonged education and earlier retirement. During 1979-81 participation rates for older males, especially aged 60-64, fell steeply, though rates for 20-54 year olds held up remarkably well. About one-third of the decline amongst those in the pre-retirement group can be accounted for by the government's Job Release Scheme, but other major factors are shake-outs and early retirement under occupational pension schemes.

Female participation rates, especially among married women, increased markedly after World War II, especially between 1971 and 1977 when the rise was nearly seven percentage points. An important reason for this is the 'cohort effect' reflecting the stronger attachment to the labour force of younger women. Since 1977, however, female participation rates seem to have levelled off, partly because of few job opportunities, though Joshi et al. (1984) suggest that increased fertility rates are a major factor.

Regional trends and outlook
Actual and projected change in regional labour participation rates for selected regions of Great Britain, 1971-91, based on similar assumptions of unemployment and early retirement to those at national level, show that for both sexes there is expected a convergence of regional experience, though patterns are not uniform (Figure 2.6) (Department of Employment 1984b). For example, trends for males are down in the West Midlands but up in East Anglia and the South-West. Female rates show less variability in trend, though generally the direction is one of convergence. The consequence for the regional labour force is also variable: although the national labour force is expected to grow by 2.8 per cent during the 1980's, those of the North and North-West regions are projected to fall while substantial growth is expected in East Anglia, the South-West and East Midlands.

While regional variations mainly reflect demographic conditions, trends in population and participation rate vary. In the North-West, for example, male participation rates are projected to fall more rapidly than in most other regions, leading to a falling male labour force despite rising population of working age (Table 2.7). In Scotland, a small fall in male participation rate together with a large increase in that for females will mitigate the effects of population increase well below the national average. Finally, though the population effect in the South-East is expected to be slightly below average, a constant male participation rate will ensure that growth in the region's labour force will be well above average.

In sum, for most of the 1980's all regions in Britain except the North and North-West are likely to have larger labour forces because demographic gains will offset reductions in participation. For women both demographic and participation rate effects are positive in all regions, so their labour will grow universally. By the end of the decade the regional pattern is likely to become more variable, with male labour forces in the more prosperous East Midlands, East

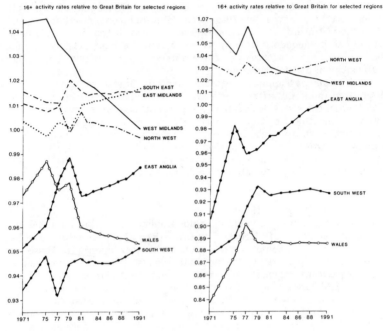

Fig. 2.6 Great Britain : 16+ activity rates by sex and selected regions

Anglia, South-East and South-West continuing to grow for demographic reasons, while those elsewhere decline. Female labour forces in all regions except the North, North-West and Scotland are projected to grow 1988-91, largely because of higher participation rates. Hence, at both national and regional levels during most of the 1980's we can expect upward demographic pressures to outweigh trends towards lower participation. The really significant fact, of course, is that at a time when demand for workers is hardly likely to increase, the number seeking jobs will continue to grow.

MIGRATION OF LABOUR

Recent and prospective changes in the labour supply component of the labour market system indicate the likely extent of imbalances. The study of Western European job markets at the present time

54

Table 2.7 Components of change in regional civilian labour
force expressed as percentage of regional
civilian labour force

	1981-88 (as percentage of 1981 civilian labour force)			1988-1991 (as percentage of 1988 civilian labour force)		
	Popul-ation effect[1]	Activ-ity rate effect[2]	Total change	Popul-ation effect[1]	Activ-ity rate effect[2]	Total change
Male						
North	-0.4	-1.6	-2.0	-1.1	-0.8	-1.9
Yorkshire and Humberside	+2.8	-1.3	+1.5	+0.1	-0.6	-0.4
East Midlands	+4.8	-1.7	+3.1	+0.9	-0.5	+0.4
East Anglia	+7.5	-1.7	+5.8	+2.7	-0.5	+2.1
South-East	+3.3	-1.3	+2.0	+0.7	-0.5	+0.2
South-West	+5.7	-1.6	+4.2	+1.7	-0.5	+1.3
West Midlands	+3.6	-2.3	+1.2	+0.2	0.9	-0.7
North-West	+1.4	-2.8	-1.3	-0.4	-0.9	-1.4
Wales	+3.4	-2.2	+1.2	+0.6	-0.9	-0.3
Scotland	+2.2	-0.8	+1.3	0.5	-0.4	-1.0
Great Britain	+3.4	-1.8	+1.5	+0.5	-0.7	-0.2
Female						
North	+0.3	+2.1	+2.4	-1.2	+0.7	-0.5
Yorkshire and Humberside	+3.0	+1.2	+4.1	-0.1	+0.5	+0.4
East Midlands	+5.6	+0.3	+5.8	+0.9	+0.4	+1.3
East Anglia	+9.4	+2.6	+11.7	+2.3	+0.8	+3.1
South-East	+2.9	+0.9	+3.8	-	+0.4	+0.5
South-West	+5.8	+2.6	+8.5	+0.8	+0.6	+0.5
West Midlands	+3.0	+1.5	+4.5	-0.3	+0.5	+0.2
North-West	+1.2	+1.3	+2.4	-0.8	+0.5	-0.3
Wales	+2.1	+2.1	+4.2	-0.2	+0.6	+0.4
Scotland	+1.4	+3.1	+4.6	-0.9	+0.5	-0.5
Great Britain	+3.2	+1.4	+4.5	+0.1	+0.4	+0.4

1. The change in the labour force that would have occurred if the activity of each
age group had remained over the period at its value in the initial year.
2. The residual change - total change less the change due to the population effect.

Source : Department of Employment (1984b)

reveals two basic structural problems, both of which imply the need for greater geographical mobility of the labour force. One is the increase in levels of national unemployment and the persistence of regional blackspots; the other stems from occupational changes resulting from the adoption of new technologies. Mismatches in the labour market result from time lags between employers seeking workers and workers seeking jobs, skill mismatches and those of location. The structural problem results especially from technological change, reflected in a reduction in the length of time over which particular types of job continue to exist, implying more frequent job changing, shifts in occupation and retraining. Such changes are likely to increase propensity to migrate. Technological changes also affect the locations of production and services: as enterprises are more footloose, decentralisation occurs and employment sites may become more dispersed. These trends require a higher degree of occupational and geographical mobility of the workforce if mismatches are not to increase.

Most western economies have experienced such problems in varying degrees, and each country has adopted measures designed in part to relocate labour geographically. The analysis of policies adopted by individual countries (Schnitzer, 1969; Klaasen and Drewe, 1973; Sundquist 1975; Johnson et al., 1980) shows a good deal of confusion about aims and direction, and also a general lack of commitment, perhaps because adoption of a migration policy might seem to indicate acceptance that all areas cannot have equal development. In view of the imbalances in the labour market and of the inability of conventional regional policies alone to reduce regional disparities, a more positive migration policy may be necessary. However, public policy for both quantitative and qualitative relocation of labour is overshadowed by the private migration policies adopted by virtually all large employers.

Government migration policy in the UK

The general approach of the British government - as with other western governments - has been to tackle local and regional imbalances in the labour market by a policy based on job creation in areas of high unemployment. The alternative philosophy of moving workers to the work has been criticized on the grounds that it may unleash cumulative forces of economic, social and political decline. The arguments have been frequently recorded (see, e.g. Dennison, 1939; Sant, 1975; Johnson et al., 1980). Economic arguments against workers moving to the work stress the possible inflationary effects of labour movements into areas of existing pressure on housing and other resources, and the further under-use of social capital and infrastructure in the origin regions. Social arguments invoke the disintegration of communities, a problem enhanced by selective out-migration. Political aspects have included the strategic disadvantages of concentrating industries in a few areas and the political attitudes associated with a brand of economic regionalism that is jealously concerned with maintaining the size of regional populations to maintain political influence. Such arguments are all open to challenge and the debate illustrates the lack of understanding of the role of migration in processes of regional growth and decline.

The work to the workers policy, adopted by successive British governments is concerned to maintain the status quo by steering jobs to the economically less fortunate areas of Britain thereby reducing unemployment and increasing their prosperity. Implicit in the policy has been the attempt to restrict out-migration and avoid the harmful social and economic effects assumed to follow selective out-migration from assisted areas and to reduce pressures on land and housing in the receiving areas, especially in Southern England. It is impossible to assess the impact of these policies. Estimates of numbers of jobs created vary: research suggests that up to the end of the 1970's a total of about half a million; but in recent years, economic depression has drastically reduced the numbers of jobs created to at best a few thousand per annum and at startlingly high cost, currently estimated as about £35,000 per job (Department of Trade and Industry, 1984a).

Paralleling regional economic policy aimed indirectly at influencing migration, a series of government schemes have been directly concerned with the movement of population by helping workers to move from areas of labour surplus to areas of labour shortage. Begun originally in 1926 as the Industrial Transference Scheme, and intended to help the unemployed move from depressed areas in the north and west to the more prosperous south and east, the policy continues, with modifications, to the present as the Employment Transfer Scheme (ETS). During the 1950's and 1960's only a few thousand were moved but in the 1970's a more active policy with higher levels of assistance increased participation (Johnson et al., 1980). The present main policy vehicle, the ETS and its associated Job Search Scheme (JSS), is designed to help unemployed people move from one part of the country to another by providing financial assistance to cover travel and removal costs, house buying and selling costs (up to a maximum of £1,150) and a transfer grant to cover settling-in costs (up to £1,350). Hence a family moving under the scheme could expect a maximum grant of around £3,000.

During the 1970's the ETS became a significant element in total migration (Table 2.8), but since the peak year of 1977-78 a steep fall reflects fewer available jobs and, perhaps more important, a general tightening-up of the rules governing the scheme since 1979 with a view to achieving greater cost-effectiveness. Assistance has always been restricted to unemployed people and those under threat of redundancy, though in the past certain rules were waived for people moving from assisted areas. With the general increase in unemployment and the reduction in public funds available, the rules now apply equally in all areas. Particularly significant in this respect is Rule 14 which states that "The employer must be able to show that he has tried and failed to attract suitable local unemployed people". More stringent application of this rule has markedly reduced the

57

possibilities for movement (even by bike!), largely explaining the fall in the proportion of ETS movers coming to London from 23 per cent in 1978-79 to 13 per cent in 1982-83.

Although there are no data on the types of labour moved, indications are that the scheme is now more concerned with encouraging particular skilled unemployed people to move to areas of skill shortage rather than seeking to direct unemployed people in general towards jobs. In performing that task cheaply (the total cost in 1982-83 of the ETS and its related JSS was £5.4 million; numbers helped under the ETS were 4,879, a cost of little more than £1,000 per person/job) moving workers to the work seems to be more cost effective than the reverse policy. Even so, the effectiveness of the ETS has been questioned on a number of grounds (Beaumont, 1976; Johnson et al., 1980; Parker 1975): in particular it has been suggested that such a scheme aids many who would have moved without ETS assistance: one study suggested 69 per cent (Beaumont, 1976), another only 42 per cent (Parker, 1975). A further problem is wastage, with 25 per cent in Beaumont's sample who failed to settle in the new area and returned home.

Table 2.8 : Number of settling-in grants paid, 1972-83

(Year ending March) ETS

Year	ETS	Year	ETS
1972-3	18557	1978-9	22897
1973-4	15237	1979-80	9785
1974-5	14333	1980-1	5668
1975-6	15701	1981-2	5637
1976-7	13436	1982-3	4879
1977-8	26539		

Source : Manpower Services Commission: private communication.

In the last few years a new policy initiative, the National Mobility Scheme (NMS), has been introduced by the Department of the Environment. Under this scheme local authorities and housing associations voluntarily place a small proportion (about 1 per cent) of their housing stock at the disposal of migrants thus helping to get around one of the main stumbling blocks to movement, the housing waiting list. In 1982-83 there were 3,438 moves between and a further 1,253 moves within regions. The pattern of movement suggests that the scheme is encouraging a general drift south. One-third of moves were for employment reasons and about three-quarters of migrants in the scheme moved from local authority housing and 93 per cent of them were re-housed at destinations by local authorities.

Currently, therefore, government migration policies operating through the agencies of the ETS and NMS are responsible for nearly

10,000 labour migrations per annum in Britain: when household members are included the numbers involved are some 30,000.

Private migration policies

These numbers of people moving under publicly developed migration policies are much smaller than the numbers who are transferred by employers. Little is known about the scale and extent of this form of labour migration though it is vastly more important than the attention so far paid to it would suggest: for example, a study ten years ago found that one-third of labour migrants to Chatham, High Wycombe, Huddersfield and Northampton who had been employed before moving did not change employer (Johnson, et al., 1974). Analysis by the author of a sample of 62 long distance movers handled by a network of estate agents, 1979-81, and for whom employer details were available, showed that 53 per cent worked for multi-location organizations before and after; omitting retirees the figure rose to 73 per cent. A survey in 1982 of 17 large removal firms, carried out by the author as part of a study of organizational labour migration, suggested that 65-75 per cent of moves beyond the local area were paid for by the employer, though not all of these will have been relocations since companies increasingly pay the removal expenses of recruits. More recently Gleave (1984), using Labour Force Survey data for Britain, has shown that 54 per cent of all inter-regional and 74 per cent of all inter-district (but also intra-regional) migration during 1974-75 was of people who did not change employer. Data for London from the 1979 and 1981 Labour Force Surveys show that of those in employment at both the time of the survey and one year before almost two-thirds of men and over half of women moving either to or from Greater London from other districts did not change employer. Use of these figures has to be guarded since many of those recorded may have moved locally across the GLC boundary. Nonetheless, the data are consistent with others in indicating that movements within the internal labour markets of large employers are now the principal type of labour migration in Britain.

Further confirmation of this comes from the author's recent findings that, despite recession, large employers continue to transfer staff (usually managerial and technical) to locations which necessitate a change of residence at surprisingly high rates. During the early 1980's internal transfers in 76 large organizations averaged 97 moves per organization per annum, ranging from 35 organizations with fewer than 25 moves per annum to 18 with over 100, of which 11 had over 200 and 3 over 500. Companies rarely transfer hourly-paid staff or clerical and lower paid technical staff, apart from married women or young females moving at their own request with husbands or parents : indeed in one bank the majority of its migrants were low grade female clerical staff. For those staff whose occupations put them at some risk of transfer annual mobility rates (transferees divided by the population at risk) are surprisingly high : eight out of 76 organizations had rates of 10 per cent or more, the highest being 24 per cent.

Organizations transfer staff for a number of reasons. A major one is rationalisation and transfer of redundant staff elsewhere; but the vast majority of movement occurs as a result of career development, though promotion does not necessarily occur: only 44 per cent of those employees for whom data were available (N = 5232) had a promotion associated with the relocation. The friction of migration is eased by the availability of relocation assistance packages, averaging about £7,000, which cover removal and rehousing costs, provide information on destination area conditions and generally ease the trauma of moving so that the company transferee has less worry than other migrants.

Since most people increasingly work for employers who operate more than one site the role of the internal labour market in redistributing labour is vital. The author's recent study of organizational labour migration shows that in the current recession internal labour markets have been strengthened as companies turn in upon themselves in recruitment: first, many organizations have increasingly followed a 'grow your own timber' policy; secondly, the investment in training and experience of existing staff has become something to be guarded, while morale is enhanced by keeping careers moving; thirdly, rationalisation ensures that resources are used to best advantage by matching staff with internal vacancies; finally, staff turnover is now more likely to lead initially to a review of where and how the work can be reabsorbed internally, leading to new posts and job structures without increasing staff, rather than to recruitment from outside. In consequence, jobs are now more likely to be filled internally than by outside recruitment.

With a few exceptions hourly paid staff are recruited and laid off locally, and there is no tradition of relocation: indeed some of those offered moves have preferred to be made redundant locally. Hence, the labour redistribution policies of employers largely leave out of account the lower paid and less skilled workers, so that an even greater polarization between a mobile elite and an immobile mass is occurring, adding to the limited ability of public migration policies to assist the lower paid.

THE FUTURE OF WORK

Looked at in traditional terms the view of people as producers presented in this chapter is depressing. Demographic pressure is being exerted on a labour force in which participation rates are higher than a generation ago, especially among married women. Marked regional disparities in ability to find work, reflecting variations in demand seem to be getting worse. Migration of workers does little to correct structural imbalances between demand and supply, and this chapter has indicated the weaknesses of traditional regional policy in the circumstances. Precisely at this juncture comes not the cavalry to the rescue but new technological hordes slashing jobs still further.

All the evidence predicts continuing and massive job losses: whether new processes and products will bring new jobs on a sufficient scale to replace them is problematical. Estimates of present (1500) and predicted for the late 1980's (5000) shortfalls of IT-trained personnel in Britain (Department of Trade and Industry, 1984b) are slight compared with current unemployment levels and prospective increases in the labour force. Indeed, total IT employment in Britain is only about 160,000, while the electronics industry as a whole, thought by many to represent the best hope for new jobs, reduced its employment between 1970 and 1980 by 7 per cent (while increasing output by 80 per cent) (Bell, 1984). The argument ultimately is less one of where and whether jobs will be lost but whether many jobs will be created elsewhere. If so, migration will become more important because job losses and job gains are unlikely to be coincident leading to geographical mismatches. If there are few new jobs, migration will still be important for the redistribution of skilled manpower within internal labour markets.

The biggest future problems are likely to be in the service and female employment sectors. Offices are generally undercapitalized, and have shown relatively low productivity increases. With high and rising labour costs the time is ripe for replacement of labour by electronic equipment: for example, the Central Policy Review Staff (1978) found that the use of one word-processor gave productivity gains of more than 100 per cent over a conventional typewriter. West German trade union studies estimate that the jobs of two out of five million typists and secretaries are threatened by word-processors (reported in Rada, 1980). Clerical and administrative staff in banks, insurance, postal services and a range of manufacturing plants are all at risk (Nora and Minc, 1978).

One response to new information technology has been a more dispersed pattern of employment. Hakim (1984) has demonstrated a vast recent increase in work at home: in England and Wales, 1.7 million people worked at or from home in 1981, and she pointed to the "inescapable conclusion" that while manufacturing at home is now relatively rare, white collar and service work is now increasingly common. For example, the 'networking' scheme operated by Rank Xerox employs 200 freelance workers using home-based computers and pooled software on sub-contracting work (Mitchell, 1984). Such straws in the wind point to the need for hard thinking about work and the use of labour in ways that are fundamentally different from those of the recent past.

It can no longer be assumed that developed economies will be able to provide jobs for all who want them, and there seems a general lack of urgency in producing the new forms of work organization required. The number of people reaching working age has been increasing (a trend that can be forecast at least 15 years in advance) and will continue to do so. Actual and potential participation rates for married women may well rise further, especially in those homes with an unemployed husband and in those regions where they are still below the national average. In some countries the second generation effects of international migration will boost labour supply still further. The tragedy in Western Europe today is that so little forward planning seems to have been done to cope with known demographic and participation trends, so that what might have been a harvest of opportunity is passing for many into a nightmare of prolonged unemployment.

REFERENCES

Beaumont, P.B. (1976) 'The problem of return migration under a policy of assisted labour mobility : an examination of some British evidence,' British Journal of Industrial Relations, 14, 82-88

Bell, D. (1984) Employment in the age of drastic change : the future with robots, Abacus Press, London

Central Policy Review Staff (1978), Social and employment implications of microelectronics, London (Mimeo)

Champion, A.G. (1983) 'Population trends in the 1970's,' in J.B. Goddard and A.G. Champion (eds.) The urban and regional transformation of Britain, Methuen, London

Commission of the E.E.C. (1984) The regions of Europe, Second Periodic Report on the social and economic situation and development of the regions of the Community, E.E.C.Commission, Brussels

Davis, N. (1982) 'Demographic trends and labour supply,' OPCS Occasional Paper 28, 1-7

Dennison, S.R. (1939) The location of industry and the depressed areas, O.U.P., Oxford

Department of Employment (1983) 'Qualifications and the labour force,' Gazette, 91, 158-164

Department of Employment (1984a) 'Labour force outlook for Great Britain,' Gazette, 92, 56-64

Department of Employment (1984b) 'Regional labour force outlook to 1991,' Gazette, 92, 165-172

Department of Trade and Industry (1984a) Regional industrial policy : some economic issues, London

Department of Trade and Industry (1984b) First Report of the Skills Shortages Committee, London

Ermisch, J., and H. Joshi (1984) Human resources and the labour force: issues for contemporary and comparative research, Centre for Economic Policy Research, Discussion Paper No.1, London

Gleave, D. (1984) The relationship between labour mobility and technical change, Technical Change Centre, London

Hakim, C. (1984) 'Homework and outwork ; national estimates from two surveys,' Department of Employment Gazette, 92, 7-12

Johnson, J.H., J. Salt and P.A.Wood (1974) Housing and the migration of labour in England and Wales, Saxon House, Farnborough

Johnson, J.H., J. Salt and P.A.Wood (1980) 'Employment transfer policies in Great Britain ' Three Banks Review, 126, 18-39

Joshi, H., R.Layard and S. Owens (1983) Why are more women working in Britain?, Centre for Labour Economics. L.S.E., Working Paper, 162

Klaasen, L.H., and P. Drewe (1973) Migration policy in Europe : a comparative study, Saxon House, Farnborough

Massey. D. (1979) 'In what sense a regional problem?' Regional Studies, 13, 233-44

Matthews, R.C O.. G H.Feinstein and J.C Odling-Smee (1982) British economic growth, 1857-1973. Clarendon Press, Oxford

Mitchell, P. (1984) 'Networking : an alternative approach to work', Topics. 17 12 13

Nora S., and A. Minc, (1978) L'informatisation de la Société. Rapport à M. le Président de la République, Paris, La Documentation Française

OECD (1983) SOPEMI. Continuous reporting system on migration, 1982, Directorate for Social Affairs, Manpower and Education, OECD, Paris

Parker, S. (1975) Assisted labour migration, OPCS Social Survey Division (unpublished)

Peach, G C.K. (1982) 'The growth and distribution of the black population in Britain 1945 80' in D.A. Coleman (ed.) Demography of immigrants and minority groups in the UK, Academic Press. London

Psacharopoulos, G., and R Layard (1979) 'Human capital and economics : British evidence and a critique', Review of Economic Studies, 46, 485-503

Rada. J. (1980) The impact of micro-electronics, International Labour Office, Geneva

Routh, G. (1980) Occupation and pay in Great Britain 1906-1979. Macmillan London

Salt, J. (1976) 'International labour migration : the geographical pattern of demand in J. Salt and H.D. Clout (eds.) Migration in Post-war Europe. O U.P., Oxford

Salt, J. (1984) Labour transfers during the recession. Paper presented at the Geography of Recession' symposium, Institute of British Geographers Annual Conference, Durham

Sant, M. (1975) Industrial movement and regional development Pergamon, Oxford

Schnitzer, M (1969) Regional unemployment and the relocation of workers, Praeger, New York

Sundquist, J.L. (1975) Dispersing population : What America can learn from Europe, Brookings Institution, Washington

Chapter Three

LABOUR FORCE AND JOB CREATION IN THE THIRD WORLD

W.T.S. Gould

INTRODUCTION

Jobs and development

One of the major potential challenges offered by population growth in
the Third World is that there will be more hands to put to work. An
increased supply of labour can in some circumstances raise levels of
output and productivity per unit of land and capital, and that increase
will contribute to rising incomes and gross national product. If the
poverty of Third World countries is - as is often argued - in part due
to inadequate use and uneven distribution of existing human, physical
and technological resources, then population growth can contribute
substantially to the development effort. However, it is generally
argued, not only by neo-Malthusians, that high rates of population
growth in Third World countries do not have such favourable effects:
" ... in most poor countries rapid population growth slows, sometimes
drastically, the rate of increase in the proportion of the labour force
in the modern, high productivity sectors of the economy" (McNicoll,
1984, p.210-11). Indeed, as countries struggle to expand modern
sector activities the rising supply of labour seems greatly to exceed
the growth in the demand as measured by the numbers of people in
recorded employment, to the extent that one of the major world-wide
issues for development is the creation of additional jobs for the
additional number of job seekers. In the countries of the Third World
that additional number of job seekers is growing very rapidly.

Historically, development in Europe and North America has
been associated with the change in productive structures from
feudalism to capitalism and to socialism, in the U.S.S.R., Eastern
Europe and China, bringing the growth of factory and formal
employment. Urban employment 'absorbed' most of the rapid growth
in population and, indeed, was in part responsible for that growth.
While the growth of the international industrial and commercial
economy brought major problems of boom and slump associated with
the trade cycle, Keynesian economic management of the 1950's and

1960's seemed to have solved the problem of cyclical unemployment, and economic growth kept unemployment at unprecedentedly low levels for a quarter of a century. Western societies are now all-too-acutely aware that the employment problem has returned as a long-term issue. However, in the Third World the immediate and long-term problem of job creation is a much greater challenge.

Whereas experience of the transformation of developed countries from rural to urban societies, where jobs were created in large numbers in urban areas, seemed in the 1960's to be a viable development strategy for newly independent countries, it is now clear that the urban sector has not been able to absorb massive rural/urban migration. The number of job seekers has rapidly outstripped the apparent ability of most economies to generate and expand urban wage employment.

Although there are major policy and planning issues raised by the relationships between population change and employment generation in the Third World, McNicoll also argues that "to reduce the consequences of rapid population growth principally to a problem of labor absorption -even a serious problem, calling for politically laden alignments for factor prices and elaborate public sector employment generating programs - would be to down-play them" (1984, p.212). As Salt has argued in the previous chapter, planning for population change with respect to employment must be concerned not only with problems associated with the size of the potential labour force but also with secular changes in age - and sex-specific participation rates. It must also consider changes in the skill levels of the population: population quality as well as population quantity. Employment planning in the Third World must recognize the particular characteristics of national population structures and dynamics, and incorporate them in overall strategies for job creation as part of the wider process of economic development.

This chapter seeks to identify some of the key ways in which population structure and dynamics affect the supply of labour in the Third World, and are reflected in the nature of the demand for labour. The argument is presented in three major sections. First, there is discussion of some of the structural characteristics of economies of different size and associated labour force in the Third World and how these are being moulded by wider processes of differentiation in the world economic system. Secondly these macro-economic processes are related to demographic factors and policies affecting the size and structure of the labour force. The third major section considers levels of skill and training and how these are reflected in plans to improve the human resource base. The concluding section brings these general features together in specific consideration of population and employment in Botswana.

Data problems
One must be keenly aware of major problems of data availability on the labour force in Third World countries. Some of these problems are essentially conceptual, in particular the concept

of 'employment' as paid, regular work which is recorded in official 'employment statistics'. Such a concept is increasingly questioned even in advanced, post-industrial societies, where much thought is currently being given to the nature of work, and it is certainly inadequate and often misleading for the Third World where much labour is self-employed in small-scale family farms or in the 'informal' sector in both towns and rural off-farm areas. Formal and full-time wage employment occupies a much smaller proportion of the labour force than it does in developed societies, and many job seekers, in some senses 'unemployed', often find part-time employment on a casual or irregular basis without any regulation of wages or pensions or other benefits by the state. Other data problems are those of practice: for example, the non-recording or under-recording of employees in labour force surveys which exclude many categories of workers from consideration.

In Kenya, for example, the number of workers in registered employment rose from just over 500,000 at Independence in 1963 to over one million twenty years later. Much of that increase is due to white-collar urban employment in the public sector (Figure 3.1). These data, derived from the Annual Enumeration of Employees, cover all public and private sector establishments in urban and rural areas but exclude all establishments employing five workers or less, thus omitting many full-time and even more part-time workers. A Survey of the Rural Labour Force, 1977/78, however, using different concepts of work and employment paints a very different picture of the structure of the labour force. Some 85 per cent of the population of Kenya lives in rural areas, and most labour is active in agriculture, but with rather different activities by age for men and women (Figure 3.2). The Kenyan situation is replicated throughout the Third World, and problems of definition and enumeration hamper meaningful international or even interregional comparisons of the numbers and structures of employment.

THE STRUCTURE OF THE LABOUR FORCE

Patterns of job creation
The industrial structure of the labour force varies considerably by level of development and per capita income (Table 3.1). Using the World Bank standard groupings of countries, it is clear that there is a regular decline in the proportion in agriculture from poorest to richest countries, and a corresponding rise in the proportion engaged in industry. Moreover, that pattern experienced considerable change between 1960 and 1980. In the Low Income group of countries there were rises in the proportion in industry and in services, but these were not as spectacular as rises in these sectors in the Middle Income countries, and particularly in some of the Newly Industrializing Countries (NICs). In South Korea, for example, the proportion of the labour force in industry rose from 9 to 29 per cent between 1960 and 1980, with equivalent rises of 15 to 24 per cent in Brazil and of 12 to

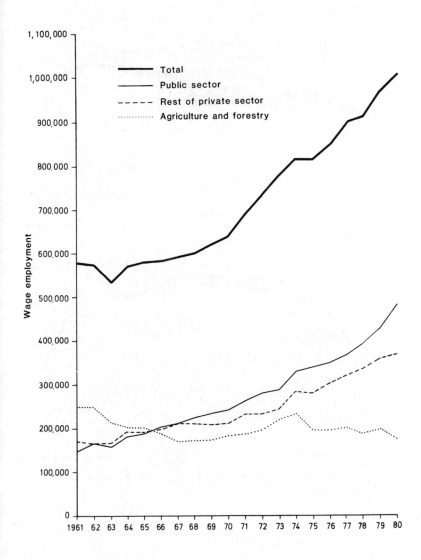

Fig. 3.1 Kenya : registered wage employment by major sectors, 1961–80

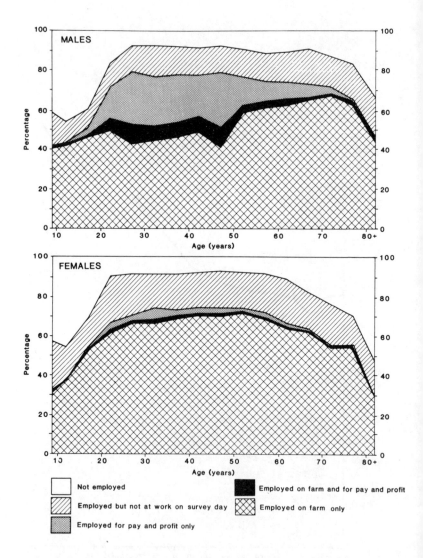

MALES

FEMALES

- Not employed
- Employed but not at work on survey day
- Employed for pay and profit only
- Employed on farm and for pay and profit
- Employed on farm only

Fig. 3.2 Kenya : employment status of rural population by age and sex, 1977/78
Source :   Mott and Mott, 1980, p. 8

Table 3.1 : Structure of the labour force, 1960 and 1980

Type of economy	Percentage of population aged 15-64		Percentage of the labour force in:					
			Agriculture		Industry		Services	
	1960	1980	1960	1980	1960	1980	1960	1980
Low income economies	55	59	77	72	9	13	14	15
China and India	56	61	NA	69	NA	17	NA	14
Other low-income	54	53	82	73	7	11	11	16
Middle income economies	55	56	67	46	15	21	23	34
Oil exporters	54	54	66	48	13	20	22	32
Oil importers	55	57	60	44	16	21	24	35
Lower middle income	54	55	71	56	11	16	18	28
Upper middle income	55	57	49	30	20	28	31	42
High income oil exporters	54	52	62	46	13	19	25	35
Industrial market economies	63	66	18	6	38	38	44	56
East European non-market economies	63	66	42	18	30	44	28	39

NA = not available

Source : World Bank, 1984, Table 21

25 per cent in Algeria. Nevertheless the proportion employed in industry in the Middle Income countries, taken as a whole, is still by the 1980's only about half that in industrial market economies and the socialist states of Eastern Europe.

Equally large increases in the proportion in service sectors in these Middle Income countries are also apparent, but this may reflect more a growth of the tertiary refuge sector, absorbing the growing numbers of urban migrants in a wide range of petty services in the informal economy, for it is in these countries, mainly of Latin America and East Asia, that the largest urban squatter populations are to be found (see Chapter 5, Figure 5.3). Nevertheless even in these countries there is still a large labour force, though not necessarily 'employed', in agriculture. However, the gap between the Upper- and Lower-Middle Income countries seems to have widened since 1960 as the employment structures of the relatively few NIC's move towards those of richer and more complex economies.

Policies for employment generation in the Third World has been focussed strongly on the industrial sector. The development strategies of most countries have an implicit bias towards industry rather than agriculture, a bias which is part of the common assumption that a modern economy must develop a structure similar to that of industrial market economies, an approach derived from linear development models based on Rostovian principles. Industrial growth is therefore taken as important evidence of development, and most countries invoke a wide range of policies to create industrial employment. In the 1960's and '70 s this involved the encouragement of import substitution and export processing industries geared towards the internal market and internally produced products respectively. By the 1970's, however, a growing number of countries had begun to export their own manufactures, often produced for a world market by multinational companies. Japanese electronics firms established major manufacturing bases in East and South East Asian countries; European and North American car firms established plants in Third World countries not only to satisfy rapidly growing internal markets but for export, often to Western countries but more particularly to neighbouring Third World countries. There is, however, a growing awareness of indigenous industrial growth in the major countries of the Third World, much of which has a considerable capacity for export. For example, Brazil and India are major world traders in heavy manufactures, including armaments and industrial machinery.

These developments have been characterized by the dependency school as further evidence of the domination of the world economic system by governments and multinational companies of the rich countries. These developments in the 'semi-periphery' are part of the global trends in the international division of labour, and essentially contribute to the maintenance of the status quo in relationships between rich and poor countries. The employment structures have changed, but the global pattern remains. Industrial employment has been created but largely in assembly manufacture using cheap, semi-skilled and unorganized labour, rather than in high technology or income-generating and demand-led service industries.

The demand for labour
While it is not the purpose here to examine the causes of changing economic and employment structures it is important to raise two issues which reflect the level of demand for industrial labour. The first of these relates to the choice of technology, whether capital- or labour-intensive. An ILO study has concluded that multinational companies tend to operate using international standards and may be more inclined to substitute capital for labour than locally-based companies, even though the technology used may not always be as sophisticated as is used for similar processes in the metropolitan country (ILO, 1981). Thus national policies for absorption of the rapidly growing labour force may need to be seen in a trade-off with company policies that may prefer more capital-intensive techniques.

A second factor concerns the size of national economies and

associated economies of scale in local markets for manufactured products. While a few Third World countries are giants and, even with low levels of per capita demand, have large economies, the great majority of Third World countries are small. The majority have a population of less than 5 million, and a large number of micro-states, especially in the Caribbean and the Pacific, have populations of less than 1 million people. The local market is too small to create viable local manufactures and the possibilities for emulating the exceptional experiences of Hong Kong and Singapore, small but now industrialized countries, are remote. There have been many attempts at regional integration in common market agreements of various kinds, but, while these may have achieved political benefits, the economic results have been disappointing. Small populations present problems as intractable for development policies as do large populations.

A major point of comparison of industrial and demographic structures is also identified in Table 3.1, that while nearly two-thirds of the population in the rich countries is in the working age-group and, due to falls in fertility, that proportion has not risen since 1960, present proportions in Low and Middle Income countries are generally below 60 per cent. Poor countries have a higher proportion of dependents and more adverse dependency ratios, but those are changing according to experiences of fertility decline. In India and particularly China, fertility declines have ensured that the dependency ratios have improved: in other Low Income countries they have become more unfavourable as high rates of population growth have been maintained. Fertility declines in many countries, though significant, have not been sufficient in the short term to alter population structures to a higher ratio of productive to non-productive population. Although the size of the economically active cohorts is growing, so is the size of those younger, school-age cohorts who will be seeking jobs in future years, exacerbating the present excess of supply over demand. In India, for example, the annual numbers of labour force entrants will double between 1970 and 2000; but in China, due to rapid fertility decline the number of labour force entrants in 2000 will be similar to that in 1970 (Figure 3.3).

THE SIZE AND DISTRIBUTION OF THE LABOUR SUPPLY

Participation rates
As was argued in the previous chapter the size of the potential labour force is not governed solely by the demand for labour, nor is it principally a function of the size of the age-group at risk. There is a complex of economic, social and cultural variables operating at different scales that affect the number of people actively seeking to participate in wage employment. These factors may be very different according to the type of economy:

"In peasant or primitive economies labour force

71

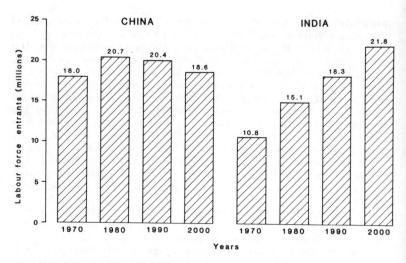

Fig. 3.3 China and India : labour force entrants, 1970–2000
Source : Brown, 1984, p. 14

participation is constrained only by health, nutrition, the
rhythms of the seasons and the demand for income. It is
when the economy changes, when wage labour becomes a
dominant feature of agriculture and when urbanization
and non-agricultural employment expand that other social
and economic factors have a greater effect on the level
and pattern of labour force participation ... with
economic growth, the participation rates of particular
groups may become more sensitive to the structure of the
labour market ..." (Standing, 1978, p. 223).

Standing argues that in early stages of development more labour than
hitherto is made available as a result of changes in agriculture and in
traditional sectors, but that change operated differentially. In the
first instance they allowed men to have much higher participation
rates than women. Women are much more rigidly tied to domestic
and traditional responsibilites for reasons of supply rather than of
demand which can be associated with cultural preferences and male-
dominated decisions within the family rather than a lower level of
demand for female labour. Women's participation rates in the
modern sector are often confined to particular occupations such as
teaching or nursing, though a growing number of women are now into
the industrial wage sector on their own account. They are strongly
represented in electronics assembly in Asian NICs (Standing and
Sheehan, 1978), and increasingly industries such as food processing in
Africa (Dennis, 1984). A further major differential is associated with

72

socio-economic status. That activity rates are higher for higher socio-economic groups is clearly directly related to that activity, but also to the differential availability of education for children (and wives) of higher status family heads. The role of education is particularly important as a differential in white-collar employment, and especially in Government Service, which provide a disproportionately large share of new jobs.

Both of these are however related to the spatial factor of regional differentials in participation rates. Most jobs are found in or near towns, reflecting an urban 'bias' in job creation that has been a feature of modern development since the eighteenth century. This is being replicated in Third World countries, where high degrees of primacy in the urban hierarchy have generated large proportions of existing and new jobs in the largest cities. The urban inhabitants and those of the areas immediately surrounding these towns, themselves usually more educated and knowledgeable and with better urban connections, are more able to have direct access to such jobs.

Internal labour migration

The mis-match between the distribution of the potential labour force and the distribution of jobs has been and remains one of the main reasons for population movements at various scales within and between countries of the Third World. The phenomenon of labour migration is a major aspect of the geography of development in all Third World countries and has been a major focus for research from a wide variety of standpoints with a wide range of approaches and conclusions (e.g. Masser and Gould, 1975; Prothero and Chapman, 1985; Sabot, 1982; Todaro, 1976). Whether from the point of view of individual rationality — that labour migration is a rational response to real and expected economic differentials — or from the point of view of the structural under-development of the periphery — that labour migration is a symptom and cause of the penetration of capitalist modes of production and associated spatial differentials - it is clear that the distribution of job opportunities has encouraged massive urban migrations. While such migrations are often into unemployment, the great majority find some means of livelihood, often in marginal activities in the tertiary sector (Table 3.2). Migration generates a massive increase in the available labour supply that is only indirectly related to population growth.

With only a few exceptions, rural-urban migration has been beyond the direct control of governments. Various indirect policy mechanisms have been formulated to try to prevent or at least slow the drift to town. These include positive incentives for the spread of jobs through growth-pole and other regional policies. In Brazil, for example, regional policy over several decades has sought to create growth poles, particularly in the North-East, to prevent the drift to the Rio de Janeiro/Sao Paulo axis. However, the actual increase in jobs in the North-East in the 1960's was substantially below the number necessary to meet demand caused by population growth and rural-urban migration within the region (Dickenson, 1980, p. 69). In

73

Table 3.2 Employment status of male internal migrants, selected studies, 1965–82

Region, Country, Date	Population	Unemployment Rate — Migrants	Unemployment Rate — Non-migrants	Skilled or Unskilled Labour, Transport	Clerical, Sales	Prof., Tech., Admin.	Service	Farming, Fishing, Mining	Other or Unspecified
AFRICA									
Ghana 1975	Migrants to urban areas of Accra Capital District	4.7	7.4	47	30	10	9	3	
Sierra Leone 1981	Lifetime internal migrants	10	NA	26[a]	11	3	6	43	10
Sudan 1977	Migrants to Greater Khartoum[b,c]	8	5/3[d]	39	16	5	26	2	11
ASIA									
India 1982	Migrants from rural areas of districts around Calcutta to urban or other rural areas	8.8	NA	28	9	15[e]	24	21	3
Indonesia 1981	Interprovincial migrants to Jakarta[f]	6	7	34	45		13	2	6
Korea, Rep. of, 1981	Migrants to Seoul	4.3	5.2	48	32	6	9	1	4
Sri Lanka 1980	Migrants to Greater Colombo[f]	7.89	5.49	40	42		13	1	4
Thailand 1981	Migrants to Bangkok[g,h]	2.2	3.9	48	26	3	11	2	10
LATIN AMERICA									
Chile 1965	Migrants to Greater Santiago	4.6	7.2	40	28		13	3	16
Colombia 1981	Migrants to Bogota[g,h]	9.7	3.9	42	32	6	2	5	14
Mexico 1978	Migrants from rural villages in Jalisco State to urban areas	12.9[i]	NA	76	9		3	12	-
MIDDLE EAST									
Turkey 1980	Migrants to metropolitan areas[b]	20.0	20.4	58	17	12	10	3	

NA = available

[a] Includes miners
[b] Resident less than 5 years
[c] Includes small number of women
[d] Total urban unemployment rate/rate for migrants resident 5 years or more
[e] Includes trader, money lender, rent receiver
[f] Resident 1-4 years
[g] Ages 15-24
[h] In first occupation
[i] Vendor or seeking work

Source : Kols, 1983, p.258

other cases measures have been more negative, such as imposing restrictions on housing and other urban infrastructure that might be thought (usually wrongly) to discourage migrants. However, there is a general feeling among governments that despite the social and physical problems associated with urbanization, the jobs must be created in urban areas. Since the sorts of jobs governments are anxious to create are mainly in manufacturing industry, there is often a compelling case for the economies of scale to be gained from location in large urban areas. Hence, the urban imperative is confirmed.

This has not prevented formulation of policies to create jobs directly in rural areas as in small towns, not merely as a mechanism for deflecting migration flows to the larger towns, but also as a means towards self-sustaining developments in these areas. Rural industrialization schemes are associated with small-scale industries, often on industrial estates and associated with 'bottom-up' development strategies in small enterprises processing local agricultural produce or else in small assembly plants (Stohr and Taylor, 1981). Other rural job creation has been in agricultural activities, notably in plantation agriculture, but agricultural jobs do not attract political or economic kudos attached to industrial and urban jobs. Nevertheless rural off-farm activities may already provide a great deal of unrecorded employment. A national survey of off-farm activities in Kenya, for example, has concluded that there may be as many people employed in this sector (about 1 million) as small repairers, merchants, providers of a wide range of services, as there were in the modern sector in the mid-1970's (Freeman and Norcliffe, 1984), though their earnings are much less.

International labour migration

Major differentials between Third World countries in economic performance and associated growth of employment have been responsible for major flows of international migrants within the Third World. The most outstanding example of international labour migration is the major flows to the oil-rich economies of the Middle East (Birks and Sinclair, 1980a). These economies have a world-wide catchment, but the majority of workers, especially in middle and lower grades, is drawn from other middle income countries in organized migrations from as far apart as South Korea and the Philippines in the East to Morocco and Senegal in the west, with some countries (e.g. Jordan, Yemen) supplying over 25 per cent of their own labour force to the oil states, while in other countries (e.g. Kuwait, Oman) more than 50 per cent of the labour force is foreign nationals (Birks and Sinclair, 1980a). Many of the wider issues in international labour migration for source and destination countries discussed above for Western Europe (Salt, chapter 2) apply also to migration between countries and the Third World, but there are also some special factors, noticeably in forms of recruitment, involving official recruiting agencies and bilateral agreements between sending and receiving governments. Most migrants are hired on short-term contracts with an obligation to return to the home country at the end of the contract, and this is relatively easy to enforce in 'island' construction sites where companies recruit their own labour force, provide accommodation and all facilities at the site maintaining isolation from the host society and repatriate the workers at the end of the contract. Such arrangements are attractive to countries like Saudi Arabia where local labour shortages (themselves exacerbated by the effective exclusion of women from the labour market) must be met by large-scale immigration of foreign workers whose lifestyles threaten traditional values.

The dilemmas of the sending countries are often more acute than they are for the sending countries of Mediterranean Europe, in particular that they are often much poorer and even more anxious for foreign exchange but have much weaker economies with very bleak prospects for generation of productive employment internally. Pakistan, for example, is now a major exporter of labour to the Gulf States and, though the returns per worker are small, aggregate remittances are now the major earner of foreign exchange. Isabelle Tsakok (1982) records how despite major disadvantages to the Pakistan economy through loss of scarce skilled labour in construction and local manufacturing and a high import content of remittance expenditures, the government is actively encouraging temporary emigration and has used its own funds to develop training programmes specifically to supply labour needs in the Gulf. The attraction of this emigration for skilled and unskilled labourers compounds the longer standing problem of emigration from Pakistan of more highly skilled workers to more developed countries, notably U.K., as part of the 'brain drain'.

International migrations within and to the Middle East provide an extreme case of the widespread migration flows that occur as a result of rather smaller, but still significant, differences in economic performance within the Third World. Other oil- and mineral-rich states attract workers to mines and oil fields from neighbours (e.g. Ghanaians to Nigeria, Cameroonians to Gabon, Peruvians to Ecuador and Bolivia) and in other cases migrants may be attracted to other rural or urban destinations. For example, in the Ivory Coast, a country with a relatively buoyant economy and surrounded by states with various degrees of environmental and economic collapse, one in five inhabitants in 1975 was an immigrant, with over one-half of these from Upper Volta and another quarter from Mali. 25 per cent of the labour force were foreigners and nearly half the immigrants, as compared with 30 per cent of Ivoirians, lived in towns (Zachariah and Condé, 1981).

EDUCATION, TRAINING AND THE LABOUR FORCE

Manpower planning
Although it is most commonly assumed that numbers of people or the rate of population growth are at the heart of most of the problems of planning for population change, in many respects the more significant and longer-term problems for the labour force in Third World countries stem from current low levels of education and training. Population problems are qualitative as well as quantitative, and planning can seek to redress what is a major bottleneck for many countries by investing directly in human resources, by improving education and health services to ensure that more people are physically able and mentally equipped to meet rising demands for skilled workers. Issues involved in planning health care and educational provision in the Third World are considered in greater detail below (Chapters 7 and 9), but it is clearly important for this discussion of the labour force to consider how investments in human resources can affect the pace and type of expansion of jobs; how the quality of the supply can affect the level of demand; and how policies to manage the quality of that supply will greatly affect the rate and type of development.

Educational planning throughout the Third World has been premised on the assumption that lack of skills has constituted a major constraint on development and that a more educated labour force will accelerate the rate of development. General and specific skills learned in school or in formal training will allow improvements in technology to be introduced and thereby generate greater efficiency at work.   Individual productivity in all industries, including agriculture, will rise with educational level of the work force, and in the aggregate investment in human capital is as necessary for development as investment in other forms of capital.   The human capital theory of development is most associated with the American economist, Theodore Schultz, whose Nobel Prize lecture in 1979, "The economics of being poor" was a plea for more investment in human capital in countries of the Third World as a prime weapon in the fight against endemic poverty (Schultz, 1981). Most countries of the Third World have been able to expand their education and training systems rapidly in recent years and the bottleneck of low levels of indigenous capacity for modern industrial development has been considerably reduced.

In theory these expansions were planned under the umbrella of manpower planning, to allow the education and training system to produce manpower appropriate to the projected needs of a rapidly expanding economy. In the 1960's many countries, particularly in Africa, embarked on elaborate manpower planning exercises, but these have proved to have been much too optimistic, for they assumed not only a fairly rigid structure of labour requirements based on historical experience elsewhere, but also continuing rates of economic growth to the end of the twentieth century. By the mid-1970's, however, it was clear that dependence on manpower planning techniques had been misplaced. Rapid technological change created new and unforeseen manpower demands and, even more serious, the rate of expansion of jobs in the formal sector of the economy had slowed with the general decline of rates of economic growth in most Third World countries. Economies were increasingly unable to absorb the secondary school leavers and higher education graduates coming onto the labour market (Hallak and Caillods, 1980).

Education and migration
These higher levels of education have created other problems of population change, in particular that they have been associated with much increased levels of rural-urban migration.   The educated everywhere have demonstrated higher propensities for migration than the uneducated or poorly educated, especially in the earlier periods of development (Caldwell, 1968; Gould 1982).   Expansion of enrolments at rates faster than the growth of jobs leads to an apparent over-supply of qualified labour and creates a class of educated unemployed or an escalation of qualifications that creates a further demand for educational attainment to reach the new level. Ronald Dore's conceptualization of 'The Diploma Disease' (Dore, 1976) encapsulated much of the problem of over-reliance on formal qualifications for jobs in countries where there is an apparent over-supply of educated labour   The real skill level of the labour force is much less than most formal qualifications would suggest and for any given job minimum formal qualifications have often been pushed

inappropriately high.

Education has allowed the labour force to grow more rapidly than the rate of population growth as more and more children have gained qualifications that could be expected to be used in the job market. Activity rates, for males and even more prominently for females, have risen very considerably, and certainly more rapidly than the number of jobs available. The result is rising levels of unemployment, particularly among young people. In Latin America, for example, "more than half the unemployed are young people. Thus in Argentina youth unemployment has been estimated to account for 72 per cent of all unemployment, in Colombia and Panama for 74 per cent and in Venezuela for 61 per cent" (ILO, 1985, p.118).

The response of Governments has been to target development programmes at the educated unemployed. These may be in projects for employment or retraining after they have left school or in curriculum adjustments in the schools themselves. Village polytechnics in Kenya, for example, offer one-or two-year courses that provide school leavers with skills such as carpentry or tailoring that they can use in their own home areas. They therefore attempt to stem the urban migration of rural school leavers as well as providing them with commercially viable skills. However, studies of village polytechnic students consistently show how their perceptions of what is desirable are consistently biased towards urban values, and their polytechnic experience will merely delay rather than prevent urban migration (Barker and Ferguson 1983). In other countries school leavers are obliged to do some form of community or military service in rural areas, to some extent with similar objectives of reducing the migration of school leavers, but with equally disappointing results.

Planning to reorientate the values and subsequent mobility of school leavers has also involved the introduction of 'relevant' education in the schools, this being taken to mean the introduction of practical and vocational subjects such as agriculture or woodwork in the curriculum. This has been the basis for educational innovation in many countries (Sinclair and Lillis, 1980), most notably in Tanzania as part of the wider restructuring of economy and society after the Arusha Declaration of 1967. All schools are obliged to inculcate values of rural self-sufficiency and each school has its own small farm which is used for instruction as well as production. However, even from its earliest days the Tanzanian experiment in 'relevant' education was a matter of sharp criticism, particularly in the vocational fallacy argument of Philip Foster - that unless and until farmers' incomes were comparable with those of white collar workers, practical education of this kind would not be of direct economic benefit and that the traditional skills of literacy and numeracy are perceived to be more 'relevant' and 'vocational' to those who aspire to white collar jobs (Foster, 1969). In other circumstances, however, there is a demand for technically trained manpower that has not elicited sufficient response from the education system. "The nature of education in the Arab world as a whole is ill suited to meet the manpower requirements of the modern industrial economies to which the governments aspire" (Birks and Sinclair, 1980b, p.22). The question of curriculum remains a major controversy in the formulation of policies to raise the educational and training standards of job seekers in the Third World, and thereby in the extent of rural-urban migration.

Internal migration of educated and skilled workers is an issue for all Third World countries, but the international migration of educated and skilled workers affects some countries very severely and others hardly at all. The Third World as a whole has been particularly affected by the brain drain to Western Europe and North America, but larger countries with a well developed education system, notably India, Pakistan, Egypt and Philippines and most of Latin America, have been much more so than countries of Africa South of the Sahara (Glaser, 1978). The changes in immigration laws in the 1960's and 1970's in U.S.A., Canada and Australia from being based on racial and national criteria to economic criteria created a demand for doctors, engineers and other highly skilled professionals that could be met from countries where there seemed to be an over-supply in salary terms (i.e. local salaries are much lower than internationally competitive levels), though the need for these professionals is much greater than in the richer countries (Abdin, 1983). Planning to control the emigration of professional workers through fiscal means or in direct remuneration have seldom been sufficient to affect the rate of emigration and many countries have been obliged to take account of emigration in making estimates for manpower planning purposes (Gould, 1985).

Any analysis of population change in the context of the size and composition of the labour market and their impact on development must integrate aspects of quality as well as quantity, and in some countries the former may be even more important than the latter. Changes in population distribution are associated with expansions of education and training, but it is often analytically impossible to separate cause and effect: does education cause differential migration propensities in level of education; or are these different propensities merely a symptom of the nature of the job market? The level of interaction (or lack of it) between quality improvements and the demand for labour will vary from country to country according to the nature of that labour demand, but will affect the way in which governments can plan to improve the skill level of the population and thereby the size and composition of the labour force.

CONCLUSION: THE CASE OF BOTSWANA

It is appropriate to conclude this overview of some of the planning problems associated with the labour force and its relationships with population change in Third World countries by specific discussion of one particular country. Botswana in Southern Africa is large in area, but its population is small, with only 941,027 inhabitants in 1981, though the de jure population, taking citizens working abroad, mostly in South Africa, into account, was 967,365. That de jure population, however, grew at an intercensal annual rate of 4.1 per cent, 1971-1981, due mainly to sharply falling infant mortality rates. Economically Botswana remains very much in the shadow of South Africa, but its GNP has expanded very rapidly in recent years the largest increases being in the mid-1970's when mineral developments were producing large returns for the first time (Colclough and McCarthy, 1980). Export of beef is also a major prop of the economy, but 6 per cent of foreign earnings in 1976 were in the form of remittances from Botswana citizens working in South Africa, a figure that has since fallen as fewer foreign workers are being recruited by South Africa (Taylor, 1982).

The Botswana Census of 1981 recorded 316,488 people out of 570,073 aged 12 years and over as 'economically active', that term being defined according to U.N. recommendations as "all individuals 12 years of age or over who, during the month preceding the census, were working regularly for cash, working in family lands or cattle posts, or were actively looking for work or doing periodic piece jobs" (Tumkaya, 1984a, p. 138). The activity rate for males was 73.2 per cent and for females 40.9 per cent. These rates vary also by age and location, though it is clear that sex and age are more important than location. For males in the main economically active age groups, activity rates are in excess of 90 per cent (Figure 3.4). However spatial variations are considerable when total economic dependency ratios (the proportion of persons of all ages who are not economically active per 100 economically active) are used. Ratios are low for urban areas, particularly Gaborone, the capital, and the mining towns of Orapa and Jwaneng, where the proportion of the young and the old is less than in the national population, but high in districts where not only are there high proportions in the non-active age groups but also high proportions of economically inactive persons aged 12 and over. The occupational structure of the economically active also varies by sex, with over half the women but only 40 per cent of the men in family agriculture, but nearly half the men and only one-third of the women in cash-earning occupations.

These rates and proportions have changed in recent years and will continue to change into the future. The 1971 census used different definitions of 'economically active' and 'employed' so that direct intercensal comparisons are not possible. However it is clear that there was a sharp increase in cash employment and a fall in the proportions engaged in family agriculture in the inter-censal decade. The annual employment surveys of the Central Statistical Office, recording formal sector employment only, record a growth in total employment from 41,300 in 1971 to 100,100 by 1982, with major structural shifts, notably a growth in proportions in mining manufacturing and in government, itself the direct employer of over one-third of all the formal labour force. There was, however, an absolute as well as proportionate fall in employment in agriculture (Table 3.3). Separately calculated estimates for traditional

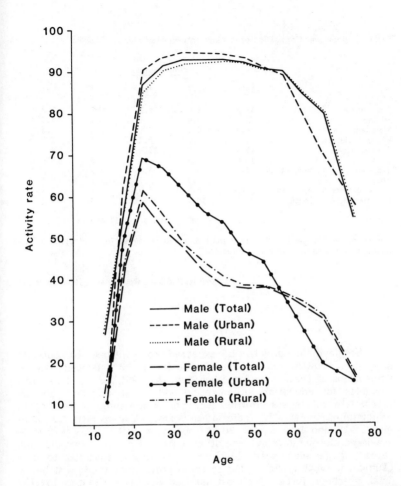

Fig. 3.4 Botswana: economic activity rates by age, sex and rural-urban residence, 1981
Source: Tumkaya, 1984a

agriculture record a fall in the present decade, associated in particular with the recurring and continuing drought (Botswana Government, 1984, p.12). Further projections based on a national macro-economic model forecast continuing growth in employment in excess of 5 per cent per year into the 1990's, with the share in government service rising to nearly 40 per cent. Manufacturing will continue to expand but mining will fall in relative terms though numbers employed will rise slightly.

Table 3.3 Botswana: Formal Sector employment, selected years, 1972-1991

	Percentages				
	1972	1977	1982	1987	1991
Agriculture	11.7	6.8	4.2	5.1	5.2
Mining	3.9	8.8	7.1	5.4	5.1
Manufacturing	6.4	6.6	7.2	10.4	11.4
Water & Electricity	n.e.s	1.5	2.2	2.1	2.5
Construction	15.4	11.0	13.6	9.3	8.4
Trade	19.0	15.9	16.6	15.3	15.6
Transport & Communications	2.7	3.0	3.7	3.7	3.6
Finance	7.6	3.7	5.7	5.9	5.8
Social & personal services	n.e.s	3.4	3.9	3.4	3.9
Government & education	32.8	39.2	35.3	39.6	39.1
Total	41300	62700	100100	132659	167709

Totals and percentages for 1971, 1977 and 1982 are as measured: for 1987 and 1991 based on national macroeconomic model forecasts

Source: Botswana Government, 1984, pp. 9 and 31

Employment growth is expected to continue to outpace population growth, but participation rates can be expected to rise. Projections of the labour force based on the 1981 Census data, with variables for education, urbanization and industrialization and an attempt to encompass informal sector growth, assume improvements in participation rates for males of 25 years, but sharp falls for 12-14 and 15-19 and less so for 20-24, due principally to more people staying on longer in school and other higher education. Participation rates for females aged 20-24 and above are assumed to rise (Tumkaya, 1984b). According to these projections there will be by 1991 a labour force of almost 600,000 but an estimated 167,709 modern sector jobs, a ratio of 30.6 per cent, compared with 276,412 and 100,100 respectively, a ratio of 36.2 per cent in 1981. Thus the rate of growth of the labour force is considerably in excess of the rate of growth of modern sector jobs, with the inevitable expectation that much of that increment will be absorbed either in the family agriculture sector or in the informal sector. The projections assume greatest expansions in the latter, doubling during the 1980's and almost doubling in the 1990's to the extent that overall activity rates improve from 1981 to 2001 (Table 3.4).

Table 3.4 Botswana: Labour force and employment, 1981, 1991, 2001

	1981	1991	2001
Labour force projections	449133	599084	836466
Employment projections			
Formal sector	97400	167713	280926
Informal sector	35487	78930	136544
Traditional agriculture	98577	102145	124515
Economy total	231464	348788	541985
Activity rate	51.5	58.2	64.8

Source: Botswana Government, 1984, p.38

This gross improvement has to be set against two major factors that suggest a note of caution. In the first place there has been and will continue to be a major expansion in school enrolments. Enrolment rates in primary schools are already by the mid-1980s above 90 per cent in many districts, despite relative under-enrolment of boys due to their being 'economically active' as herd boys looking after cattle, and it is government policy to achieve universal junior secondary enrolments by the mid 1990's with an expansion from 10,800 in the first year of secondary school in 1985 to 23,000 by 1991. This will inevitably increase expectations of a modern sector job that cannot be realized, but will not, on the other hand, in itself reverse the current deficit in high level manpower that requires the employment of 15,000 expatriate workers in 1984, almost all in jobs for which there are insufficient trained citizens. Rapid expansion of high-level training is also planned to reduce dependence on foreign skilled manpower. Even for jobs requiring a degree or higher it is expected that there will be a surplus of local manpower in 1997 (Botswana Government, 1984, p. 48).

A second factor concerns the sharp fall in numbers of citizens recruited to work in South Africa. From a peak of 40,000 in 1976 this had fallen by half by the mid-1980's and the fall is likely to continue. It is entirely due to policies of the South African Government ensuring recruitment of its own internal labour force much more than had been the case in the past, but with the implication that potential international migrants will henceforth be expected to seek jobs within Botswana. These, as has been seen. are unlikely to be found in mining, and will add to the ranks of the unskilled and poorly educated job seekers in the formal and informal sectors (Taylor, 1985).

The major impact of the increasing labour force will be in accelerated rates of internal migration, and particularly rural-urban movement on a temporary or permanent basis. In 1971 there were five designated urban areas with a total population of 54,416, 9.5 per cent of the national population; by 1981 there were eight designated urban areas with 146,264 people, 17.7 per cent of the national population.   Gaborone, the capital, has experienced spectacular growth to 59,657 in 1981 at an average annual growth rate of 12.9 per cent, 1971-81, and is now the largest settlement, having been second largest in 1971.   This growth is a response to the growth of employment in government service and in a growing range of industries, many of which are essentially market-oriented and import substituting, such as the country's only brewery. It is also the centre for financial and business services, headquarters of the country's many foreign firms, mostly South African, in the country. While the sex ratio of 106 males per 100 females is more balanced than it is in many other African capital cities, the age structure reflects migration with only 30 per cent of the population aged less than 14, compared with 47.3 per cent for Botswana as a whole; conversely 67.6 per cent of the population compared with national 45.7 per cent is aged 15-59.   The town has attracted young adults, both male and female, from all parts of the country, and 85.2 per cent of them were in cash employment. Only 10.7 per cent were 'seeking work' in 1981, a lower proportion than the 14.7 per cent in Francistown and 18 per cent in Lobatse, the second and third largest towns respectively (Taylor, 1984).

The understanding of patterns and processes of population mobility in Botswana has been considerably enhanced by the National Migration Survey, 1978/79, based on a series of surveys of a national sample over a period of 12 months.   The NMS investigated, amongst many other topics, the relationship between mobility and economic activity.   Morag Bell's (1982) analysis of some of the economic data in the survey concludes that "it would seem unlikely that in the short term a significant slowing down of the rural-urban trend among job seekers will take place.   As a result a substantial proportion of new jobs will have to be found in the formal and informal sectors in the towns" (p. 493).   She illustrates how the detailed analysis of patterns and types of population change as revealed by the surveys, and in particular through the filters of sex and education, have important implications for national employment policy in its spatial aspects as well as aggregate structure.

Changes in population structures, by age, sex and education and in its distribution, are vital ingredients for the formulation of policies in job creation, policies that must be central to the economic and political strategies in Botswana, as in all Third World countries. The Government of Botswana has sponsored a wide range of data collection and research initiatives in population studies that have been and are being actively integrated into economic policy. Economic planning has been informed by a substantial understanding of many of the processes of population change, but it can also use these studies to anticipate some of the demographic impacts of policies that are formulated.

REFERENCES

Abdin, R., et al. (1983) A world of differentials: African pay structures in a transnational context, Hodder and Stoughton, London

Barker, D , and A.G. Ferguson (1983) 'A goldmine in the sky faraway: rural-urban images in Kenya', Area, 15, 185-91

Bell, M. (1982) 'Education, mobility and employment', in C. Kerven (ed.) Migration in Botswana: patterns, causes and consequences. Final report of the National Migration Survey Vol. 2, Central Statistics Office, Gaborone, 442 97

Birks, J.S., and C.A. Sinclair (1980a) International migration and development in the Arab region, ILO, Geneva

Birks, J.S., and C.A. Sinclair (1980b) Arab manpower: the crisis of development, Croom Helm, London

Botswana Government (1984) National manpower development planning, Employment Policy Unit, Ministry of Finance and Development Planning Gaborone

Brown, L. (1984) 'Must prosperity be a bitter dream?', People, 11, 12-14

Coale, A.J., and E.M. Hoover (1958) Population growth and economic development in low income countries: a case study of India's prospects. Princeton U.P., Princeton, N.J.

Caldwell. J.C. (1968) 'Determinants of rural-urban migration in Ghana' Population Studies, 22, 361-96

Colclough, C.H., and S.J. McCarthy (1980) The political economy of Botswana, O.U P , Oxford

Dennis, C. (1984) 'Capitalist development and women's work: a Nigerian case study', Review of African Political Economy, 27/28, 109-19

Dickenson, J.P. (1980) 'Innovations for regional development in Northwest Brazil: a century of failures', Third World Planning Review, 2, 57-74

Dore, R. (1976) The diploma disease: education, qualification and development, Unwin Education Books, London

Foster, P. (1969) 'Education for self-reliance: a critical evaluation' in R. Jolly (ed.) Education in Africa: research and action, East African Publishing House, Nairobi 81-102

Freeman, D.B., and G.B. Norcliffe (1984) 'National and regional patterns of rural non-farm-employment in Kenya', Geography, 69, 221-34

Glaser, W. (1978) The brain drain: emigration and return, Pergamon Press, Oxford, for U.N. Institute for Training and Research, Research Report, no. 22

Gould, W.T.S. (1982) 'Education and internal migration' International Journal of Educational Development. 1, 103-26

Gould, W.T.S. (1985) 'International migration of skilled labour within Africa', International Migration, 23, 5-27

Hallak, J., and F. Caillods (eds.) (1980) Education, work and employment: Vol.I: Education, training and access to the labour market, UNESCO: International Institute for Educational Planning, Paris

International Labour Office (1981) Employment effects of multinational enterprises in Developing Countries, ILO, Geneva

International Labour Office (1985) World labour report: 2, ILO Geneva

Kols, A. (1983) 'Migration, population growth and development', Population Reports, Series M, no. 7, Population Information Program, Johns Hopkins Univ.

McNicoll, G. (1984) 'Consequences of rapid population growth: an overview and assessment', Population and Development Review, 10, 177-240

Masser, I., and W.T.S. Gould (1975) Interregional migration in Tropical Africa, Institute of British Geographers, Special Publication No. 8, London

Mott, F.L., and S.H. (1980) 'Kenya's record population growth: a dilemma of development; Population Bulletin, 35, 1-43

Prothero, R.M., and M. Chapman (1985) Circulation in Third World countries, Routledge and Kegan Paul, London

Sabot, R. (ed.) (1982) Migration and the labour market in developing countries, Westview Press, Boulder, Co.

Schultz, T.W. (1981) Investing in people: the economics of population quality, University of California Press, Berkeley, Los Angeles, London

Sinclair, M.E., and K. Lillis (1980) School and community in the Third World, Croom Helm, London, in association with the Institute of Development Studies, Sussex

Standing, G. (1978) Labour force participation and development, ILO, Geneva

Standing, G., and G. Sheehan (eds.) (1978) Labour force participation in low-income countries, ILO, Geneva

Stohr, W.B., and D.R.F. Taylor (eds.) (1981) Development from above or below? The dialectics of regional planning in developing countries, Wiley, New York and London

Taylor, J. (1982) 'Changing patterns of labour supply to the South African gold mines', Tijdschrift voor Economische en Sociale Geografie, 73, 213-20

Taylor, J. (1984) 'Migration', in Botswana Government, 1981 Population and Housing Census, Central Statistics Office, Gaborone, 36-74

Taylor, J. (1985) 'Some consequences of recent reduction in mine labour recruitment in Botswana', Geography, 70

Todaro, M.P. (1976) Internal migration in developing countries, International Labour Office, Geneva

Tsakok, I. (1982) 'The export of manpower from Pakistan to the Middle East, 1975-85', World Development, 10, 319-25

Tumkaya, N. (1984a)   'Economic activity and labour force', in Botswana Government, <u>1981 Population and Housing Census</u>, Central Statistical Office, Gaborone, 138-80

Tumkaya, N. (1984b)   'Labour force projections, in Botswana Government', <u>1981 Population and Housing Census</u>, Central Statistical Office, Gaborone, 214-28

World Bank (1984)   <u>World Development Report, 1984</u>, O.U.P., New York and London

Zachariah, K.C. and J. Condé (1981)   <u>Migration in West Africa: demographic aspects</u>, O.U.P. for the World Bank, OECD, London

Chapter Four

DEMOGRAPHIC CHANGE AND SOCIAL PROVISION IN WESTERN
EUROPE

Paul L. Knox

Set against the problems of 'planning for people' in other regions of
the world, the situation in Western Europe is rather distinctive. The
relative magnitude and sophistication of social welfare expenditures
in West European welfare states means that an unusually large
component of the economy must be acutely sensitive to demographic
changes of all kinds. Furthermore, rather than having to cope with
social provision within the context of economic and demographic
growth, West European policymakers are now faced with the
unprecedented combination of demographic stagnation and sharply
restricted rates of economic growth.

On the other hand, patterns of demand for social provision must
be understood, as in any other region, as a product of past patterns of
socio-economic development. Part of the legacy of the various
overlays of past economic surges, shifts and declines are populations
with distinctive profiles in terms of age, marital status, educational
status, household structure, social class, and so on, all of which are
important determinants of such needs as housing, education, medical
care, pension programmes and personal social services of all kinds.
The economic base from which these populations derive their
livelihood is also a major determinant of the ability of communities
to finance such services; and of their disposition towards public
provision of various kinds. Moreover, the economic base is not simply
an independent variable in these relationships. Demographic change
has a significant effect on local economic development in a variety
of ways: by determining labour supplies and by affecting potential
demand for housing and consumer goods, for example. Similarly,
some aspects of demographic change not only affect the relative
need for various kinds of social provision but also the relative ability
and willingness of a community to pay for them.

Theory in the social sciences is beginning to cope with the
complexities of these inter-relationships in which, as Professor
Lawton has argued (Chapter 1 above), public policy must be grounded
if rational strategic choices are to be made about patterns of social
provision. The objective in this chapter is to review the broad sweep
of demographic change in Western Europe since 1945 and to draw out

the major consequences for spatial aspects of public service provision. In this context, the overarching dimension of demographic change is the relative stagnation of population size resulting from the low levels of mortality and fluctuating levels of fertility which have characterised the post-war period and which have caused a progressive ageing of the population. At the same time, there has been a significant redistribution of population within West European countries as a result of several interdependent processes. These include the continuing (though locally variable) phenomenon of rural-urban migration, together with more specific flows of migrant labour, return migrants and retirees, all of which have been overlain in most of Western Europe by the decentralization of population from metropolitan areas.

POPULATION STAGNATION AND ITS IMPLICATIONS

Fertility decline
Because of relatively high birth rates and declining death rates, most West European nations experienced fairly healthy rates of natural population growth in the early post-war period (Knox, 1984). In 1964, the peak year for natural increase in many countries, there were over one million births in West Germany and less than 650,000 deaths: a natural increase of 420,000. Yet by 1975 this had been converted to a natural decrease of 150,000 a year as the number of births had fallen to less than 600,000 and the number of deaths had risen to 750,000. In Great Britain, over the same period, a natural increase of nearly 400,000 per year had changed to a small net decrease and a similar, though numerically less dramatic, change occurred in many other countries (Davis, 1978). In 1981, the excess of births over deaths almost everywhere was so slight as to amount to almost no change in population numbers; only in Ireland was population growing at a rate of more than one per cent per annum, though in Greece, Portugal and Spain it was growing at 0.55-0.65 per cent (Table 4.1).

Table 4.1: Natural change in population in Western Europe, 1981

	Rate Per Cent		Rate Per Cent
Austria	0.01	Norway	0.22
Belgium	0.14	Portugal	0.56
Denmark	-0.06	Spain	0.65
France	0.46	Sweden	0.06
Greece	0.55	Switzerland	0.23
Ireland	1.16	United Kingdom	0.12
Italy	0.14	West Germany	-0.16
Netherlands	0.44		

The key to this widespread stagnation of population is the striking fall in fertility from the mid-1960's which, as a number of writers have shown (Bourgeois-Pichat, 1981; Coleman, 1980; Monnier, 1981), was the product of complex changes in the pattern of family formation and reproductive behaviour, changes which themselves have significant implications for patterns of social provision. The initial decline in fertility rates in the 1960's is attributable to a number of factors. New and highly effective means of contraception became available and were readily adopted in many countries; thereafter the size of completed families was relatively rigidly controlled. There also appears to have been a widespread shift in preferences away from familism towards consumerism: a change which was undoubtedly fostered by the knowledge of reliable methods of birth control (Roussel and Festy, 1979). Also, whatever the intentions of young couples at marriage, delayed parenthood inevitably fostered a taste for life-styles based on the availability of two incomes; and as time passed the social and financial costs of starting a family began to outweigh, for some, the less tangible benefits of having children. What started as the intention to defer having children thus became, for many, cancelled births. At the same time, changing social attitudes about the status of women came to be reflected in improved educational opportunities and a wider choice of employment, both of which fostered the development of non-familistic life-styles. The consequent decline in birth rates was reinforced soon afterwards in many countries by abortion legislation which made it easier to terminate unwanted pregnancies. In addition, changed attitudes toward sex and procreation set in motion further trends reflected in fertility levels. The social value of marriage decreased, with a consequent decline in the rate of marriage, an increase in the average age at marriage, an increase in divorce, an increase in cohabitation without marriage, and a decrease in the rate of illegitimate births. These trends, which conspired to depress the fertility rate still further (Van de Kaa, 1980), appeared first in Denmark and Sweden around 1965 and have since spread progressively to Switzerland, West Germany, Great Britain, Norway, France and Italy.

The critical question for the future is whether this spiral of downward fertility will be checked. In several countries there has recently been a modest upturn in fertility, but the limited evidence at present available suggests that this is mainly the result of a rise in the fertility rates of women in their late twenties and early thirties (Muñoz-Perez, 1982), and it must be doubtful whether the supply of these presumably deferred births will be sufficient to counterbalance the decreased fertility resulting from post-war changes in the overall pattern of family formation (Westoff, 1983). Meanwhile, in every Western European country except Greece, Portugal and Spain total fertility rates in 1980 were less than 2.1, the current level of replacement fertility. This has renewed speculation about the existence of a fifth stage in the demographic transition: a senile stage with fertility falling consistently below the death rate, leading to population decline.

France has nurtured the darkest and most obsessive fears about population decline, largely as a result of its exceptional demographic history. The early onset of fertility control in France meant that, while Britain's population grew by 43 per cent and that of the German Empire grew by 58 per cent between 1871 and 1911, France experienced an increase of less than ten per cent in that period (Dyer, 1978). Following the loss of over 1.4 million people during the First World War, the French were frightened by rising birth rates in Nazi Germany and Fascist Italy and dismayed when the death rate in France began to exceed the birth rate in 1935. A wide spectrum of pro-natalist groups had already developed and, in 1939, the institution of the Code de la Famille reinforced restrictive measures against contraception, extended family allowances, introduced tax allowances to encourage bigger families and imposed restrictive legislation relating to abortion. After the Second World War there was a general increase in fertility in Western Europe as a result first of the 'baby boom' and then of changing patterns of nuptiality; but it has been suggested that the vigorous pursuit of pro-natalist policies and propaganda in France may have raised fertility by as much as ten per cent (Calot and Hecht, 1978). Nevertheless, the French continue to alarm themselves with statistics, constructing elaborate projections of the consequences for the population if a particular level of fertility were to be maintained: "As soon as fertility falls below replacement level, there is a rush to calculate the day on which the last Frenchman will be born" (Ogden and Huss, 1982, p.284). Not surprisingly, French demographers have been prominent in the debate surrounding the possible onset of a new 'senile' stage in the demography of Western Europe. But although the French have retained some of their fears about the impact of slow population growth on the role of their culture and political influence in the world, the focus of concern elsewhere has shifted towards issues concerning economic development, the maintenance of welfare systems, and the changing patterns of household composition (Council of Europe, 1978; United Nations, 1975).

Labour supply
Some of the most important aspects of population decline in Western Europe relate to the supply of labour, since the rate at which the labour force is able to renew itself is a crucial aspect of economic health (see Chapters 2 and 3). Since the mid-1970's the increase of women in the labour force, the availability of migrant labour and the international economic recession have more than made up for any shortages of labour, but Guilmot (1978) has shown that the underlying trends point to many West European countries eventually being unable to replace their labour force. The general rise in fertility in the early post-war period, however, ensures that there will be no immediate problem of replacement. Indeed, the cohort of the peak birth rates in the mid-1960's, which has only recently entered the labour market, represents a 'disadvantaged cohort' of European

population which is likely to find greater competition not only in the labour market but also in housing markets and many other spheres of life.

The changing <u>composition</u> of labour supply has, however, already brought pressing problems explicitly related to the shifting age structure of the labour force (Chapter 2). While it is very difficult to weigh the occupational experience and reliability of the 'old' against the dynamism and innovation of the 'young' - especially when technological change and structural economic trends are taken into account - it is generally accepted that the productivity of both 'young' (an increasing component of the workforce in the recent past) and 'old' (an increasing component of the workforce in the near future) is significantly lower than that of 20 to 50 year-olds (Guilmot, 1978). Another immediate problem arising from the changing age structure of the workforce centres on the issue of career structures. The workforce in slow-growing or stable populations tends to suffer from an acute restriction of opportunities for promotion at intermediate levels, thus increasing the number of cases in which careers reach an 'early peak', followed by a long stationary or declining period (Keyfitz, 1973). This, in turn, is likely to have important implications in terms of life-styles and for the profile of demand for various kinds of goods and services.

Dependents

The corollary of changes in the size and composition of the labour force may be seen in the changing size and composition of the dependent population: schoolchildren, housewives without paid employment and retired persons. For some time a widespread trend within Western Europe towards prolonged education and training and earlier retirement has tended to increase the size of the dependent population (Kirk, 1981). The regional pattern of dependency, measured by the ratio of the economically active to the inactive population (Figure 4.1), shows that throughout most of Western Europe there is at least one dependent for each economically active (but not necessarily employed) person; though in southern Italy, Sicily, Sardinia, southwestern Spain, eastern Austria and the northern Netherlands the dependency ratio is twice as high.

Because of postwar trends in fertility, the dependency ratio began to fall after 1970 and will continue to do so at least until the year 2000 (Guilmot, 1978). Nevertheless, present levels of dependency already represent a considerable burden on the economically active population and have proved to be a considerable strain on the state welfare systems which have been established in many countries since 1945 (Wirz, 1977). Moreover, much of the anticipated decrease in dependency ratios will result from a reduction in the proportion of children, who cost only half as much as the elderly in terms of public expenditure (Bourgeois-Pichat, 1981). It follows that any such decrease in dependency ratios will not be matched by proportional decreases in the burden they impose. On the contrary, the dependent population will almost inevitably exert an

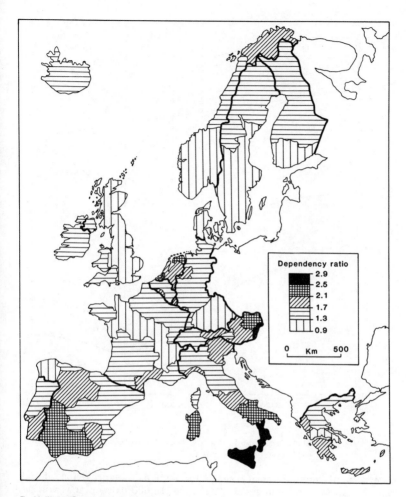

Fig. 4.1 Western Europe : dependency ratios
Source: Knox, 1984

increasing burden as it becomes increasingly concentrated in the
older age groups which are more expensive to maintain (Figure 4.2).
This issue has attracted a good deal of attention among social
scientists and policy-makers (Abrams, 1979; Eversley, 1979;
Feichtinger, 1975; Guillemard, 1983; Stearns, 1977). One major
concern especially for national welfare systems and large-scale
private pension schemes has been the question of 'who will pay our
pensions?' (Chadelet, 1975).

Many of the implications are at the community level, however,
where ageing populations impose increasing demands on a wide

93

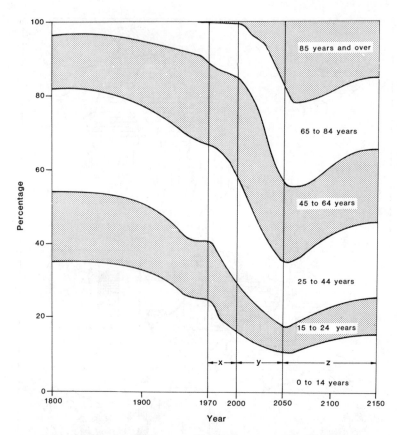

Fig. 4. 2 Actual and projected age composition of the European population, 1800–2150
Source: Bourgeois–Pichat, 1981, p. 41

spectrum of local authority services, such as the provision of old people's homes. In Denmark, for instance, 16,000 extra places will be required in old people's homes by the year 2000 if the 1980 levels of provision are to be maintained. Should mortality among the elderly continue to decline at the overall post-war rate, 27,000 extra places will be needed (Leeson, 1981). These trends are not simply quantitative, but also have a qualitative dimension, involving an increased number and proportion of the geriatric elderly for whom specialist services are expensive and, as yet, generally limited. Such aspects of public service provision for the aged include specialised health facilities and health care delivery systems, specialised housing and domiciliary services, transportation and environmental design, and neighbourhood and community care (Amman, 1981; Bergman, 1979; Millas, 1980). All involve not only increased levels of expenditure, but also changes in social priorities and in the nature

94

and organisation of service delivery. This, in turn, adds an important dimension of political decision-making to the whole issue.

Meanwhile, the school-age population in much of Western Europe will fall. From a strictly demographic viewpoint, some of the costs of educational provision should be alleviated; but other trends - extensions to the period of compulsory schooling and the increased need for vocational and recreational education for all ages, for example -provide a strong imperative for educational provision even during a period of falling numbers of school-age children (see Chapter 8, below).

Household composition
While it must be accepted that changing patterns of household composition are a product of a variety of factors. it is clear that demographic trends exert a strong influence on patterns of family status (see, for example, Haavo-Manila and Kari, 1979). Two particular consequences of this relationship are relevant here, since they are both related to population sub-groups which are not only socially and economically vulnerable but which have also become localised in specific regions and neighbourhoods.

The first of these sub-groups involves the lone elderly. Because of the differential between male and female mortality (a gap of up to six years in terms of life expectancy at birth), stationary or declining populations include increasing numbers of widows. For example, if 8 per cent of married women are widows in a population growing at a rate of 2.8 per cent per annum, the figure will be 25 per cent in a stationary population having the same rate of mortality (Le Bras, 1974). Post-war trends away from familistic lifestyles and the consequent attenuation of kinship systems have left the lone elderly increasingly isolated, personally and socially. Moreover, they are increasingly concentrated in such areas as inner-city neighbourhoods, inter-war housing developments and small villages and, due to differential migration, in particular regions such as South-West England.

The second sub-group, the single-parent family, is of increasing importance because of ideological, economic and technological changes in society as well as post-war demographic trends (Clason, 1980). The single most important factor, however, is that, over the last ten years or so, the incidence of divorce has doubled or even tripled in many parts of Western Europe (Festy, 1980). While a fair proportion of divorcees with children eventually remarry, the increased rate of divorce has produced much greater numbers of single-parent families, especially in North-Western Europe. Together with lone unmarried mothers, these families represent a particularly vulnerable group: in Britain, for example, 45 per cent of all single mothers have to rely on the welfare state's income maintenance programme (Pierce, 1980). Like the single elderly, they also tend to become localised, particularly in inner-city environments, contributing to distinctive syndromes of stress and deprivation and requiring careful consideration in relation to the provision of amenities such as pre-school facilities (Pinch, 1984).

POPULATION MOBILITY

Rural-urban migration

Although the long-standing flow of rural-urban migration has necessarily slowed as the 'stock' of rural population has fallen, most rural areas of Western Europe continue to experience a net loss of population through migration. These losses are still pronounced in parts of Southern Europe. In terms of service provision, such migration has potential implications for both sending and receiving areas. For the most part, however, the scale of rural-urban flows relative to urban size means that the implications for service provision in urban areas are less serious than for the areas of rural decline. The exceptions are the rapidly-growing metropolitan areas of Southern Europe. In Barcelona, for example, large-scale in-migration has resulted in large service-dependent populations in inner-city districts and among the substantial squatter population of the barracas. In Barcelona as a whole there was a deficit of 100,000 hospital beds and nearly 180,000 school places in the 1970's; and in some peripheral neighbourhoods even such basic services as electricity, water, drainage, road surfacing and flood control have had to be organised and paid for by the residents themselves since the city government has been unable to cope with the costs of urban growth (Naylon, 1981).

Ironically, it is in the rural regions of North-Western Europe, where the numbers of out-migrants involved are relatively small, that the problems of service provision can be most intense. Past flows of out-migrants have reduced many communities to the critical threshold population necessary to support even basic amenities and services, so that the loss of even a few families may mean the withdrawal of key services. Moreover, because of the selectivity of rural-urban migration, the residual population tends to contain disproportionate numbers of the elderly, who have less to spend (making it more difficult to sustain local shops and amenities) and little to contribute to local taxes but are more demanding in terms of specialised public services. In much of rural Europe, the future of such small communities hangs by a thread, since the arguments for maintaining the high levels of subsidy required to support basic services such as schools, post offices and bus services seem increasingly thin as economic recession prompts successive waves of fiscal retrenchment. In more prosperous times the arguments in favour of preventing depopulation - the preservation of distinctive ways of life and the maintenance of attractive landscapes for the benefit of urban populations - may seem reasonable, but the case for giving priority to public service provision in rural areas and small towns during periods of high unemployment and national recession is far from self-evident. In the final analysis, therefore, the future of marginal communities is likely to depend very much on their political significance and electoral strength.

Migrant labour

At the beginning of the 1980's there were an estimated 14 million aliens living in Western European countries, half of whom were young adult males who originally emigrated to seek work on a temporary basis. The rest were wives and families who had joined them (see Chapter 2, above). At the heart of this influx lies the labour needs of the more developed countries. The demographic 'echo effect' of low birth rates in the 1930's and 1940's produced a sluggish rate of growth in the post-war indigenous labour force of North-Western Europe (McDonald, 1969; Drewer, 1974). As the demand for labour expanded, so indigenous workers found themselves able to shun low-wage, unpleasant and menial occupations (Böhning, 1972; Castles and Kosack, 1973). Such jobs represented welcome opportunities to many unemployed and underemployed workers of Mediterranean Europe and former European colonies, however. At the same time the more prosperous countries felt that foreign workers might provide a buffer for the indigenous labour force against the effects of economic cycles - the so-called konjunkturpuffer philosophy.

The demographic impact of immigrant labour has been localised within larger urban areas, reflecting the immigrants' role as replacement labour for the low-paid, assembly line and service sector jobs vacated in inner-city areas by the upward social mobility and outward geographical mobility of the indigenous population (Salt, 1976). The subordinate position of immigrants in the labour market is of course partly self-inflicted: for many the objective is to earn as much as possible as quickly as possible before returning home. Many take on hourly wage jobs with overtime and even a second job. In any case, most immigrants do not have the skills or the qualifications to compete for better jobs. They do tend to be kept at the foot of the economic ladder, however, by a combination of official restrictions and social discrimination (Castles and Kosack, 1973). In West Germany in the mid-1970's, for example, only one per cent of migrant workers held non-manual jobs (King, 1976).

In housing markets immigrants are similarly disadvantaged. Cheap accommodation in camps, factory hostels, hotels meublés (immigrant hotels), bidonvilles (suburban shanty towns) and inner-city tenements is reinforced by restrictions and discrimination which concentrate immigrants in an environment which creates problems both for themselves and for the indigenous population. Trapped in limited niches of the housing stock, they are vulnerable to exploitation. A study of the Ruhr, for example, showed that immigrant workers pay an average of 30 per cent more rent than do German nationals for better accommodation (Böhning, 1972). One response, the notorious 'hotbed' arrangement, has two or even three workers on different shifts taking turns at sleeping in the same bed. In France, a more common response has been to retreat to the cardboard and corrugated iron bidonvilles where, although there may be no sanitary facilities, immigrants can at least find cheap accommodation amongst their fellow countrymen (Granotier, 1970; Hervo and Charras, 1971). In such circumstances, problems of health and welfare proliferate, further polarising the immigrant community in terms of social well-being.

Yet most foreign workers do not have the same civil rights as the indigenous population (Rose, 1969); nor are local social services adequately geared to deal with their problems (De Haan, 1976). Educational problems have become acute as a second generation of immigrants makes its presence felt (Beyer, 1980; Bilmen, 1976). There are already over 800,000 foreign children in the educational system of both France and West Germany and more than 250,000 in Switzerland. In some cities, such children represent over 20 per cent of the total school population; in some school catchment areas, they form an overwhelming majority. Educational systems and educational resources have so far failed to deal with the special problems of language and culture faced by immigrant children, and educational issues have become a common focus for the mistrust and resentment felt by local residents towards immigrant communities (Kane, 1978).

Return migration

After the onset of economic recession in 1973, return migration become a major feature of European migration streams. In France, a donation of £1,100 and a free ticket home was offered as an inducement to repatriation (Kennedy-Brenner, 1979); and 650,000 foreign workers left West Germany in 1975 as the konjunkturpuffer approach took effect. As a result, there was a reversal of the flows between many European and former exporting countries. The major suppliers of gastarbeiter (guestworkers) to West Germany experienced a dramatic turnround between 1973 and 1974 when they all became net importers of labour, despite their persistent problems of rural unemployment.

Return migration is not simply a product of adverse economic conditions, however. Most returnees cite non-economic factors such as discrimination, homesickness, family ties, children's education and the desire for enhanced status on return (Gmelch, 1980). Return migration is a long-standing phenomenon (Ravenstein, 1885) and most recent inter-regional migration streams within European countries have generated a counter-stream. A study of migrants from West Durham to the English Midlands during the 1960's, for instance, found that nearly 20 per cent of the families returned within a few years (Taylor, 1979). Similarly, intercontinental emigration from Europe has generated a series of reverse flows: for example from Australasia (Price, 1963), Canada (Beyer, 1961; Richmond, 1968) and the United States (Backer, 1966; Handlin, 1956; Saloutos, 1956; Vagts, 1960). Such flows have given rise to a number of local economic and social problems, including the tendency for returnees, after a spell in more prosperous environments, to act as catalysts in articulating demands for a wider range and a higher quality of public service provision (Knox, 1984).

98

Retirement migration
This phenomenon is by no means new, but since 1950 it has gained considerable momentum and has had a considerable impact in particular regions. Some retirement moves involve a return to the place or district of origin; others involve migration on retirement to 'places of reward and repose', often to an area visited during vacations. Both trends have a clear urban rural component, though it is the second which carries the greatest spatial impact, creating regional concentrations of the elderly which, together with the spas and coastal resorts which have traditionally attracted the elderly, represent a distinctive dimension of European social geography which has received surprisingly little attention from geographers. Although most of these regions, resorts and spas exhibit some common attributes, there exists a wide spectrum of 'retirement communities' (Law and Warnes, 1980).

Retirement migration is complex in its selectivity. Françoise Cribier's (1975) study of French retirement migration, for example, found a strong correlation between education and propensity to migrate on retirement. However, whereas one in three of those in higher-status groups in Paris tended to stay on, three out of every four lower-status Parisians left, mainly because of the difficulties of living on modest pensions in a high-cost area. In contrast, the higher-status elderly in provincial cities were more likely to migrate than their working-class neighbours, partly because they had the means to seek wider geographical horizons. Retirement migration creates localised concentrations of particular sub-groups within the elderly population and unique settings for, first, the profile of community needs for local authority services; secondly, the political disposition of the community to pay for particular kinds of services (policing is generally given high priority, for example, whereas expenditure on family welfare services tends to be discouraged); thirdly, the ability of the community to sustain the range of services needed and/or wanted (see, for example, Newton 1984; Sharpe and Newton 1984).

Metropolitan decentralization and the rural turnaround
A number of recent studies of post-war changes within the European urban system (Hall and Hay, 1980; Klaasen, Molle and Paelinck, 1981; Pumain and Saint-Julien, 1979; van den Berg et al., 1982) point to a slowing-down of growth rates in metropolitan areas. All major cities of Northern Europe reported heavy population losses by the mid-1970's, and there was evidence of a radical reduction of growth rates of larger cities in Southern Europe (Vining and Kontuly, 1978). Hall and Hay (1980) conclude from an analysis of cities in fifteen European countries that a 'clean break' in urbanisation trends occurred during the late 1960's and early 1970's:

"The urban cores, which had as much as two-thirds of net population growth in the 1950's, and less than one-half in the 1960's - and a negligible share in the early 1970's. The [suburban] rings, conversely, took only one-third of the

growth in the 1950's, over one-half in the 1960's - and the
whole of the net share in the early 1970's" (ibid, p.87).

But, they note that on balance, population was still leaving rural for
urban areas. One reason for this is the continuing increase in the
growth rates of smaller towns: in nine of the ten Western European
countries studied by van den Berg et al. (1982), for example, between
70 and 100 per cent of population growth between 1960 and 1980 took
place in towns with less than 50,000 inhabitants. Intermediate-sized
cities also grew relatively rapidly: in Belgium, Denmark and Great
Britain cities of 50,000-100,000 grew fastest; while in Italy and
Sweden the most rapid growth took place in cities of 100,000-
250,000. Only in France did cities of more than 250,000 outpace
smaller settlements.

Recent evidence suggests that parts of Europe may also be
experiencing the so-called rural turnaround which Beale (1977)
claimed to recognise in North America. Some of the most
spectacular rates of in-migration have occurred in areas relatively
remote from metropolitan influences. In Britain, for example,
peripheral rural areas in Wales and in the Borders and Highlands and
Islands of Scotland grew by about ten per cent between 1971 and 1981
whereas they had previously lost population; in contrast, the more
prosperous rural areas of southern and eastern England experienced a
sharp fall in their rate of growth (Champion, 1981; 1982). Such
changes in rural migration seem to have involved two very different
groups - returnees and incomers with very different aspirations,
orientations and skills. There are, therefore, important differences
between their socio-economic impacts while the tensions between the
indigenous population, returnees and incomers are in many ways the
key to the contemporary social geography of many Western European
rural communities.

The net effect of metropolitan decentralisation and the growth
of small and medium-sized cities, coupled with the turnaround in
population trends in some rural areas, has been described as
counterurbanisation (Fielding, 1982; Koch, 1980; Vining, 1982).
However, while there is widespread (but by no means universal)
evidence for a reversal of the positive overall relationship between
settlement size and net migration which obtained until the early
1960's, the arrival of 'counterurbanisation' does not mean that the
European urban system is somehow likely to be 'drained' towards rural
areas. Rather, it portends a shift in relative importance within the
urban system towards smaller cities and their adjacent countryside
and away from saturated major metropolitan regions. Moreover,
systematic statistical analysis of urban growth patterns reveals
important regional variations, most of which are attributable to the
realignment of the urban system rather than to the effects of the
rural turnaround on urban populations.

The differential momentum of urbanisation is also reflected in
regional variations in the degree of urban centralisation and
decentralisation. In broad terms, capital cities and cities founded

during the industrial revolution have come to experience the highest levels of decentralisation, while the larger cities of 'peripheral' Europe are still experiencing centralisation. Within Italy, for example, such industrial cities as Milan, Genoa and Turin have become heavily decentralized, with some growth spilling over into smaller towns nearby; meanwhile, cities in central and southern Italy together with parts of their immediate hinterland have continued to experience significant levels of in-migration.

THE SUM OF THE PARTS: REGIONAL CHANGE, DEMOGRAPHIC CHANGE AND SPATIAL ASPECTS OF SERVICE PROVISION

This selective review of demographic change in Western Europe demonstrates the variety of trends - sometimes cumulative, sometimes cross-cutting - which must be considered in the assessment of local implications for service delivery. While such a task is beyond the scope of this review, in two particular types of spatial setting - inner city areas and peripheral rural areas - the implications of demographic change for social provision are of particular interest. These settings share similar syndromes of social and economic problems which stem, fundamentally, from the same structural economic roots (Moseley, 1980): both involve high levels of unemployment, low wages and restricted job opportunities resulting from local economic stagnation. These problems lead in turn to depopulation, leaving behind the aged and the socially and economically vulnerable who become 'trapped' in the worst of the housing stock. Meanwhile, privately-organised facilities and services decline or disappear, and public-sector services struggle with the dilemma of an increasingly indigent population coupled with a progressively smaller tax base (Figure 4.3). Such a squeeze on local resources, both fiscally and in the individual household, precipitates a downward spiral of further deterioration in amenities and services, further out-migration, and disinvestment. Similarly, both inner urban and peripheral rural areas experience parallel social consequences of economic restructuring and regeneration. While inner urban areas sustain a variety of conflicts arising from the colonisation of some neighbourhoods by migrant labour and of others by 'gentrifiers', rural areas find themselves the arena for the conflicts and socio-economic dislocations surrounding a variety of incoming streams - the purchasers of second homes. return migrants, and the 'neo-rurals' who constitute the vanguard of the 'rural turnaround'. All of these groups have very different priorities for service provision from the 'local' population.

The differences between the two settings, in terms of issues related to service provision, stem largely from basic contrasts in the physical and social environment (Knox and Cottam, 1981). In inner-city areas these issues are compounded by problems of environmental decay, class and ethnic conflict, overcrowding, delinquency,

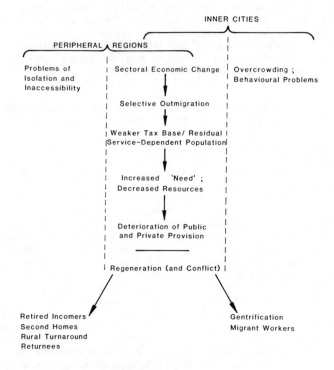

INNER CITIES

PERIPHERAL REGIONS

Problems of Isolation and Inaccessibility	Sectoral Economic Change	Overcrowding ; Behavioural Problems
	↓	
	Selective Outmigration	
	↓	
	Weaker Tax Base/ Residual Service-Dependent Population	
	↓	
	Increased 'Need' ; Decreased Resources	
	↓	
	Deterioration of Public and Private Provision	
	Regeneration (and Conflict)	

Retired Incomers
Second Homes
Rural Turnaround
Returnees

Gentrification
Migrant Workers

Fig. 4.3 The overlap of urban and rural problems
Source: After Moseley, 1980

criminality and social disorganisation. The issues in peripheral rural areas are intensified by problems of inaccessibility, social isolation and the lack of a sufficiently large threshold population to retain basic services, let alone attract higher-order services and amenities. On the other hand, the problems of inner-city areas have to be set against the richer opportunity environment of cities, while those of peripheral rural areas must be set against the advantages of higher environmental quality and social stability.

Against this overall framework it is possible to identify two major themes relating to the geography of service provision: the physical accessibility of services, and the question of service-dependent areas versus service-dependent households. There is now a considerable body of literature dealing with the problems associated with the inaccessibility of particular sub-groups of the population to different kinds of services and amenities. Such problems are most pronounced in rural areas: indeed, it can be argued that isolation and inaccessibility are at the heart of the so-called rural deprivation problem (Knox, 1985). Social well-being in peripheral rural areas is heavily conditioned by the limited opportunities available to households as a result of the prohibitive costs of service delivery to thinly scattered populations. In addition, rural households face significantly higher prices for basic foodstuffs and consumer goods (thus compounding the problems of low wages associated with economic decline and high unemployment), largely because of the combination of low turnover and local monopoly conditions imposed by physical isolation and inaccessibility (Cottam and Knox, 1982). Where rural depopulation is the dominant demographic trend, these problems are intensified.

In urban areas, physical accessibility is much less central to social well-being. Nevertheless, there are certain aspects of service provision which do give cause for concern. The failure of such services as doctors' surgeries (Jones and Kirby, 1982; Knox, 1978) and pre-school facilities (Pinch, 1984) to keep pace with metropolitan decentralisation has resulted in serious under-provision in many suburban areas. Meanwhile, the apparently generous levels of provision in many of the demographically depleted inner-city districts must be seen in relation to the quality of accessible services. It has been shown that inner-city residents in Glasgow, Liverpool and London have high levels of accessibility to family doctors' surgeries, but many of them staffed by elderly practitioners working single-handedly in unpleasant and poorly-equipped conditions (Knox, 1979).

Finally, we must confront the issue of whether service provision should be viewed on an area or household basis. In this review it has been implicitly assumed that demographic changes producing localised changes in patterns of need and demand for service provision will require at least some area-based policies to complement across-the-board policies geared to specific population sub-groups. The validity of this assumption, however, rests on whether or not service-dependent populations are sufficiently localised to represent an efficient or an equitable 'target' group. This is an issue which has been aired at some length in relation to housing and planning policies (Agnew, 1984; Taylor, 1980; Wolch, 1981). There is very little firm evidence on which to make judgements, however, mainly because most census authorities do not provide multivariate data which identify the overlap of needs at the household level (see, for example, Norris, 1983). An exception is provided by recently-released data from the 1981 Census of Scotland, which show the overlap of six different kinds of disadvantage at the household level (single-parent households, elderly-only households, overcrowded households, low-income households, head-of-household unemployed, sick or disabled, and households with more than three dependent children), aggregated to several different spatial scales. Detailed analysis of these data shows that multiply-disadvantaged households - the most needy in terms of a broad spectrum of service provision - are indeed concentrated disproportionately in the worst-

Table 4.2 : Scotland: disadvantaged households[a], 1981

Region or District	Households with no disadvantages		Households with 2 disadvantages		Households with 3 or more disadvantages		Total households	
	Number	Per cent	Number	Per cent	Number	Per cent	Number	Per cent
Borders	15,620	1.9	5,910	1.9	380	0.8	36,290	2.0
Central	44,250	5.6	14,270	4.7	1,620	3.7	92,900	5.2
Dumfries & Galloway	22,160	2.9	7,520	2.5	980	2.3	50,170	2.8
Fife	54,790	7.0	18,180	6.0	2,030	4.7	115,890	6.5
Grampian[b]	45,140	5.8	12,090	4.0	1,070	2.5	80,280	5.0
Highland	30,630	3.8	9,510	3.1	900	2.1	63,160	3.6
Lothian[c]	48,370	6.2	15,800	5.2	1,790	4.2	100,400	5.7
Strath- clyde[d]	251,770	31.9	90,590	29.8	13,650	31.8	546,190	30.8
Tayside[e]	34,420	4.3	11,320	3.7	920	2.1	74,830	4.2
Islands	10,870	1.4	3,940	1.3	410	0.9	23,610	1.3
Aberdeen	35,330	4.5	11,010	3.6	1,360	3.2	74,880	4.2
Dundee	37,040	3.4	14,979	4.6	1,790	4.2	66,960	3.8
Edinburgh	77,960	9.9	24,550	8.1	3,280	7.6	163,730	9.2
Glasgow	89,190	11.3	65,030	21.4	12,770	29.7	272,170	15.3
Scotland	787,540	100.0	303,790	100.0	42,990	100.0	1,770,460	100.0

(a)   projected from 10% sample

(b)   excluding Aberdeen

(c)   excluding Edinburgh

(d)   excluding Glasgow City

(e)   excluding Dundee

Source: Census of Scotland, 1981

off areas, though not overwhelmingly so (Table 4.2). For example, there is a marked localisation of multiply-disadvantaged households in Glasgow and the Strathclyde region. To a large extent, this reflects the distribution of population within Scotland: the Strathclyde Region contains over 46 per cent of all Scottish households. But is also contains a disproportionately large share of multiply-disadvantaged households: 52.5 per cent of all those with two or more disadvantages and 61.5 per cent of all those with three or more. Table 4.2 shows that most of this proportional share is localised within the City of Glasgow itself (Glasgow District), which accounts for 22.4 per cent of all households with two or more disadvantages and 29.7 per cent of those with three or more but only 15.3 per cent of all Scottish households.

Within Glasgow there is also a localisation of multiply-disadvantaged households, with an incidence of more than 50 per cent on the fringes of the inner city around the East End district (Figure 4.4). What is most striking about the overall pattern, however, is that there are substantial numbers of multiply-disadvantaged households in many of Glasgow's neighbourhoods (postcode sectors), including most of those in the peripheral suburbs to the northwest, east and southwest of the city. In short, there is little evidence of multiple disadvantage as an overwhelmingly 'inner-city' phenomenon in this particular case. The explanation for this, to a large extent, is to be found in the distinctive ecological structure of Scottish cities. Public housing forms a major component of the Scottish urban mosaic, so that 'normal' processes of residential segregation are restricted to rather less than half of the urban area. Moreover, the eligibility roles and allocation mechanisms of the public sector are such that multiply-disadvantaged, service-dependent households are given priority, so that public housing contains a disproportionately high share of such households. The dispersed pattern of multiply-disadvantaged households in Glasgow can, therefore, be seen largely as a function of the way in which public housing is scattered throughout the city.

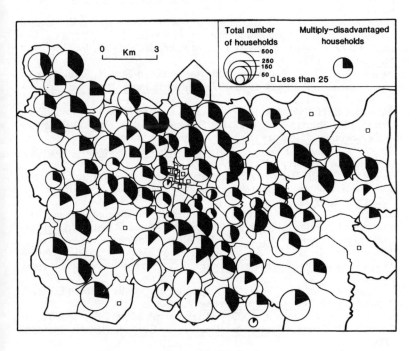

Fig. 4.4 Multiply-disadvantaged households in Glasgow, 1981

Only in relation to detailed patterns such as these can 'planning for people' be effective. The geographer's contribution to such planning must be at two levels. The first is in isolating the facts and trends at every spatial scale: international, regional, and intra-regional, whether urban or rural. The second is in integrating the evidence within a framework of theory which can accommodate the complex interactions between demographic change, economic and social change, political disposition, and the resources available for service provision.

REFERENCES

Abrams, M. (1979) 'The future of the elderly', Futures, 178-84
Agnew, J. (1984) 'Devaluing place: 'people prosperity versus place prosperity' and regional planning', Environment and Planning D, 2, 35-46
Amman, A. (1981) 'The status and prospects of the ageing in Western Europe', Eurosocial Occasional Papers, 8, Vienna
Backer, J.E. (1966) 'Norwegian migration, 1856-1960', International Migration, 4, 172-85
Beale, C. (1977) 'The recent shift in United States population to nonmetropolitan areas, 1970-1975', International Regional Science Review, 2, 113-122
Bergman, S. (1979) 'The future of human welfare for the aged', in H. Orimo, K., Shimada, M. Iriki and D. Maeda (eds.), Recent Advances in Gerontology, Excerpta Medica, Amsterdam, 44-48
Beyer, G. (ed.) (1961) Characteristics of overseas migrants, Government Printing Office, The Hague
Beyer, G. (1980) 'The second generation of migrants in Europe: social and demographic aspects', European Demographic Information Bulletin, 11, 49-72
Bilmen, M.S. (1976) 'Educational problems encountered by the children of Turkish migrant workers', in N. Abadan-Unat (ed.) Turkish workers in Europe, 1960-1975, Brill, Leiden, 235-52
Böhning, W.R. (1972) The migration of workers in the United Kingdom and the European Community, Oxford University Press, London
Bourgeois-Pichat, J. (1981) 'Demographic change in Western Europe', Population and Development Review 7, 19-42
Calot, G., and J. Hecht (1978) 'The control of fertility trends', in Council of Europe, Population Decline in Europe, Arnold, London, 178-96
Castles, S., and G. Kosack (1973) Immigrant workers and class structure in Western Europe, Oxford University Press, London
Chadelet, J.-F. (1975) Who will pay our pensions in 1990?, Council of Europe Working Paper, Strasbourg
Champion, A.G. (1981) 'Population trends in rural Britain', Population Trends, 26, 20-23

Champion, A.G. (1982) 'Rural-urban contrasts in Britain's population change, 1961-1981' in A Findlay (ed.) Recent National Population Change, Institute of British Geographers, Population Study Group, London, 4-17

Clason, C. (1980) 'The one-parent family: the Dutch situation', Journal of Comparative Family Studies, 11, 3-16

Coleman, D.A. (1980) 'Recent trends in marriage and divorce in Britain and Europe', in R.W. Hiorns (ed.), Demographic patterns in developed societies, Taylor and Francis, London, 83-124

Cottam, M.B., and P.L. Knox (1982) The Highlands and Islands: A Social Profile, Occasional Paper No. 5, Department of Geography, University of Dundee

Council of Europe (1978) Population decline in Europe, Arnold, London

Cribier, F. (1975) 'Retirement migration in France', in L.A. Kosinski and R.M. Prothero (eds.), People on the move, Methuen, London, 361-74

Davis, N. (1978) 'Population trends: a European overview', Population Trends, 12, 10-12

De Haan, E. (1976) 'Foreign workers and social sources in Federal Germany', in N. Abadan-Unat (ed.) Turkish workers in Europe, 1960-1975, Brill, Leiden, 346-62

Drewer, S. (1974) 'The economic impact of immigrant workers in Western Europe', European Studies, 18, 1-4

Dyer, C. (1978) Population and society in Twentieth-Century France, Hodder and Stoughton, London

Eversley, D. (1979) 'Welfare', in Council of Europe, Population Decline in Europe, Arnold, London, 115-42

Feichtinger, G. (1975) Are economically dependent groups likely to become a significantly larger proportion of the population as a whole?, Council of Europe, Seminar Paper AS/PR/Coll.75(2), Strasbourg

Festy, P. (1980) 'On the new context of marriage in Western Europe', Population and Development Review, 6, 311-15

Fielding, A.J. (1982) 'Counterurbanisation in Western Europe', Progress in Planning, 17, Pergamon, Oxford

Gmelch G. (1980) 'Return migration', Annual Review of Anthropology, 9, 135-59

Granotier, B. (1970) Les travailleurs immigrés en France, Maspero, Paris

Guillemard, A.M. (ed.) (1983) Old age and the welfare state, Studies in International Sociology, No. 28, Sage, London

Guilmot, P. (1978) 'The demographic background', in Council of Europe, Population Decline in Europe, Arnold, London, 3-49

Haavo-Manila, E., and K. Kari (1979) 'Demographic background of changes in the life patterns of families in the Nordic countries', Working Paper, 11, Department of Sociology, University of Helsinki, Helsinki

107

Hall, P., and D. Hay (1980) Growth centres in the European urban system, Heinemann, London

Handlin, O. (1956) 'Immigrants who go back', Atlantic, 198, 70-74

Hervo, M., and M. Charras (1971) Bidonvilles, Maspero, Paris

Jones, K., and A. Kirby, (1982) 'Provision and well-being: and agenda for public resources research', Environment and Planning A, 14, 297-310

Kane, T.T. (1978) 'Social problems and ethnic change: Europe's "guest workers" ', Intercom, 6, 7-9

Kennedy-Brenner, C. (1979) Foreign workers and immigration policy -the case of France, OECD, Paris

Keyfitz, N. (1973) 'Individual mobility in a stationary population', Population Studies, 27, 210-27

King, R.L. (1976) 'The evolution of international labour migration movements concerning the EEC', Tijdschrift voor Economische en Sociale Geografie, 67, 66-82

Kirk, M. (1981) Demographic and social change in Europe: 1975-2000, Liverpool University Press, Liverpool

Klaasen, L.H., W.T.M., Molle, and J.H.P. Paelinck (eds.), (1981) Dynamics of urban development, Gower, Aldershot

Knox, P.L. (1978) 'The intra-urban ecology of primary medical care: patterns of accessibility and their policy implications', Environment and Planning A, 10, 415-35

Knox, P.L. (1979) 'Medical deprivation, area deprivation and public policy: a review', Social Science and Medicine, 13D, 111-21

Knox, P.L. (1984) The Geography of Western Europe: a socio-economic survey, Croom Helm, London

Knox, P.L. (1985) 'Methodologies and the poverty of theory', in P. Lowe (ed.) Deprivation and welfare in rural areas, Geo Books, Norwich

Knox, P.L. and M.B. Cottam (1981) 'Rural deprivation in Scotland: A preliminary assessment', Tijdschrift voor Economische en Sociale Geografie, 72, 162-175

Koch, R. (1980) 'Counterurbanisation auch in Westeurope?', Informationen zur Baumentwicklung, 2, 59-69

Le Bras, H. (1974) 'Le mythe de la population stationnaire', Prospectives, 3, 71-82

Leeson, G.W. (1981) 'The elderly in Denmark in 1980: consequences of a mortality decline', European Demographic Information Bulletin, 12, 89-100

Law, A., and A. Warnes, (1980) 'The characteristics of retired migrants', in D.T. Herbert and R.J. Johnston, (eds.), Geography and the urban environment, 3, Wiley, Chichester, 175-222

McDonald, J.R. (1969) 'Labour immigration into France, 1946-1965', Annals, Assocation of American Geographers, 59, 116-34

Millas, A. (1980) 'Planning for the elderly within the context of a neighbourhood', Ekistics, 47, 273-76

Monnier, A. (1981) 'L'Europe et les pays developées d'outre-mer: données statistiques', Population, 36, 885-96

Moseley, M.J. (1980) 'Is rural deprivation really rural', The Planner, 66, 97

Muñoz-Perez, F. (1982) 'L'évolution de la fecondité dans les pays industrialisés depuis 1971', Population, 37, 483-512

Naylon, J. (1981) 'Barcelona', in M. Pacione (ed.) Urban problems and planning in the Developed World, Croom Helm, London, 223-57

Newton, K. (1984) 'Public services in cities and counties', in A. Kirby, P. Knox and S. Pinch (eds.) Public service provision and urban development, Croom Helm, London

Norris, P. (1983) 'Microdata from the British Census', in D. Rhind (ed.) A census user's handbook, Methuen, London, 301-19

Ogden, P.E., and M.-N. Huss, (1982) 'Demography and pro-natalism in France in the nineteenth and twentieth centuries', Journal of Historical Geography, 8, 283-98

Pierce, S. (1980) 'Single mothers and the concept of female dependency in the development of the Welfare State in Britain', Journal of Comparative Family Studies, 11, 57-86

Pinch, S. (1984) 'Inequality in pre-school provision: a geographical perspective', in A. Kirby, P. Knox and S. Pinch (eds.) Public service provision and urban development, Croom Helm, London, pp. 231-82

Price, C.A. (1963) Southern Europeans in Australia, Oxford University Press, Melbourne

Pumain, D., and T. Saint-Julien, (1979) 'Recent transformations in the French urban system', L'Espace Geographique, 8, 203-10

Ravenstein, E. (1885) 'The laws of migration', Journal of the Royal Statistical Society, 48, 167-227

Richmond, H.A. (1968) 'Return migration from Canada to Britain', Population Studies, 22, 263-71

Rose, A.M. (1969) Migrants in Europe: problems of acceptance and adjustment, University of Minnesota Press, Minneapolis

Roussel, L., and P. Festy, (1979) Recent trends in attitudes and behaviour affecting the family in Council of Europe Member States, Population Studies, 4, Council of Europe, Strasbourg

Saloutos, T. (1956) They remember America: the study of repatriated Greek-Americans, University of California Press, Berkeley

Salt, J. (1976) 'International labour migration: the geographical pattern of demand', in J. Salt and H. Clout (eds.), Migration in Post-War Europe, Oxford University Press, London

Sharpe, L., and K. Newton, (1984) Does politics matter?, Oxford University Press, Oxford

Stearns, P.N. (1977) Old age in European society, Croom Helm, London

Taylor, P. (1980) 'Policies for deprived areas or deprived people?', Discussion Paper No. 8, Policy Analysis Research Unit, Glasgow College of Technology, Glasgow

Taylor, R. (1979) 'Migration and the residual community', Sociological Review, 27, 475-89

United Nations (1975) Economic survey of Europe in 1974. Part II: Post-war demographic trends in Europe and the outlook until the year 2000, United Nations, New York

Vagts, A. (1960) 'Deutsch-Amerikanische Ruckwanderung', Beuhefte zum Jahrbuck für Amerikastudies, No. 6, Heidelberg

Van den Berg, L., R. Drewett, L.H. Klaasen, A. Rossi, and C.H.T. Vijverberg (1982) Urban Europe: a study of growth and decline, Pergamon, Oxford

Van de Kaa, D.J. (1980) 'Recent trends in fertility in Western Europe', in R.W. Hiorns (ed.), Demographic Patterns in Developed Societies, Taylor and Francis, London, 55-82

Vining, D.R. (1982) 'Migration between the core and the periphery', Scientific American, 247, 44-53

Vining, D.R., Jr., and T. Kontuly, (1978) 'Population dispersal from major metropolitan regions: an international comparison', International Regional Science Review, 3, 49-73

Westoff, C.F. (1983) 'Fertility decline in the West: causes and prospects', Population and Development Review, 9, 99-104

Wirz, H.M. (1977) 'Economics of welfare: the implications of demographic change for Europe', Futures, 9, 45-52

Wolch, J. (1981) 'The location of service-dependent households in urban areas', Economic Geography, 57, 52-68

Chapter Five

SERVICE PROVISION IN THE THIRD WORLD : A DEMAND-BASED
PERSPECTIVE

W.T.S. Gould

THE DEMAND FOR SERVICES

Introduction

One of the features of the countries of the Third World that sets
them apart from developed countries is the low level of provision of
social services and associated physical infrastructure. Not only are
there fewer roads per area of land or per 1000 people and fewer jobs
(Chapter 3) and less income per person, but also fewer medical
centres or schools. Piped water supplies and electricity grids are less
common and less extensive, and levels of housing provision, both in
terms of living space per person and the quality of that space in
materials and services provided, are lower. Global patterns of
indices of per capita provision of most social services, public and
privately provided, even if they could be measured or if sufficient
comparative data were available, would all point to the
differentiation between high levels of provision in the developed
world and low levels in the Third World, symptoms and to some
extent also causes of global disparities in levels of living.

The problems associated with low levels of provision are
exacerbated by population growth. Since services are essentially
consumption goods, the more people there are the greater the
theoretical demand for services. Furthermore, the demographic
impact of population growth on age structures means that there are
disproportionately more people in younger age-groups, and they are
even more obviously consumers rather than producers, at least in the
short-term. Though there are fewer people in the older age groups,
dependency ratios are distinctly more adverse than they are in
Europe or North America (Chapter 4), with more dependents than
working-age population in some countries (Chapter 3). In an
economic context people produce, and more people may produce
more goods and services. However, these services are provided to be
consumed, and, unless production can create disproportionately more
wealth that can be used to increase the resources available to the
State or private agencies to maintain these services, per capita
availability of services will fall.

111

Recent development, therefore, has necessitated a great desire and a great effort on the part of governments and of the population at large to redress imbalances in service provision. The revolution of rising expectations has meant that a stronger demand has been felt for the wide range of social and economic facilities that were by the mid-twentieth century commonplace in developed countries, valued as a symbol of and a means to development, but also much prized in their own right. It seems that every village has been clamouring to government or to local politicians for a primary school, if not a secondary school; for a dispensary if not a hospital; for a motorable track, if not a tarred road; for a clean water supply; for a diesel generator if not mains electricity. Since people have become more aware of the possibilities of having welfare services, social security payments and improved housing, per capita demand has risen to further aggravate the problems caused by low levels and weak structures of most current service provision.

Governments have been anxious, for directly developmental as well as more cynically political reasons, to accede to these rising demands. Before the 1960's, social policies both in poor, independent countries as in the colonies of the time were generally formulated in isolation from the more general stream of economic and other developmental policies, and provision was very strongly biased both socially, towards the elite, and spatially, towards urban and favoured rural areas. While the legacy of these imbalances remains and in some cases may have been aggravated in recent years, the trend has generally been reversed as social policy has moved into a more central role in development strategies (MacPherson, 1982). Objectives of development are defined in social as well as economic terms, and this has been associated in particular with the widespread adoption of a 'basic-needs' approach to development. Providing basic needs of water, education, health care and housing, particularly to the rural poor, is both socially desirable and economically justified, for better health and education, clean water supply and rural electrification will not only be purely social services that improve the quality of life for their consumers, but will enable these consumers to themselves become more productive. In international organizations such as the World Bank investments in services are normally justified in strictly economic terms. Expanding school enrolments is 'investment in human capital'; evaluation of the provision of clean water supply in rural areas is not only a technical and engineering matter but must invoke economic criteria (Cairncross et al., 1980; Saunders and Warford, 1976). In practice, therefore, it is often difficult to clearly differentiate economic and social provision.

In almost all sectors in almost all countries, there have been massive expansions in the number and range of services. Each sector has its own problems and issues (two of which, health and education, are specifically dealt with in Chapters 7 and 9 respectively), but generally there have been very considerable efforts and expenditures to expand the size and improve the impact of the service delivery system. These expansions have normally been sufficiently large to considerably outstrip population growth and per capita provision has improved, often by a substantial factor. They have also normally been quantitatively more impressive than improvements in economic and income levels, though seldom sufficient to adequately satisfy demand. As Jackson (1979) has clearly pointed out for Papua New Guinea, governments are less able to control the pattern and type of economic expenditures than they are to build social facilities, with the result that social expenditures have not only been greater in quantity than economic expenditures, but have been able to be more equitably distributed regionally and locally. Governments can therefore gain 'credit' or political kudos more readily from building a school or community centre or improving the local water supply than from less tangible investments in, for example, agricultural extension or improved seeds, and investments in social overhead capital therefore assume greater short-term importance than do investments in directly productive activities.

Levels and models of provision

The most immediately apparent need in the Third World is for the level of provision to at least keep pace with population growth. Given low levels of provision in the first instance, this is not normally difficult to achieve. Much more important, however, is the fact that the per capita levels need to rise substantially so that, given the high rates of national population growth that remain characteristic features of many countries and especially the poorest, gross expansions of provision may need to be often in excess of 5 per cent p.a. over several years if they are to have any long term impact on levels of provision.

The western model of provision for all or even most facilities should not be assumed to be either appropriate or expected. The particular case for a radical restructuring of health care facilities in favour of low technology care and maximum access and away from high technology specialist services is discussed below (Chapter 7), but similar sorts of issues arise in other sectors. De-schoolers see the institution of the school as undermining the real education of children in the Third World, inculcating anti-rural and neo-colonial values, to the extent that traditional schools systems, arranged in a spatial hierarchy from primary school to university to provide maximum access, are inappropriate. Such a view is seldom held by Governments who tend to view and use space within the positivist frameworks enshrined in western planning practice.

It should be remembered, however, that population growth need not impose additional burdens on services. Some services could, without any increase in the number or type of facilities, under certain circumstances be provided without any real decline in access or the standard of service. This is particularly the case with large capital investments with low recurrent costs, such as a road. A road once built might be able to carry twice the number of people or cope with twice the traffic density for which it was built. One of the potential benefits of having a larger population is that facilities and other fixed assets can be more intensively used. More commonly, however, population growth will require additional facilities to maintain the quality and range of service provided, especially since existing facilities in most countries of the Third World are used well beyond the capacity for which they were designed. Oversized classes in schools, long queues at clinics or standpipes are familiar enough, and often cannot further absorb the continuing growth in population served, even within the same catchment area. Where there is an absolute shortage of facilities, any supply will elicit a strong demand, but planning must ensure that the demand that can be met from available resources is maximized. Hence demand-based rather than supply-based planning criteria for the level and type of provision are more appropriate to policies for meeting basic needs.

Supply and demand and population change

It is because of the direct link between the service provided at the delivery points and the consumers of the service, the population at large or specific sub-groups within it, that the planning of services is premised on a major concern for population and population change. The better the service, the more accessible it is to the population for which it satisfies the demand. However, since population change is such a major feature of that demand, the extent of any correspondence between supply and demand in a spatial or even in an aggregate sense is dependent on the supply being responsive to that changing demand.

In this chapter we adopt a demand-based perspective to consider how the pattern of responses on the supply side can be affected by changes in level and types of demand, and in particular by changes in the geographical distribution of demand required by changing population distributions at various scales. The next section deals with some general aspects of population change for the planning of the nature and type of social services in the Third World, and is followed by three more specific sections that deal in some detail with contrasting issues: problems of service delivery to rural populations, with particular reference to Africa; housing provision in rapidly expanding cities, with particular reference to Latin America; and practice in the planning of fertility reduction, with particular reference to Asia.

DEMOGRAPHIC STRUCTURES AND THE PATTERN OF DEMAND

Provision for the elderly

If there is an area where western institutions that have been developed in response to the type of demographic evolution of developed countries seem to have had little relevance in the Third World, it is with respect to the elderly. It is certainly true that the elderly remain a small proportion of the population of Third World countries, overshadowed by the massive proportions in the younger age groups and with corresponding demands for more schools and child care in the health sector. In the Third World as a whole the elderly (aged 65+) are about four per cent of the population but that proportion has risen from just below 3.8 per cent in 1975, and is expected to be about 4.6 per cent by 2000 (equivalent proportions for developed countries are 10.6 per cent in 1975 and 13.1 per cent respectively). In 1975 50 per cent of the world's elderly lived in the Third World, and by 2000 this may be 58 per cent. The numbers of old people are growing rapidly as life expectancies rise. Even though the sharp fall in infant mortality rates has been the major factor in mortality reduction, better nutrition and working conditions have meant that adults are living longer.

The demographic basis for major expansions of facilities for the elderly is evident, but the social situation can warrant a very different emphasis from the type and level of provision in Western societies, or in Japan where the proportion aged 65+, currently 9.1 per cent is likely to rise to over 14 per cent by the first quarter of the 21st century when it will be the highest of any country (Steslicke, 1984). Throughout most of the Third World family and kin ties remain much stronger than they are in the developed world, with a stronger sense of caring for the old within traditional social relationships notably in multi-generation households. Alienation and the demand for institutional care for the growing number of old people are therefore correspondingly less. Undoubtedly social change in many countries, and particularly in urban areas, is bringing the major changes in family structures that may have an impact on the demand for care facilities for the elderly, yet there is substantial evidence of considerable resistance to the principle of institutional provision for the elderly. In Hong Kong, for example, where the proportion of the population aged over 65 was 6.6 per cent in 1981 and is expected to rise to over 10 per cent by 2001, old people are of disproportionately low socio-economic status, but tend to live with a son or daughter. In 1981 only 15.4 per cent lived alone and 15.2 per cent in a two-person household with another old person, but 69 per cent lived in households with three or more people. Not surprisingly, therefore, the distribution of old people in the colony was similar to the distribution of the population as a whole (Lo, 1984). Hong Kong is, of course, a rather special case, but in general it would appear that change in numbers of old people in Third World countries may not elicit the kind of supply response that has been the norm in developed countries.

The problem of the elderly is heightened in countries where fertility has been falling rapidly and life expectancies have been rising rapidly so that the proportion of the old rises. In China, 1980, life expectancies for men are 67 and for women 68 years, and over 70 years for both in towns, double the expectancies in the 1930's (Banister, 1984). Urban workers in China receive retirement pensions of 60-90 per cent of their working wage, and many 'retire' on that pension to voluntary work such as looking after children of working mothers. The strength of traditional family support systems in towns has declined. Some rural communes may also pay retirement pensions (about 15 per cent of the total population is covered), but their working children are expected to support the elderly. However, with the pressure for the one-child family, traditional structures of three-generation households are breaking down, even in rural areas. Important as these short-term implications of this policy may be (see below), the very sharp fall in fertility of recent years and its continuation will carry through to a very adverse ratio of working age:elderly by the second quarter of the 21st century when it is estimated that 21 per cent of the population will be aged over 65 (World Bank, 1984, p.104). There will then be a very great demand for health care and social support, including institutionalized housing, that will need to be maintained by wealth created by the smaller proportions of the working age groups.

The Chinese case is exceptional, but there is a more general problem of poor countries being able to support pensions schemes. In Africa in 1981 about 50 countries had introduced some form of old age protection, either in the form of social insurance, social assistance or a national provident fund (Ewane, 1981). However, these affected only a few people in favoured, generally white-collar occupations.

Provision for children

It is, however, in the lives of the greatly increased numbers of children that there are major problems of quality of life in the Third World, not only in direct peri-natal and post-natal health care, but also in the quality of nutrition and social and economic security during childhood. A major study mounted by UNICEF, with many case studies in a wide range of countries, both developed and developing, has concluded that children have fared disproportionately badly in the current international recession. A range of structural and short-term variables operating at various scales from the household to the global economy all affect child welfare services (Figure 5.1), and an analysis of several kinds of indices reveals that:

> ". . the decline in incomes and resources for children is general, unmistakable and, in certain cases, extremely severe. The decline in quality and quantity of available basic needs, goods and social services also appears to be very general ... The impact on child survival and welfare seems, on the contrary, more composite. Risk of death for children has increased in those cases where declines in household incomes and cuts in social services have been particularly severe. One does not observe, however, a general worsening of infant and child mortality even in countries experiencing moderate recession. Rather, infant mortality rates and some social indicators have continued to improve - although at much reduced rates. In most countries one observes, however, a serious deterioration in indicators of nutrition, health status and

STRUCTURAL VARIABLES ──────────────▶ DIRECT INFLUENCES ──▶ CHILD WELFARE

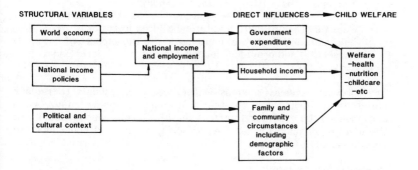

Fig. 5.1 Linkages affecting child welfare
Source: Cornia, 1984, p. 394

school achievements, and it is quite evident that if this process is not reversed it will lead to more dramatic deteriorations which will then be reflected in a higher rate of infant and child mortality" (Cornia, 1984, p.390).

Many of the issues raised are related to basic health care and provide powerful support for the sorts of policies suggested by 'Health care for all by 2000' (see Chapter 7) but also require more general effort by individual governments and the international community for redistribution of national and global incomes. "In Brazil, for example, 60 per cent of the children live in the poorest 40 per cent of households, households that between them have just 10 per cent of total income" (World Bank, 1984, p.53). Improving the quality of life for children is clearly not simply a matter of the poor having smaller families and governments providing more small scale services directed at the vulnerable groups, important though these may be in the short term.

Older children in the Third World do themselves provide services and at an earlier age than in developed countries. These services may be in the home, notably in the laborious and time-consuming tasks of fetching water (for girls), tending cattle and protecting crops from animal pests (for boys) and weeding crops (for boys and girls). More important for hard pressed families at the margins of existence are children's incomes from providing these and other services for other families. The children's meagre addition may make a valuable contribution to the household economy (Fawcett, 1982). The net economic benefit of children is generally positive, even in the poorest countries, one of the factors contributing to the persistence of high fertility:

"Beyond the fifth child, economic considerations predominate (in couples' attitudes to their family). Parents speak of sixth and later children in terms of their helping round the house, contributing to the support of the household, and providing security in old age" (World Bank, 1984, p.122).

Provision of services such as water supply or schools to replace childrens' contributions to the household economy may, as a consequence, be expected to affect fertility levels. Supply conditions the level of demand for services as surely as demand conditions the level of supply of services.

Provision for the family

The relationships between dependents, the old and young, and the labour force in the economically active age-groups are cemented in the family. Not only is mean family size (as a demographic rather than a social measure) falling in many parts of the Third World, but also changes in the structure of the family are occurring and have occurred in many countries. Generally the trend is from traditional forms of extended, multi-generation families and households towards nuclear families and two-generation households of parents and their dependent children. This change can be expected to have major demographic implications, in particular to alter patterns of inter-generational wealth flows in the family from younger to older in the traditional pattern to older to younger in the Western pattern. In traditional societies the old of the family were supported by the produce and income of the younger members, but the crucial decisions about the creation and allocation of that wealth were made by the elders or household heads. In the modern family the income earners spend proportionately more on children than hitherto for education and in delayed earnings as a result. If they do support older, retired people, it is on their terms. Jack Caldwell (1977), the Australian demographer, sees changes in inter-generational wealth flow in the family as a prime cause in the fertility transition from high to low rates. The persistence of high fertility, particularly in Africa and India, is because family structures have not changed and traditional structures are still dominant, even in many urban areas, e.g. in Nigeria. In East Asia, on the other hand, family bonds have been loosened, and in these circumstances the costs of children are considerably greater, so the economic rationality of lower fertility and smaller families is so much more evident. However, even here the net value of children to the household may be positive.

The smaller family directly reduces aggregate demand for publicly provided services, but it has major consequences for the overall demand for services. With the smaller nuclear family there is a greater need for baby-minding services, traditionally available within the extended family, and there is also an increased need for retirement benefits and other services for the elderly, who are no longer assured of support and shelter by younger members of the household. Fertility reduction, as explained by Caldwell's hypothesis, implies a cost for social services that may be serious and growing, and may outweigh any short-term savings that accrue from postponed or cancelled births.

For similar sorts of reasons associated with persistence of traditional family relationships, the demand for certain types of family provision that are typical in countries where the nuclear family is the norm has been much lower in the Third World. Children of single parents and these parents themselves are usually supported within the wider circle of the extended family. Indeed in many areas, e.g. in the Caribbean, single mother families may be the norm but kin relationships can ensure support for their children even though the mother has a job outside the home. While the demand for public family welfare services may be lower, the need for the economic support of family income, through tax benefits directly or through the wide range of children's services, e.g. dental care and eye testing, is so much greater. However, these are much less available than in richer societies, and in many countries direct economic and fiscal support for families is non-existent.

Hitherto 'family planning' has been associated only with the regulation of family size, directly affecting fertility and associated aspects of child and maternal care (Population Reports, 1984). But clearly family planning can be extended into the more general realm of planning for change in family structures, and currently volatile family relationships in the Third World might suggest that this wider conceptualization of 'family planning' may be more directly appropriate to the needs of those involved and certainly of greater longer term significance to economic and social planning.

THE PROBLEM OF SUPPLY

Facility provision in rural Africa
Absolute and per capita levels of social provision throughout sub-Saharan Africa are generally low, whether in levels of health care, education or water supply or any other available index (Figure 5.2). Yet this is the world region with the highest levels of poverty and the greatest need for more and better facilities, exacerbated by the demands imposed by continuing high rates of population growth, rising to an estimated 4 per cent per year in Kenya but nowhere less than 2 per cent per year. Critically the spatial pattern of provision within African countries is heavily biased towards urban areas, even though Africa is the least urbanized continent with only 21 per cent of its population in 1980 in urban areas. The rural/urban inequalities have their origins in the colonial period when social provision based on the western formal model of fixed-site facilities was introduced and diffused hierarchically and unequally through the national space (Riddell, 1970; Soja, 1968). Furthermore, social expenditures had low priority for that was seen to be "inevitable that in a poor country like Nigeria, in which essential expenditure on administration and security

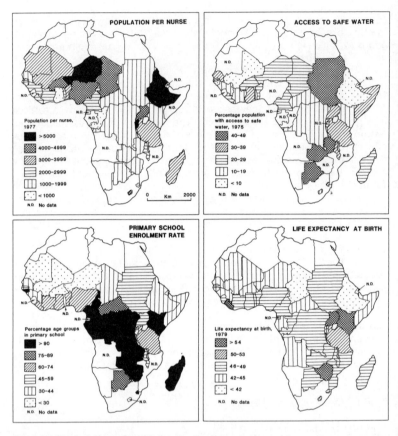

Fig. 5.2   Tropical Africa : Social indices by country
Source : World Bank, 1981

and in the service of the public debt must absorb an unduly large
percentage of available revenue" (Nigerian Government Printer,
1944, p.34).

Expansion in the number of facilities and type of provision has
been very rapid in most areas of social expenditure since
independence and guided by rather different sets of assumptions,
principally the objective of promoting greater equality of provision
and access. The 'basic needs' thrust, especially in the 1970's, was
encouraged by international agencies, such as the World Bank and
ILO, who were in a very strong position to influence impoverished
national governments anxious for external funds and willing to bend
their own objectives for social provision to those of the funding
agencies. Thus there was, for the first time, a systematic concern

for the level and type of rural provision.

However, the supply problem in Africa was not simply to be solved by providing capital for more facilities, or in massive training programmes for doctors. nurses, teachers, water engineers or community officers, though these were and still are essential and were certainly attempted. There were more fundamental problems associated with how supply and demand were to be matched. However desirable it is in theory to provide every citizen with easy and equal access to all services, in practice resource constraints necessitate a compromise between equity and efficiency, and patterns of provision have evolved within the efficiency constraints of each sector. The ideas of efficiency have certainly changed, most notably in the health sector where more low threshold facilities are deemed to be more efficient as well as more equitable. In terms of rural water supply much attention has been paid in recent years to developing low-cost technologies such as hand pumps instead of expensive pipe networks and using plastic well linings instead of steel. In Malawi, for example, there has been a major focus on improving rural water supplies at a cost of only $6 per person served (World Bank, 1981, p.90).

Changed assumptions meant that the population threshold for many facilities fell; instead of regional allocations of one dispensary per 50,000 people it may have fallen to one per 10,000 people. Efficiency became to be defined not only in technical terms of least-cost but also in terms of the planning objectives. Due to population change, however, the planning of the supply could not assume a static pattern of demand. Population growth itself affected the assumptions that could be made about the size and useage of facilities. Schools could be more 'efficient' with more potential pupils in the catchment area, and efficiency could be further improved when real rates of enrolment were rising. Population growth allowed for more intensive use of facilities, and has been particularly important in supporting the case for extending provision to low density areas of rural Africa.

Locally, the problem of low effective demand in areas of low population density is compounded by the distribution of that population, for in many areas of Africa, and in particular throughout most of Eastern and Southern Africa the traditional rural settlement pattern is highly dispersed, with isolated family groups living on their own land without the economic and social cohesion that is important in nucleated villages. For this reason in many countries, both in the colonial period (Kay, 1967) and since independence, the planning of social facilities has become strongly associated with planning of population change in the form of settlement planning. In part for ideological reasons associated with the development of socialist forms of production (e.g. in Tanzania, Mozambique and Zimbabwe), in part for more directly technical reasons of improving access, governments have encouraged nucleation of settlement, with provision of facilities at central points operating as both stick and carrot for the nucleation.

Villagization policies have been at the heart of the Tanzanian attempts to develop a socialist society and economy based on ujamaa. Aggregate population densities are low and settlement was traditionally highly dispersed, but by 1974 over 7,000 nucleated villages had been created, often by coercion, with the expectation that government services would be provided in these villages (Maro and Mlay, 1982). The villages have involved permanent migrations of family groups over short distances to the village sites, even though temporary residences may persist for occasional use at times of major agricultural activity on well-scattered plots. Even though villagization has allowed better provision of low order facilities, e.g. one dispensary per 10,000 people (Thomas, 1982), it has created several problems. Some of these are largely implementational, e.g. inappropriate siting of new villages away from water supplies (Moore, 1979), but others are more fundamental to the long-term viability of the villages, ignoring much of the environmental basis for dispersed settlement as a risk-minimising strategy in areas of low and annually and spatially variable rainfall and poor soils. Nucleation breaks the direct link between the household and the land worked and imposes severe pressures on resources of water and wood for fuel near the large village (Kjekshus, 1977).

In other cases in Africa there has been planned resettlement in new areas that have perhaps been freed from tsetse fly infestation or other disease or provided with water supplies. In such areas social facilities are normally provided as part of the resettlement programme and will contribute to its success, even though that success may be defined primarily in terms of agricultural output and increased farmers' income. Particularly important in Africa in recent years has been provision in refugee settlements, for Africa has about 5 million refugees, many of whom live in organized rural settlements. UNHCR and other organizations have sought to provide these settlements with basic facilities, and the provision itself is a further attraction to refugees outside the formal settlements.

In rural Africa social facilities are scarce but much needed, and can be used as important tools for managing population distribution at the local level (Prothero and Gould, 1984). However it is clear that achieving better social provision cannot depend on population distribution alone, for population concentration can bring problems. In other cases planning can assume a relatively static population distribution, such that service provision adjusts to that population distribution, and not vice versa, by having more and better distributed facilities, each serving fewer people. In other circumstances, there is planning for population deconcentration. In Botswana, for example, government policies in agriculture encourage more people spending longer away from the large agro-villages, the traditional settlement patterns. However such a policy means a spread of facilities that until recent years have been concentrated in the large villages. Here there is a continuing and unresolved tension between planning that seeks to manage the distribution of supply of facilities and planning that seeks to manage the distribution of demand for their use.

Housing in Latin American cities

The problems of social provision in rural areas of the Third World are very different from those in urban areas, for in urban areas facilities are normally available and access is not normally constrained by distance, except for the lowest order facilities, notably running water, but rather by cost, whether directly in a fee to be paid for the service as it is used, e.g. drugs at a clinic, or indirectly in political or social pressure. Within cities of the Third World there are gross inequalities in spatial and social access to all facilities even though in aggregate terms cities are usually much better provided than surrounding rural areas. For this reason, if for no other, a rural bias in social (and other) expenditures may adversely affect the urban poor.

The contemporary problems of urban social provision are very much associated with large-scale urban migration, and particularly to the largest cities in most countries. The proportion of national populations living in urban areas has grown rapidly in all parts of the Third World and the increase is disproportionately of poor people for whom an urban life is, at best, precarious, with limited job opportunities and little job security. This is associated with a very fragmentary system of social security or state unemployment benefit. Measured rates of unemployment are high among the urban poor, for whom the informal sector may be a permanent or temporary source of income and can itself provide a wide range of social and economic services from traditional medicine to water carrying and general porterage.

Housing, however, is the most crucial provision for the urban poor. Rural housing is certainly a concern of governments, but that concern is for quality associated with such matters as health and could certainly be improved to raise the quality of rural life. Urban housing, on the other hand, raises issues of quantity as well as quality, as the stock of urban housing fails to keep up with population growth. Planning to house the burgeoning urban populations needs to recognise both the extent to which the existing stock can absorb growth and, conversely but increasingly likely given continuing growth, the need for additional housing of various types. If additional housing is needed, how might this best be provided - by the public sector, by the private rented sector or by private ownership or by some combination of each of these? In the absence of forward planning the private sector has in most instances become dominant in urban housing markets, despite self-help housing everywhere and government interventions of various kinds from complete provision in housing estates of varying qualities of housing appropriate to local markets to minimal provision of basic infrastructure (water, sewerage and site layout) in site-and-service schemes. Issues and policy choices for the overall stock of housing need to be informed by discussion and projection of rates and types of urban migration and their likely effects on the structure of the urban population. The

123

differences, for example, between a city fed by mostly permanent migrants, such as families dispossessed of a rural livelihood (as would be typical of most cities in Latin America), and a city that attracted a high level of temporary circulation, often unmarried young men and women or, if married, leaving their family at 'home' in the rural area (as is typical of most African cities), have clear implications for the urban housing market. Even in Africa, however, where there are high proportions of temporary residents and traditions of high absorptive capacity of existing housing stock, e.g. in many West African towns where urban compounds resemble rural extended family compounds open to rural kin, the need for additional housing is very apparent, since up to 80 per cent of the population of some cities live in slum or squatter settlements (Figure 5.3). But governments have failed to respond sufficiently to the rising demand, and the inevitable consequence is more overcrowding in squatter settlements and other low-income housing.

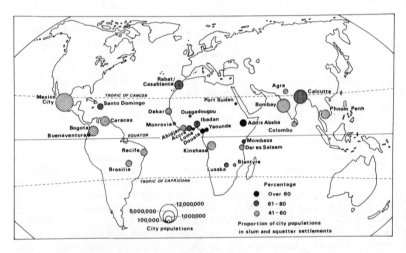

Fig. 5.3 Proportions of slum and squatter populations in some Third World cities
Source : Dickenson et al., p. 189

It is in the cities of Latin America that the relationships between planning and housing provision have been thrown into sharpest relief. The demographic as well as economic impacts of urbanization have overwhelmed the national and municipal planning apparatus, and have led to the characteristic growth of low income residential areas of informal and often illegal housing - the favelas of Brazil, barriadas of Peru, barrios of Colombia, colonias proletarias and ciudades perdidas of Mexico, each city offering different mixes of rented and owned accommodation, differing degrees of planning control, a wide variety of building styles and family and social arrangements (Dickenson et al., 1983, pp. 185-192). It is now generally accepted that these settlements need to be integrated more fully into the urban fabric, rather than rejected as undesirable and unplanned, but the process of how that integration might be best achieved remains a matter of some dispute that rests upon current inadequate knowledge of not only the growth and demographic structures of current and future populations, but also their residential patterns. both at initial entry to the city and subsequently as they become established.

The most familiar model, associated in particular with the work of John Turner in Lima and Rio de Janeiro, emphasizes migrant choice in a two-stage model in which initial settlement of 'bridgeheaders' was in or near the centre of the city, while subsequent moves of 'consolidators' were to more peripheral locations. However in more recent and more detailed studies in 13 low-income settlements in Valencia, Venezuela, Bogota, Colombia, and Mexico City, Alan Gilbert and Peter Ward have concluded that:

"residential patterns in Latin American cities are less the outcome of migrant choice as the Turner theory argues, and more the product of constraints imposed by the land and housing markets. Given that the private sector largely controls these markets, supply is determined by a range of factors such as changing land values and rents, alternative land uses and government legislation. The availability and range of housing opportunities is an outcome of the socio-political structure of the city. The differences between Bogota, Mexico City and Valencia are explained not by differences in the preferences of the poor but by differences in the availability of land and differing kinds of accommodation. We accept that a newly-arrived migrant may desire access to centres of employment and may find renting an acceptable housing solution. On the other hand, we are unconvinced that he would take up immediate ownership were it possible. In short, it is the absence of alternatives more than the preferences of the poor which shapes the housing market. Insofar as the Turner model stresses the latter it fails to explain adequately the low-income housing market" (Ward, 1983, p.12).

Furthermore these data suggest that subsequent moves within the city are strongly sectoral outwards as the city expands and its transportation system adjusts radially to that expansion. There is some residential concentration according to area of origin of the migrants, but it is not great and seems to be less than at an earlier period of urban growth. Occupational concentrations, on the other hand, are apparent for a few industries, e.g. construction, and may be related to the geography of employment opportunities within the city. "Governments should be aware of this tendency, and attempt to ensure adequate distribution of basic services and employment opportunities throughout the city" (Ward, 1983, p.15).

Family planning in Asia
Of all aspects of planning for population change considered in this book, the most directly relevant is the planning directly to engineer population change, and occurs most obviously through the planning of services that will promote fertility reduction. But successful family planning is not simply a matter of infrastructural provision: providing access to the service by having appropriate facilities at the right place at the right time. Blaikie (1975) has amply illustrated the reality of planning family planning services in India, and in particular has questioned the viability of a technocratic, normative delivery structure based on western models of spatial rationality. A successful service needs to get to grips with the economic and cultural bases of resistance to and suspicion of fertility reduction. In the absence of parallel changes and incentives in wider aspects of economy and society, mere provision of facilities will not have the desired impact (see also Fuller, 1984).

In India officially sponsored family planning campaigns seem to have been relatively successful, by world standards, since they began in the early 1950's, though their impact relative to other economic and social changes is a matter of very considerable contention (Cassen, 1978; Gulhati, 1977). Fertility reduction seems to have been greatest in areas of most rapid economic development (e.g. Punjab) or greatest social equality (e.g. Kerela) rather than in areas with most intensive family planning campaigns. These campaigns involved propaganda in their early years, but fiscal and monetary incentives grew, targetted at villages or areas as well as families, and were linked to family welfare packages that incorporated maternal health care, reductions in infant mortality and general improvements in rural environments, notably in availability of clean water. But physical provision and propaganda were not felt, by 1976, to be achieving the objectives of national policy, so major coercive measures were introduced. These very unpopular measures quickly backfired and were in no small way responsible for the downfall of the government in 1977. Family planning remains part of India's national policy, but due to massive resistance to fertility reduction national policy objectives cannot be realized without mass coercion (Vicziany, 1982).

China experienced a remarkable fertility decline of 34 per cent between 1965-70 and 1975-80 (a figure exceeded only by Cuba at 47 per cent in that period) with the annual rate of natural increase falling from 3.4 per cent in 1963 to 2.3 per cent in 1971 and 1.2 per cent by 1978. This is exceptional by any standards, but has been further intensified since 1979 by the 'One-Child' policy in which couples are encouraged to have only one child. This is expected to further reduce fertility to allow an annual rate of natural increase of 0.5 per cent by 1985 and zero by the end of the century, and in doing so further improve per capita income from $410 in 1980 to a target of $1000 by 2000 (Goodstadt, 1982; Saith, 1984). The reduction in fertility is often attributed to effective provision of services of contraception, of information and propaganda and reliance on group decision making and peer pressure, but Aird argues that the Chinese media "leaves little doubt that the single most important factor is direct administrative pressure on individual Chinese families by family planning centres and other officials. The pressures range from strong persuasion to outright coercion" (Aird, 1982, p.283). According to an editorial in the authoritative People's Daily:

> "To ensure the smooth implementation of the population policy it is necessary to institute certain rewards and restrictions. Conditions must be created to show consideration for only sons and daughters with regard to child care services, admission into schools, medical service, chances of becoming workers, chances of being enrolled in institutions of higher education, housing assignment in the urban areas, obtaining plots for housing construction in the rural areas, and so forth" (14th March, 1982; reported in Population and Development Review, 1982, vol. 8, p.355).

Implementation details vary from province to province. A national sample survey in 1982 found 42 per cent of couples with a 'one-child' certificate (Caldwell and Srinivasen, 1984); this was reported to be 56 per cent of married couples with fewer than two children in 1980 (Goodstadt, 1982)). Once a certificate has been issued, there are penalties imposed if the couple has more than one child. For a second child there may be loss of privileges of various types (e.g. free schooling) and for a third child 10 per cent may be deducted from parents' earnings. As suggested in the People's Daily editorial there are also positive incentives. Pensions are provided for parents of a single child, thus seeking to overcome the problems of having little support in old age, and fees for health and schooling may be waived. In rural areas one-child families may get the same size plots as two-child families. With such measures as these it is little wonder that fertility has fallen. Out of 17 million births in 1978 half were of a third or higher child, but by 1979 this had fallen to one quarter. The 1982 survey recorded 44 per cent of births being first births, 24 per cent being second births, but still 32 per cent were third or further births (Caldwell and Srinivasen, 1984). This varied very considerably within the country: 86 per cent of urban births were first births but only 40 per cent of rural births.

The prevention of births has meant extensive use of contraception organized as part of basic health care, particularly in rural areas where 90 per cent of birth control is one-time methods (vasectomy or IUD), with only 7 per cent using a contraceptive pill or condom, proportions that are generally similar to those in rural India. In urban China, on the other hand, only 62 per cent of contraception is vasectomy or IUD, with 29 per cent pill or condom (Caldwell and Srinivasen, 1984). But still one-third of Chinese women do not use any form of birth control, and abortions, though officially not encouraged, are a common practice of the last resort when contraception has failed.

It is quite clear, however, that the success in fertility reduction has been achieved despite some major resistance on the part of many families. Croll (1983) reports that less than 5 per cent of women would prefer to have only one child, whereas 51 per cent would prefer two, 28 per cent three and 16 per cent four. In a country where labour is the chief factor of production, family incomes, especially in rural areas, are linked positively to family size. The direct and indirect public pressures on couples to have less than the preferred number of children are clearly effective and have been a major feature in the implementation of the main thrust of population policy. In this sense, therefore, the social provision is not primarily of an infrastructural or enabling kind, though adequate public health services clearly help, but is operating on a wide front through many aspects of society and economy.

Planning for population change also operates on the basis of similar premises in the very special demographic and economic conditions of Singapore, dominated by ethnic Chinese, but also having experienced a major fertility decline from 38/1000 in 1960 to 17/1000 in 1983, and encouraged by the kinds of factors evident in China, with major economic penalties on large families and massive public social pressure to conform to national policy. But fertility differentials have an educational dimension. The 1980 census showed that women with no education have an average of 3.50 children, but this falls to 1.65 for women with tertiary education (Mukerjee, 1984). Recent events have taken policy one step further along a dangerous eugenic path by offering incentives for University graduates to have more children than the less educated in order to improve the 'quality' while controlling the quantity of births. Mothers under 30 with no 'O' levels and a monthly family income below $1,500 are currently offered $10,000 if they agree to be sterilized after their first or second child. There is also differential access to education, for children of parents without secondary level education qualify for priority places in schools only if one of the parents has been sterilized after the first or second birth. There are also tax incentives for graduates with families (Fincancioglu, 1984). Policies in Singapore are attempting to change population 'quality' as well as its quantity.

CONCLUSION

Expansion of the scale of service provision and improvements in its delivery in a wide range of economic and social contexts in the Third World are major tasks for public and private agencies. However, service provision affects and is affected by the rate and pattern of population change. Demand for services and supply of services are interdependent, and population change is one of the major filters through which that interdependence is channelled. The theory and practice of social planning must therefore be informed by close analysis of demographic variables. This is more likely where the collection and analysis of population data are integrated with planning to achieve social objectives, and where decision-making is done within communities from which the demand comes or at least with the active participation of the communities from which the demand comes. An integration of population analysis and social planning should be seen as part of the wider objectives of encouraging community participation in defining and meeting 'basic needs'.

REFERENCES

Aird, J.S. (1982) 'Population studies and population policy in China', Population and Development Review, 8, 267-97

Banister, J. (1984) 'Analysis of recent data on the population of China', Population and Development Review, 10, 241-72

Blaikie, P.M. (1975) Family planning in India : diffusion and policy, Edward Arnold, London

Cairncross, S., I. Carruthers, D. Curtis, R. Feachem, D. Bradley and G. Baldwin (1980) Evaluation for village water supply planning, Wiley, Chichester

Caldwell, J.C. (1977) The persistence of high fertility, Australian National University Press, Canberra

Caldwell, J.C., and K. Srinivasan (1984) 'New data on nuptuality and fertility in China', Population and Development Review, 10, 71-79

Cassen, R. (1978) India : population, economy, society, Macmillan, London

Cornia, G.A. (1984) 'The impact of world recession on children : a summary and interpretation of evidence', World Development, 12, 381-91

Croll, E.J. (1983) 'Production versus reproduction : the threat to China's development strategy', World Development, 11, 467-81

Dickenson, J.P., et al. (1983) A geography of the Third World, Methuen, London

Ewane, E. (1981) 'Speech given to African Regional Meeting of the International Social Security Association, Lomé, Togo', African News Sheet, 4, p.5

Fawcett, J.T. (1982) 'Value of children', in J.A. Ross (ed.) International encyclopedia of population, Free Press and Macmillan, New York and London, Vol. II, 655-71

Fincancioglu, N. (1984) 'Singapore's controversial incentives', People, 11, p.33

Fuller, G.A. (1984) 'Population geography and family planning', in J.I. Clarke (ed.) Geography and population : approaches and applications, Pergamon, Oxford, 103-10

Goodstadt, L.F. (1982) 'China's one child family : policy and public response', Population and Development Review, 8, 37-58

Gulhati, R. (1977) India's population policy : history and future, World Bank, Staff Working Paper, no. 265

Jackson, R. (1981) 'Running down the up-escalator : regional inequality in Papua New Guinea', Australian Geographer, 14, 175-84

Kay, G. (1967) Social aspects of village regrouping in Zambia, University of Hull, Department of Geography, Miscellaneous Series, no.7

Kjekshus, H. (1977) 'The Tanzanian village policy : implementation lessons and ecological dimensions', Canadian Journal of African Studies, 11, 269-82

Lo, C.L. (1984) 'The geography of the elderly in a modernizing society: the Hong Kong case', Singapore Journal of Tropical Geography, 5, 1-20

MacPherson, S. (1982) Social policy in the Third World : the social dilemmas of underdevelopment, Wheatsheaf Books, Brighton

Maro, P.S., and W.F.I. Mlay, (1982) 'Population redistribution in Tanzania', in J.I. Clarke and L.A. Kosinski (eds.) Redistribution of population in Africa, Heinemann, London, 176-81

Moore, J.E. (1979) 'The villagization process : rural development in the Mwanza Region of Tanzania', Geografiska Annaler, 61B, 65-80

Mukerjee, D. (1984) 'Graduates urged to be mothers', People, 11, 32-33

Nigerian Government Printer (1944) Ten Year Development Plan, Sessional Paper, No. 6 of 1944

Population Reports (1984) Healthier mothers and children through family planning, Johns Hopkins University, Population Information Program, Series J, no.27

Prothero, R.M., and W.T.S.Gould (1984) 'Population geography and social provision', in J.I. Clarke (ed.) Geography and population : approaches and applications, Pergamon, Oxford, 111-18

Riddell, J.B. (1970) The spatial dynamics of modernization in Sierra Leone, Northwestern U.P., Evanston, Ill.

Saith, A. (1984) 'China's new population policies : rationale and some implications', Development and Change, 15, 321-58

Saunders, R.J., and J.J. Warford (1976) Village water supply : economics and policy in the developing world, World Bank Research Publication, Johns Hopkins U.P., Baltimore

Soja, E.W. (1968) The geography of modernization in Kenya, Syracuse U.P , Syracuse, N.Y.

Steslicke, W.E. (1984) 'Medical care for Japan's ageing population : an introduction', Pacific Affairs, 57, 45-52

Thomas, I.D. (1982) 'Villagization in Tanzania : planning potential and practical problems', in J.I. Clarke and L.A. Kosinski (eds.) Redistribution of population in Africa, Heinemann, London, 182-91

Vicziany, M. (1982) 'Coercion in a soft state ; the Family Planning Program of India : Part I : the myth of voluntarism', Pacific Affairs, 55, 373-402

Ward, P.M. (1983) Residential movement among the poor : the constraints on housing choice in Latin American cities, Paper presented at the Annual Meeting of the British Association, Brighton, August

World Bank (1981) <u>Accelerated development in sub-Saharan Africa :</u>
<u>an agenda for action</u>, Washington, D.C.
World Bank (1984) <u>World Development Report</u>, Washington D.C.

Chapter Six

PLANNING FOR HEALTH CARE PROVISION IN BRITAIN: THE
LOCAL DIMENSION

John Whitelegg

INTRODUCTION

Health care planning in Great Britain is firmly rooted in demographic
analysis.   From the organisation of G.P. lists to the provision of
hospital beds for various specialities, the National Health Service
works to norms based in units of population and tries to bring about
some balance of provision between areas.   The methods and
procedures for allocating and funding 'X' beds to 'Y' population units
are crude and do not always work well, but they do allow for 'Y' to be
weighted in various ways, for example for the elderly, who may make
more demands on health services, or for those who live in
disadvantaged areas.   However, health care planning suffers from
long lead times and the matching of facilities with population can be
very difficult, not least because of the pace of demographic change
in many parts of the U.K.   The rapid growth of many smaller urban
areas and the decline of larger cities destroys the logic of the
Victorian hospital system, the locational pattern of which still
dominates hospital provision in the 1980's.   With considerable
resources tied up in existing locations and a generally negative
attitude to increased health expenditures it is very difficult for the
Health Service to respond quickly to major shifts in the size,
composition or location of the population.   One of the consequences
of this inertia is growing travel distances to hospital facilities, made
easier or more difficult according to whether or not people depend on
public transport.
      The composition of the population is a vital factor in health
care planning, particularly with respect to the distribution of the
elderly.   Changes in the location of the elderly in the U.K. have
produced a very distinctive spatial pattern that is heavily influenced
by retirement migration to seaside locations and other areas of great
attraction (Warnes and Law, 1984).   The provision of maternity and
gynaecological services is similarly influenced by composition and, in
this case, birth rate.   Whilst national population change is
approximately zero and birth rates are declining, there are marked
local variations of considerable significance to the task of health

care planning. It is not unusual, however, for such local factors to be neglected and for medical facilities to be centralised some distance from localities of obvious need (Whitelegg, 1983).

The relationship between health care provision and population characteristics is well understood at the basic mechanistic level, and health care planning can respond, where resources are made available, to varying demands in space and time imposed by population changes. There is, however, very little understanding of those structural characteristics of the population which have a direct connection with the incidence of specific health problems. The particular health problems of women, both physical and psychological, have been identified in the literature (Doyal, 1979). There is a suggestion that these problems are rooted in the societal roles ascribed to women and the relative failure of male-dominated, technocratic medicine to respond to these specific needs. Similarly the provision of health care facilities for ethnic minorities represents a challenge to health service planners in their response to specific spatial distributions and their ethnic composition of local populations. The relationship between health and social class has been the subject of a detailed report (DHSS, 1980) which graphically describes the poorer health and higher mortality of lower social classes. The authors of the report, generally known as the Black Report, show how the health characteristics of particular population sub-groups have shown no relative improvement since the inception of the National Health Service; indeed they have in some cases declined relative to higher social classes. The reasons for this poorer health record are not difficult to find in general terms but are probably too far outside the scope and philosophy of contemporary medicine for there to be any real chance of significant improvement for what is seen to be a societal condition. If health care planners pursue goals related to the structural characteristics of the population, such as eliminating a social class/health gradient, a different set of problems will inevitably arise, for the origins of much ill-health are more likely to be found in poor housing, poor diet, inadequate environments and occupational hazards than they are in a bodily malfunction which can be corrected by the routine administration of drugs or by earlier diagnosis. Furthermore, additional health care services, should they be made available, will not necessarily be accessible to those most in need. Geographical studies of accessibility problems show clearly how access becomes increasingly difficult as income declines, car ownership declines or long-term unemployment increases (Whitelegg, 1982).

The Black Report did a great deal to expose an important relationship and to identify child poverty as a key area for action, but it did very little to point the way to changes in the professional and geographical organisation of health services which might contribute to a solution. Five years after the Black Report there are few signs of any action from within the medical profession or from government. The incorporation of this important structural dimension of population analysis into local health care planning in Great Britain remains to be achieved.

LOCAL HEALTH CARE PLANNING

Health care planning in Britain is still based on a pattern of hospital provision largely established in the nineteenth century when population structure and distribution and health problems were markedly different from those of the 1980's. The pattern of centralised provision based on the district general hospital and the domination of health care provision by a hierarchy of hospitals has, if anything, been accentuated over the years by the application of new technology and the strong influence of a consultant-based hierarchical profession. These factors constrain health care provision within an ideological framework of managerial centralism and a dependence on past decisions which shapes a planning system based on greater centralisation and technologically more advanced medicine at fewer sites. The pattern of provision within a health authority in any one year will differ little from previous years except for periodic bouts of public expenditure restraint which tend to have their impact on the jobs of the low-paid and the length of the hospital waiting list rather than the pattern of provision or the system of reward and remuneration for medically qualified staff.

In the face of the formidable institutional and organisational obstacles which impede the implementation of the kind of health service reform that will serve the interests of consumers rather than of producers, there are many practical issues to be addressed and solutions to be found. More than at any time in the past, the concern of the health service planner is now with the pattern of service delivery and the degree to which this satisfies demand, reduces the measurable incidence of morbidity and mortality, and conforms with the particular local circumstances of the area for which it is being planned. In this the characteristics of the population are crucial and it is these that impose patterns of demand for health care that differ markedly from one area to another. The proportion of the elderly in the population as a whole is one important consideration, as is the proportion in the 0-4 age group; but these structural characteristics do not outweigh those social composition characteristics that were identified in the Black Report as major dimensions of variability in the health of the population. There are also geographical considerations. Health service planners are acutely aware of locational considerations and problems of accessibility (Grime and Whitelegg, 1982). Service delivery, whilst clearly influenced by economic criteria as perceived by the producer and by public expenditure restraint, cannot ignore the use made of facilities by different groups in the population, each of which have different mobility characteristics, and the accessibility problems posed by different locations for hospitals, clinics, day care centres, etc.

134

Health service planning is a very imprecise science. It encounters all those problems which are at the centre of planning for different groups in any population, problems which are both theoretical and practical and are not adequately recognised within N.H.S. decision-making structures. They include the lack of an adequate mechanism for monitoring health within a population and for relating changes in health patterns to policy initiatives: moreover, we simply do not know the likely outcome of different policies. A second problem relates to a lack of understanding of the relationship between supply and demand in health care services. The provision of high-quality, technological medicine at a small number of sites requires longer travel distances and creates more obstacles in making contact with the centre. An alternative pattern of distribution based on a larger number of sites with less advanced technology, but geared to easier access with earlier diagnosis and treatment of problems, may well improve 'health' defined in its broadest sense. Centralised medicine may increase demand, whereas decentralised medicine, because of early diagnosis, may have the opposite effect. We simply do not know.

It is clear that such problems can only be resolved at the local level and that at this level it may be possible to specifically identify health care priorities. The N.H.S. organisational structure facilitates local planning at the level of the health authority and invests a degree of responsibility for this planning in the person of the District Medical Officer (DMO), formerly the District Community Physician. There are approximately 190 health authorities in England and Wales, each planning for local need on the basis of local population characteristics and geographical circumstances. They provide an adequate framework for tackling health care problems at a level where local variation can be appreciated and incorporated into appropriate health care policies.

In the remainder of this chapter this scale of planning will be examined in more detail. From particular examples it will be argued that variations in the population and the changes which that population may experience are important in the health care planning process.

HEALTH CARE AND THE ELDERLY

Between 1951 and 1971 the pensionable population of the U.K. increased by 30 per cent to reach 9 millions, and by a further 6.4 per cent to 9.58 millions in 1981 (Table 6.1). However, as Warnes and Law (1984) point out, the size of this group as a whole is not expected to increase substantially for some decades although the numbers of the very old will do so (see Chapter 1). The distribution of pensionable populations varies considerably from region to region. The South-West, East Anglia, Wales and the South-East have the highest levels of pensionable population in Britain, ranging from 17 to 20 per cent. Within regions an important characteristic for health care planning of the elderly is its increasing concentration into a relatively few areas. Warnes and Law (1984) show that the percentages of pensionable population in the 15 lowest and 15 highest local authorities ranged from ten per cent or over 30 per cent. A more precise way of measuring such concentrations for planning purposes is the signed chi-square statistic (Gattrell and Cole, 1983) and it is this that has been used to measure spatial concentration at the local scale for the Lancaster local authority area (Maguire et al ,

Table 6.1: Great Britain population of pensionable age living alone, 1951-91 (thousands)

	1951	1971	1981	1991*
Males, 65 years+		352	516	
Females, 60 years+		1,781	2,255	
Total (Males 65+/Females 60+)	917	2,233	2,771	(3,600)
Percentage of pensionable population	13.4	24.8	28.9	(36.3)
Total pensionable population (millions)	6.84	9.00	9.58	9.78

Sources: Central Statistical Office, Social Trends 13, 1982, HMSO, Table 2.2; Office of Population Censuses and Surveys Census 1971 G.B. Persons of Pensionable Age, HMSO, 1974, Table 3; OPCS, Census 1981 G.B. National Report part 1, HMSO, 1983, Table 41.

* 1979-based projection.

Based on Warnes and Law, 1984, p.39

1983). The maps show Lancaster District in its regional setting (Figure 6.1) and the distribution of the retired population within it (Figure 6.2). There are marked spatial variations within both rural and urban areas of the Lancaster Local Authority and many of the crude percentages exceed those given for the highest local authorities listed by Warnes and Law (1984), even though the Lancaster District does not figure among them. For example, the coastal resort of Morecambe has wards with values ranging from 25-

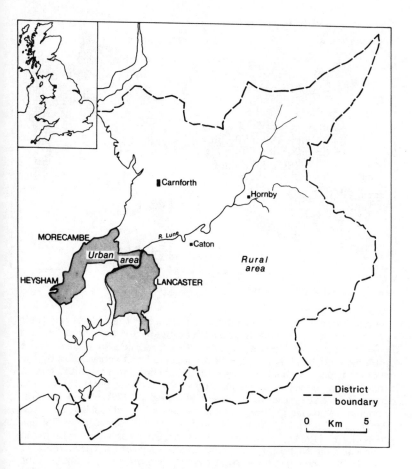

Fig. 6.1 Lancaster District and its urban and rural areas

41 per cent while the rural areas range from 15-21 per cent, not too dissimilar from the urban area of Lancaster. Such local variations are of real importance and stress the danger of using averages which mark variations at a more detailed or disaggregated spatial scale. More importantly in health planning and resource allocation, the existence of these variations is an important consideration given the way resources are allocated and re-distributed in the N.H.S. (Eyles, Smith and Woods, 1982).

It is an assumption of most health care planning that the elderly are heavy users of medical facilities. At any one time elderly people occupy nearly half of the N.H.S. beds in hospitals and about 40 per cent of all acute beds are occupied by elderly patients (DHSS, 1981).

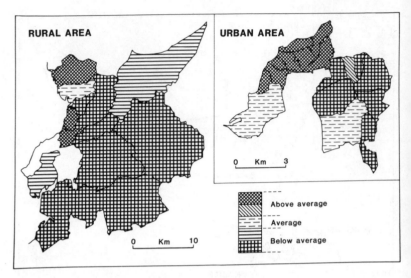

RURAL AREA

URBAN AREA

0   Km   3

▨ Above average

⊟ Average

⊞ Below average

0   Km   10

Fig. 6.2 Retired population in the Lancaster District

The combined effect of spatial concentration of the elderly and their
demand for services clearly presents problems for health authorities
in their attempts to locate and promote appropriate facilities. These
problems have been exacerbated over a period of twenty years by the
concentration of health care facilities in larger units and a
concomitant reduction in actual numbers of service points. This has
occurred in both general services (Whitelegg, 1979) and in hospital
provision (Whitelegg, 1982). In a survey of rural parishes by the
Exeter and District Community Health Council reported by Phillips
and Williams (1984), 75 per cent of the parishes reported problems in
gaining access to hospitals. In a detailed survey of the effects of
accessibility on general practitioner consultations, out-patient
attendances and in-patient admissions Haynes and Bentham (1982)
found that all rates of consultation fell with decreasing accessibility
(Table 6.2). General practitioner consultation and out-patient
attendance rates in areas far from Norwich and without a surgery,
expressed as percentages of the corresponding rates in areas near
Norwich with a surgery and with no long-standing illness, show
marked discrepancies between accessible and remote rural areas.
They also show an increase in the disparity for some groups when out-
patient attendance rates are compared with G.P. consultation rates.
They state: "...the greatest diminution [is for] the elderly, for males
and for those from manual worker households ..... groups with
generally a high relative need for health care" (Haynes and Bentham,
1982, p.568).

138

Table 6.2: Consultation and attendance rates in areas far from Norwich without a surgery as a percentage of those near Norwich with a surgery. for persons with no long-standing illness

Group		General Practitioner rate	Out-patient attendance rate
Age:	18-44	39	30
	45-64	46	47
	65+	126	72
Sex:	Male	74	21
	Female	47	77
Car:	Car-owning	47	43
	Not car-owning	80	73
Social:	Manual	56	30
	Non-manual	54	67
TOTAL		57	49

Source: Haynes and Bentham, 1982, p.567.

HEALTH CARE AND SOCIAL CLASS

It has been established that the health of social groups seems to vary directly with occupational class (The Black Report, DHSS, 1980). What is not so clear, however, is how this relates to use made of facilities, though Haynes and Bentham (1982) have provided useful information on male manual workers. The use of the term 'class' in this context presents some problems because of confusion over definition, although as Doyal (1979) has shown it is a useful concept in understanding health. The authors of the Black Report, which overcame the problem by substituting the concept of occupational class, presented its conclusions in clear and unambiguous language:

"Most recent data show marked differences in mortality rates between the occupational classes, for both sexes and at all ages. At birth and in the first month of life, twice as many babies of 'unskilled manual' parents (Class V) die as do babies of professional class parents (Class I) and in the next eleven months four times as many girls and five times as many boys. In later childhood the ratio of deaths in Class V to deaths in Class I falls to 1 5 2.0 but increases again in early adult life, before falling again in middle and old age. A class gradient can be observed for most causes of death, being particularly steep in the case of diseases of the respiratory system. Available data on chronic sickness tend to parallel those on mortality. Thus self-reported rates of long-standing illness (as defined in the General Household Survey) are twice as high among unskilled manual and $2\frac{1}{2}$ times as high among their wives as among the professional classes. In the case of acute sickness (short-term mental health, also defined in the General Household Survey) the gradients are less clear" (DHSS, 1980; Para. 3, p. 355).

Even more forcibly, it states:

"The extent of the problem may be illustrated by the fact that if the mortality rate of Class I had applied to Classes IV and V during 1970-72 (the dates of the latest review of mortality experience) 74,000 lives of people aged under 75 would not have been lost. This estimate includes nearly 10,000 children and 32,000 men of working age" (op. cit., Para. 4, p. 356).

Death rates by sex and social (occupational) class for 1971 show a gradient from Social Class I through to Class V, demonstrating the deterioration of life chances directly related to occupational class (Table 6.3).

The class gradient evident in the level of deaths from such causes as cancer, heart and respiratory disease, and diseases of the digestive system is also evident in accidental deaths. Deaths attributable to accidents at work, which form 20 per cent of the total of deaths recorded as accidents, and road traffic accidents (54 per cent of the total) also demonstrate a steep class gradient with a much greater incidence in the lower socio-economic groups. Many diseases are sex specific. Endocrine, nutritional and metabolic diseases of the digestive system demonstrate steeper class gradients amongst women and many carcinomas have quite different patterns of occurrence as between men and women, as can be seen from the maps of cancer mortality compiled by Gardner, Winter, Taylor and Anderson (1983). Such marked class and sex differentials point to the need for different levels of provision of medical services in different types of social area and also where there are marked contrasts in demographic structure.

140

Table 6.3: Death rates per 1000 by sex and social occupational class
(15-64 years), England and Wales, 1971

Social (occupational) class		Males (All)	Female (Married, by husband's occ.)	Ratio (M:F)
I	(Professional)	3.98	2.15	1.85
II	(Intermediate)	5.54	2.85	1.94
IIIN	(Skilled non-manual)	5.80	2.76	1.96
IIIM	(Skilled manual)	6.08	3.41	1.78
IV	(Partly skilled)	7.96	4.27	1.87
V	(Unskilled)	9.88	5.31	1.86
Ratio V:I		2.5	2.5	

Source: Occupational Mortality Tables, 1970-72 (DHSS, 1980,
Chapter 2).

Furthermore, age is also a significant factor in differences of
occurrence of various causes of death. The elderly, as we have seen,
are particularly susceptible to many diseases and health problems,
and areas with high numbers of elderly need special levels and types
of medical services. The young suffer disproportionately from traffic
accidents both as children and young adults leading to a loss of life
which is heavily biased against lower social classes and greater than
that arising from some serious diseases (Smith, 1981) At very young
ages the incidence of neonatal and perinatal mortality is also class
specific as the Black Report states:

"Below the age of one year, class differences in survival
are at their greatest during the post neonatal phase of life
... we may hypothesise that any factors which increase
the parental capacity to provide adequate care for an
infant will, when present, increase the chance of survival,
while their absence will increase the risk of premature
death.   The most obvious such factors fall within the
sphere of material resources: sufficient household
income, a safe uncrowded and unpolluted home, warmth
and hygiene, a means of rapid communication with the
outside world..." (DHSS, 1980, Para. 6.41, p. 173-174).

In reviewing trends in class inequalities the Black Report concludes:

"Perhaps the most important general finding in the chapter is the lack of improvement, and indeed in some respects deterioration, of the health experience, not merely of occupational Class V but also Class IV in health, relative to occupational Class I, as judged by mortality indications, during the 1960's and 1970's...

(i) mortality rates of males are higher at every age than of females and in recent decades the difference between the sexes has become greater.

(ii) For men of economically active age there was greater inequality of mortality between occupational Classes I and V both in 1970-72 and 1959-63 than in 1949-53" (Ibid., Para. 3.56, p. 91).

The Black Report does not clearly recognise a spatial dimension in its work. While this is not a vital omission, given the significance of the task actually achieved, in terms of implementing measures to bring about improvements or allocate resources the spatial dimension becomes very important indeed. Varying social and area characteristics can be directly related to the demand for N.H.S. facilities. Examining the demand for accident and emergency facilities as it varied between different areas of Lancaster, Dyer (1978) identified "correlations between socio-economic conditions and the occurrence of certain incidents", and pointed to ways in which understanding the structure of the town could result in "a better deployment of the services to suit the real needs of the community".

THE LOCATION OF HEALTH CARE FACILITIES

While there are considerable difficulties in using spatial units and spatial policies as vehicles for the reform of social and health problems (Eyles, 1979) there remains a large area for manoeuvre in the ways policies and practice can be made more responsive to local geographical circumstances and particularly to the characteristics of populations in the health authority administrative areas. A good deal of geographical research on health care facilities has been further advanced in recent years through the analysis of problems of accessibility to such facilities. Since this literature is reviewed at length in Whitelegg (1982) and this section will focus more specifically on the application of such studies to health service planning.

The location of health facilities is obviously an important factor in determining whether or not people make contact with the services they require. In a plan for reorganising health services within the Blackburn Health District, the impact on the amount of travel which would have to be undertaken for consumers to make contact with the same services as were available prior to reorganisation was examined (Whitelegg, 1982). The plan provided for a high degree of centralisation of health care facilities at the District General Hospital, but also incorporated provision for community hospitals at points some distance from the District General Hospital. Such centralisation clearly detracts from the ease with which people can make contact with health care facilities, particularly acute facilities, and no information is (or was) available to the health authority on the likely consequences of such changes for out-patients, visitors or the health of the populations concerned. At this level, where least is known about the effectiveness of health care provision, the factors which influence patient contact with facilities and the vulnerability of certain groups to ill-health provide the greatest potential for incorporating locational strategies into a broader attack on specific health care problems.

The Blackburn study was not able to make much progress with such strategic considerations but was able to show that a pattern of community hospital development was of particular value to the elderly. By reducing the length of stay in large centralised hospitals and locating continuing care for geriatric and elderly, sick and mentally infirm (ESMI) patients in community hospitals, patients would be located nearer their home communities for more of the time, would be able to receive more visitors and, under this stimulus, would be less likely to suffer accelerated mental deterioration. The importance of visitors to long-standing patients has been argued in the medical literature, yet in large centralised institutions the elderly receive few visitors. The Blackburn study showed that over 30 per cent of the travel savings arising from the reorganisation, occurred from trips generated by ESMI and geriatric patients (including visitors). Unfortunately, other specialities which were to be concentrated in Blackburn would generate longer trips and add to the travel burden for health service consumers (measured in passenger kilometres). Health service decisions which benefit one group of consumers may well lead to disbenefits for other groups, particularly when centralisation affects acute services and 'out-stations' become more like community hospitals concentrating on passive care. The Blackburn reorganisation does provide an improved service for one large group of users but at the expense of emphasising spatial and functional hierarchies which reduce accessibility to maternity services, paediatric, gynaecological and other specialisms at locations other than Blackburn. Questions of the appropriate balance of services across a health authority require political decisions about resource allocation between competing groups rather than decisions about medicine and medical provision.

This political dimension has come to the fore in the Rossendale Valley of Lancashire where the main hospital, Rossendale General, has been under threat of closure (Whitelegg, 1983). The hospital is well linked to the local community in terms of transport, has a good range of specialities available, has short waiting lists, and is well supported by the local G.Ps. It is not, however, supported by consultant groups. The Rossendale Valley also has a relatively healthy population as compared with much of North-West England (personal communication from District Medical Officer). It is clear from the geographical pattern of settlement and communications in this part of Lancashire that the loss of this hospital as a whole, or of its maternity unit, will impose serious additional costs on its users and deter groups of consumers from making use of facilities. Many of those consumers fall into known categories at risk including those using maternity services and those in lower social classes.

CONCLUSION

This chapter describes how health care planning might be more responsive to the needs of the target population. Areas with differing population characteristics will make different demands on health care provision as the needs of the elderly and the several occupational classes clearly illustrate. It is also known that there are relationships between the incidence of disease and environmental factors which have distinctive spatial patterns, as identified by Giggs (1973) in his studies of the distribution of schizophrenics and by Girt's (1972) work on chronic bronchitis. What is not clear is how one may construct causal linkages between population and environmental factors and the explanation of disease aetiology. This is not a simple matter and is fraught with difficulties associated with problems of measurement, the shape and size of areal unit to be served, the level and nature of population mobility and the danger of being misled by previous ecological relationships (the 'ecological fallacy' referred to by Mohan and Rhind (1984)).

Of more general importance is the problem of allocating resources to compensate for known deficiencies in the health of populations. Eyles, Smith and Woods (1982) show that previous attempts at ameliorating social and economic problems through spatial resource allocation have been less than successful, and go on to show how the Revenue Allocation Working Party (RAWP) may actually exacerbate the problem through its neglect of G.P. and community services and its concentration effect on acute beds in the London area. More fundamentally we are not yet in a position to relate inputs to known effects of outputs:

> "The clearly enunciated distributive principle of equity to each [place] according to need - becomes weak if not impotent in the absence of even the most skeletal technical theory of production capable of relating resource inputs to health outcomes via specific local levels of services of various types" (Eyles, Smith and Woods,1982, p. 251).

Mohan and Rhind (1984) show that there are no insurmountable technical problems in relating information on population variability in small areas to N.H.S. data. Previous work by these authors (Rhind,

Mohan and Fielden, 1982) used 1971 census data to relate specific spatial variations in mortality in County Durham to variations in environmental and social conditions. Greater accessibility to small area data from the 1981 census, together with sophisticated file matching programmes opens up considerable possibilities for this kind of exercise. In combination with computer mapping techniques (Maguire et al., 1983) it becomes possible to make a vast amount of planning information available to health care planners in a form which illuminates their task: but such technical improvements, however necessary and desirable, will not solve health care problems of those in lower social classes in poor housing or in vulnerable groups.

The reasons for this are many. Doyal (1979) points out that, in the first instance, many health care problems are products of the way society is structured and improvements of relevance to those most in need are only likely if conditions are improved in workplaces and in the quality of housing, incomes and diet. Secondly, health care planning is still largely concerned with the location and organisation of hospitals even though much illness is detected and treated at lower levels of the hierarchy. The relative neglect of G.P. and community medicine, lack of its association with most regional and district N.H.S. planning and its financially inferior status, render relatively ineffective those aspects of health care of most significance to most people.

This should not be taken as an excuse for inaction. The failure of much health care planning to make a significant impact on the health of the people should be the starting point for a new approach involving the introduction of more sensitive methods at smaller geographical scales, matching inputs with outputs and monitoring changes in this relationship over time. This is not likely to be achieved within the present framework of N.H.S. planning and will be contingent on decentralised management and a revaluation of the relative roles of hospital and technological aspects of health care vis-a-vis community medicine and specific provision for identifiable groups at risk.

REFERENCES

DHSS (1980) Inequalities in Health Care (The Black Report)
DHSS (1981) Growing older, H.M.S.O , Cmnd. 8173
Doyal, L. (1979) The political economy of health, Pluto Press, London
Dyer, J., et al. (1978) 'The demands made on emergency room facilities by an urban population', Publ. Hlth. Lond., 92, 79-85.
Eyles, J. (1979) 'Area-based policies for the inner city: context, problems and prospects', in D.T. Herbert, and Smith, D.M. (eds.) Social problems and the city: geographical perspectives, O.U.P., London

Eyles, J., D.M. Smith and K.J. Woods (1982) 'Spatial resource allocation and state practice the case of health service planning in London', Regional Studies, 16, 239-253

Gardner. M.T , et al. (1983) Atlas of cancer mortality, John Wiley Chichester

Gattrell, A., and K. Cole, (1983) 'Quantitative, geographical explanations of small area census data, University of Salford, Campus Census Project Research Note, No. 2

Giggs, J (1973) 'The distribution of schizophrenics in Nottingham. Transactions, Institute of British Geographers, 59, 55-76

Girt, J. (1972) 'Simple chronic bronchitis and urban ecological structure' in N. McGlashan, (ed.,) Medical geography: techniques and field studies, London, Methuen

Grime, L.P., and J. Whitelegg (1982) 'The geography of health care planning: some problems of correspondence between local and national policies', Community Medicine 4, 201-208

Haynes, R.M., and C.G. Bentham (1982) The affects of accessibility on general practitioner consultations, out-patients attendances and in-patient admissions in Norfolk, England', Soc. Sci. Med. 16, 561 69.

Maguire, D.J., et al. (1983) Lancaster District: a computer drawn census atlas (1981), Department of Geography, University of Lancaster

Mohan, J., and D.W. Rhind (1984) 'The geography of the census and N.H S. planning', in I. Diamond and M. Slattery (eds.) Population perspectives in N.H.S. planning, OPCS, London

Phillips, D , and A. Williams (1984) Rural Britain. A social geography, Blackwell, Oxford

Rhind, D.W., J.F. Mohan and D. Fielden (1982) Integration and analysis of mortality and census data for County Durham. Report to DHSS

Smith, T. (1981) 'Death on the roads', New Scientist, 92, 1276, 260-61

Warnes, A.M., and C.M. Law (1984) The elderly population of Great Britain: locational trends and policy implications', Transactions Institute of British Geographers, N.S , 9, 37 59.

Whitelegg, J. (1979) 'Access to health care facilities in Cumbria', in D.A. Halsall and B J. Turton (eds.) Rural transport problems in Britain, Transport Geography Study Group. Institute of British Geographers, Keele

Whitelegg, J. (1982) Inequalities in health care : problems of access and provision, Straw Barnes, Retford

Whitelegg, J. (1983) 'Health care planning and the politics of reorganisation in the Rossendale Valley', Paper presented to 'Public provision and urban politics' Conference, University of Reading, July, 1983

Chapter Seven

HEALTH POLICIES AND POPULATION IN THE THIRD WORLD

Maggie Pearson

INTRODUCTION: INADEQUATE AND INAPPROPRIATE SERVICES

Death and illness are common features of daily life in the countries
of the Third World. Whilst there has been a slow, overall
improvement in world health over the last 20 years, the gap is
steadily widening between the industrialised developed countries and
those of the Third World, where the basic health needs of the
population remain unsatisfied although the majority of ill health is
primarily preventable (WHO, 1974). Life expectancy at birth is
generally considered to be the best single indicator of a population's
health status. In the 25 least developed countries, life expectancy is
less than 40 years, whereas a person can expect to live to 72 years in
England and Wales. At least one in six live-born babies dies before
the age of one in India and Nepal, compared with one in eighty in
England and Wales or the USA.

Until the early 1970's, health policies and strategies adopted in
the Third World were based on the technological model of medical
care exported from western countries. Personnel and finance to
establish hospitals with the latest equipment and drugs with which to
cure disease were an important component of overseas trade and aid.
Such a wholesale transplant of western medicine was generally
accepted uncritically, and assumed to be both appropriate and
desirable. In 1974, Dr. Mahler, the then Director-General of the
World Health Organisation (WHO), expressed the concern that "in
many countries, the health services are not keeping pace either in
quantity or quality with the changing populations, and many are even
getting worse ..." (Mahler, 1974a, p.209, emphasis added). His
concern was that the health services were inadequate, inappropriate
and lacking in the flexibility needed to tackle the majority of health
problems, particularly in the Third World. The increasing failure of
established health services to meet the basic needs of the majority of
the world's population was in stark and glaring contrast to the radical
improvements in health achieved by countries such as China, Cuba
and Tanzania which had adopted alternative approaches to health
care in which there is an emphasis on primary health care and

147

paramedical workers (Djukanovic and Mach, 1975). This growing awareness of the need to reorientate services to adequately satisfy basic health needs was an integral part of development strategies in the 1970 s which focussed on basic needs and the marked inequalities in their being met.

The concept of Primary Health Care, in which essential health care would be universally accessible to people and acceptable to them, was the keystone of the WHO's strategy to meet the world's basic health needs. Referring to the WHO definition of health as " .a state of complete physical, mental and social well being, and not merely the absence of disease or infirmity" (quoted fully in Soddy, 1961), Dr. Mahler announced WHO's goal to achieve "Health for All by the Year 2000". He was acutely aware of the prevailing and increasing inequalities in health and access to health care and of the enormity of the task. He warned that

> "the challenge is immense if WHO's definition of health is to be taken seriously ...What is more, this definition considers health to be a right for everybody without discrimination. All this....may seem like a bad joke when set against the realities of the health service today" (Mahler, 1974b, p.1).

He drew attention to the ideology behind the inappropriate nature of those scarce services, focussing particularly on the situation in the Third World, and continued:

> "Countries further down the scale are busy initiating this kind of perversion ..Paradoxically, with such stupendous cost increases and disease addiction has gone increasing dissatisfaction with the health care system on the part of its consumers because serving champagne to the few while the many do not get their daily bread is hardly promoting confidence" (ibid, p.2)

Such a damning indictment makes it abundantly clear that health policies which are inadequate and appropriate to meet the basic needs of the people are not a simple matter of providing more of the same -more expensive hospitals and doctors. Recognition that such expensive services were ineffective in providing access to health care by the majority of the population culminated in a fundamental change in policy. In 1978 WHO and UNICEF (United Nations Children's Fund) produced a joint report on Primary Health Care (WHO-UNICEF, 1978) which formed the basis of the WHO strategy for attaining its goal of Health for All by the Year 2000. Embodied in this radical policy shift was a recognition that resources and power must be diverted from expensive and technologically-based medical centres, disproportionately serving an urban elite minority, to provide accessible and flexible primary health care for the majority, both the rural and urban poor.

The essence of any effective health policy is that it should be appropriate and relevant to local health care needs, incorporating services which are acceptable and accessible to the local population, and feasible within existing physical and financial constraints. Several components fundamental to effective implementation of such a policy may in themselves be problematic within prevailing cultural norms and socio-economic, political and professional structures. They include:

a) a comprehensive definition of need, based on the epidemiology, demography and spatial distribution of the local population;

b) the formulation of policies, strategies and service plans appropriate and relevant to local needs; and

c) the provision of services which are physically, socially and financially accessible to those who need them.

Each of these will be considered in turn in this chapter as they relate to the Third World, illustrating the need for urgent and radical action to approach, let alone achieve, the WHO goal of universal health care by the year 2000.

DEFINITION OF HEALTH CARE NEEDS

The charge made by Mahler and others, that health services are inappropriate, refers not only to their technocratic and professional ideology, but also to their epidemiological and demographic assumptions. The shift in WHO policy embodied an explicit acknowledgment that the epidemiology and demography of the Third World are qualitatively different from those of the 'developed' industrialised North. The particular model of curative medicine that had been exported from the North reflected the priorities and experience of those responsible for its development, and the resulting services highlight the pitfalls of transplanting rigidly defined blueprints from central offices, rather than formulating flexible principles of health care which can be tailored to local needs and constraints.

Epidemiology in the Third World

It has long been acknowledged that health and socio-economic development are interrelated (WHO, 1974). The relationship is neither clear cut nor simple, though higher living standards have, in general, been associated with better health. Life expectancy has progressively risen in all countries (Figure 7.1), and has been associated with a marked reduction in mortality from infectious diseases such as measles and tuberculosis (McKeown and Lowe, 1974). In England and Wales, the decline in such disease was well underway as living conditions improved in the late nineteenth century, many years before chemotherapy and immunisation were introduced.

The association between health and socio-economic factors is not only a feature of the past. Inequalities in mortality persist between

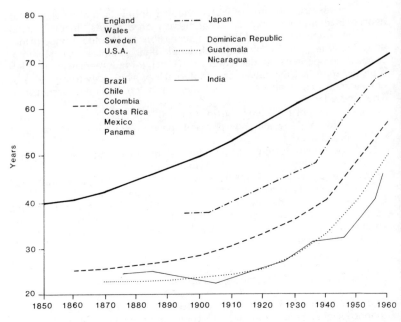

Fig. 7.1 Life expectancy at birth in selected countries, 1850–1960
Source: U.N. Demographic Yearbooks

social classes within countries (Townsend and Davidson, 1980) and between rich and poor nations. In the absence of morbidity data, mortality rates are commonly used as surrogate indices of a population's health. In particular, infant mortality rates (deaths within the first year of life) and life expectancy at birth are commonly quoted in comparative studies. Striking geographical variations in both are evident between countries (Figures 7.2 and 7.3) and there is a broad association with socio-economic status as represented by estimated per capita income or Gross National Product. A closer look at the demographic structure and mortality patterns of individual countries will elaborate the nature of the disparities between countries of different kinds of socio-economic development. Two countries in the Third World, Guatemala and Thailand, have data bases regarded by the United Nations and WHO as largely complete. Such comprehensive data bases are atypical, but in the absence of any alternatives, they have been selected to illustrate general points. Information quoted here from Nepal is less comprehensive and reliable, but is included because local studies and author's fieldwork have provided valuable information relating to general trends (Institute of Medicine, 1977 and 1979 a,b,c; Pearson, forthcoming).

150

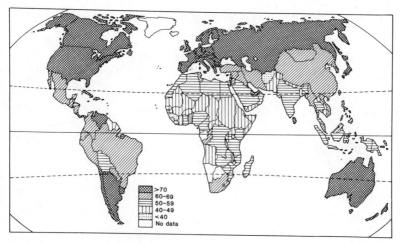

Fig. 7.2 Life expectancy at birth (in years), 1981

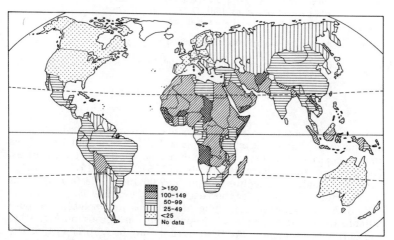

Fig. 7.3 Infant mortality rates (per 1000), 1981

The reliability of any population and mortality data is a contentious issue, but particularly in the Third World where few countries are able to support comprehensive and reliable systems of data collection and recording. These general problems of data reliability are further compounded in health statistics by the use of non-comparable disease classification systems, the under-reporting of morbidity and mortality, and inconsistent or incomplete recording of the cause of death (MacMahon and Pugh, 1970). Most published data refer to reported mortality, apart from notifiable diseases such as

Table 7.1:   Selected indices of health and socio-economic development for selected
countries, circa 1978

Country	Live births (a)	General deaths (a)	Natural increase (a)	Infant mortality (b)	Life expect- ancy at birth (c)	GNP per capita (d)
USA	15.8	8.7	7.1	13.8	73	9,770
England & Wales	13.0	12.1	0.9	12.8	72	5,720
Thailand (e)	23.3	5.2	18.1	14.2	61	630
Guatemala	41.6	9.8	31.8	69.2	58	930
India (f)	32.9	14.7	18.2	122.0	50	180
Nepal (f)	42.6	17.1	25.5	152.0	44	120

Sources: World Bank Atlas, 1980; UN Statistical Year Book, 1979;
WHO Annual Statistics. 1981; ODA, 1978;
Central Bureau of Statistics, Kathmandu, Nepal, 1979

Notes: a: Annual rate per 1000 total population
b: Annual rate per 1000 live births
c: Years (Male and Female combined), 1978
d: US Dollars per annum, 1978
e: Incomplete data
f: Estimates of unreliable sample data

cholera.   To ensure maximum possible comparability of data, an
International Classification of Diseases (ICD) is used, but there have
been successive revisions which may not be applied in all countries.
The most recent revision, the ninth (ICD 9), was in 1975.   Selected
indices of health and socio-economic development in a few countries
use a variety of sources for the years 1977-79 (Table 7.1).

The data on Thailand, some of which is incomplete, are more
reliable than that for India and Nepal which are based on estimates
and unreliable samples.   At first sight it may be surprising that the
crude death rate in England and Wales is higher than in Thailand but
this is to a large extent accounted for by an age structure in England
and Wales with a high proportion of old people, among whom
mortality is high.   The infant mortality rate in Thailand is similar to
that of some 'developed' nations despite markedly lower per capita
income and life expectancy.   Despite a per capita income almost
twice that of Thailand, Guatemala scores 'badly' on all health indices,
and has a high natural population increase of 31 per thousand per
annum.   Such apparent disparities highlight the variety of situations
prevailing in the Third World, though most have the general pattern
of high indices of ill health associated with lower per capita income
illustrated in an extreme form by India and Nepal.

Table 7.2 : Mortality patterns in three selected countries : age specific death and percentage of deaths due to specific causes

AGE	GUATEMALA				THAILAND				ENGLAND & WALES			
	Death [a] Rate	% infect. parasit.	% chest [c] inf.	% ill-defined	Death [a] Rate	% infect. parasit.	% chest [c] inf.	% ill-defined	Death [a] Rate	% infect. parasit	% chest [c] inf.	% ill-defined
0 [b]	7226.6	29.3	13.0	10.4	1415.8	16.9	17.8	27.7	1281.8	1.8	6.6	10.8
1 - 4	1352.0	53.4	11.1	16.4	293.4	18.0	21.0	40.5	50.3	6.9	8.9	1.6
5 - 14	238.2	32.6	7.7	15.4	121.0	17.6	13.9	34.0	26.0	2.4	5.1	0.3
15 - 24	251.2	20.6	6.0	14.9	215.5	8.9	6.6	21.4	62.2	1.1	2.5	0.3
25 - 34	365.7	23.7	6.5	16.3	257.1	21.2	5.8	21.6	76.7	1.4	2.3	0.4
35 - 44	530.4	21.7	7.0	14.9	478	9.9	6.1	25.1	168.0	1.1	2.4	0.3
45 - 54	795.2	21.9	6.6	15.5	864	10.9	6.2	29.8	538.7	0.7	2.4	0.1
55 - 64	1578.0	21.1	6.6	16.5	1534.8	9.6	5.6	42.9	1414.9	0.5	3.0	0.1
65+	5677.0	15.1	9.3	12.2	4895.1	3.5	2.2	9.1	6263.5	0.3	19.8	0.1
All ages	966.6	29.8	10.1	13.5	523.4	9.2	7.2	24.4	1206.0	0.4	9.4	0.2

a Death Rates per 100,000 population
b Infant Mortality Rate per 100,000 live births
c Chest infections include pneumonia

Source: WHO Annual Statistics, 1981

Table 7.2 shows age specific mortality rates from all causes for the three selected countries, and the proportion of deaths due to certain causes. In Thailand 24.4 per cent of all deaths were classed as due to 'symptoms and other ill-defined conditions' compared with 13.5 per cent for Guatemala and only 0.2 per cent for England and Wales. The large proportion of 'ill-defined' deaths in Thailand highlights the problems of data reliability and imprecise reporting. In both Guatemala and Thailand the major recorded cause of death was infectious and parasitic disease, being 30 per cent of all deaths in Guatemala and 9.2 per cent in Thailand but only 0.4 per cent of all deaths in England and Wales. It is possible that the significant proportion of 'ill-defined' deaths in Thailand might account for low reporting of infectious and parasitic disease. Pneumonia was recorded as the cause of 9.6 per cent of deaths in Guatemala; 9.2 per cent in England and Wales; and 1.9 per cent of deaths in Thailand. In total, 40 per cent of all deaths in Guatemala were recorded as being due to infectious and parasitic diseases and chest infections, compared with 16.4 per cent for Thailand and 9.8 per cent for England and Wales (Table 7.3).

The high proportion of Third World deaths attributed to infectious disease and chest infections is reflected in morbidity data from community health surveys in four districts of Nepal (Institute of Medicine, 1977 and 1979a,b,c) which found that between 29 and 36 per cent of reported illness was due to respiratory disease, and between 15 and 21 per cent due to gastro-intestinal diseases (Table 7.4). These surveys also found that within a 14-day period up to 10 per cent of the population was prevented by illness from undertaking 'normal activities', and between 22 and 45 per cent of the population reported feeling ill.

153

Table 7.3: Percentage of all deaths due to infections and ill-defined
            causes: selected countries, circa 1978

Country	Recorded Causes of Death		
	Infectious and Parasitic Disease	Respiratory Infections and Pneumonia	Symptoms and ill-defined Causes
Guatemala	29.8	10.1	13.5
Thailand	9.2	7.2	24.4
England & Wales	0.4	9.4	0.2

Source: WHO Annual Statistics. 1981

Table 7.4: Reported morbidity in Nepal

| Cause of Morbidity (% all reported illness) | Selected Districts | | | |
	Surkhet	Nuwakot	Tanahu	Dhankuta
Respiratory Disease	29	26	33	36
Diarrhoea/Dysentery/GI	15	19	18	21
Fever	9	4	6	5
Acute Disability (% of population)	10	3	10	2
'Illness Rate' per 14 days (% of population)	32	34	45	22

Source: Institute of Medicine, Kathmandu, 1977 and 1979 a, b, c.

Most illness and mortality in the Third World is clearly of an
infectious nature, largely preventable by education and basic public
health measures, or eminently curable by chemotherapy if detected
early. Such illnesses are not most appropriately dealt with by
hospital-based care.

Demographic structure and change
The proportion of the total population in broad age groups partly
reflects the level of socio-economic development, but has clear
implications for health policy. The rate and nature of demographic
change will affect projections of the future structure and health care

needs of the population, both quantitatively and in their emphasis. 'Young' populations need extensive maternal and child health services, whilst ageing populations need more geriatric care. As compared with 21 per cent of the population of England and Wales aged under 15, Thailand and Guatemala have over 40 per cent of the total population in that age group (Figure 7.4). The majority of health care needs for such a young population are for pregnancy, childbirth and child health services focussing on immunisation and the prevention and treatment of infection which contributes to currently high infant mortality rates (Table 7.2).

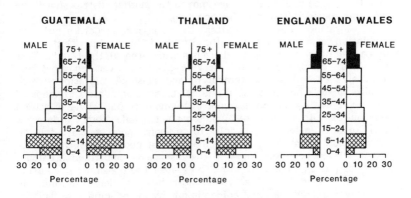

N.B. The 0-4 age group is half the range of the other age groups; proportions are correspondingly small

Fig. 7.4 Guatemala, Thailand, England and Wales : Age structure c.1980

Spatial distribution of the population
In the absence of detailed information for specific countries, general statements on the differential distribution of population between rural and urban areas in the developed and Third World are risky. In more developed regions such as North America and Europe, over three-quarters of the total population may be in urban areas, compared with approximately 25 per cent in 'less developed regions' such as South Asia (Basch, 1978). Whilst such a crude urban-rural distinction serves as a useful guideline, it masks the rush to the cities and the plight of shanty town dwellers in the Third World. There is also considerable and continuing rural-rural migration in many Third World countries. In Nepal, for example rapid recent migration to the recently cleared forests of the southern jungle (terai) has led to an estimated annual population growth 4.2 per cent in these districts compared with a national annual rate of 2.6 per cent (Blaikie et al., 1980). Basic health posts in these areas are unable to cope with the rapidly increasing demand for their services. Resource allocations

155

and service plans have not taken the above-average population growth into account and health-post staff, equipment and drugs are under-supplied (Pearson, 1983). This has particularly worrying implications for squatter settlements where sanitation is virtually non-existent, living conditions are overcrowded and unventilated and diseases spread quickly. Hookworm, passed in faeces and contracted through the skin of bare feet in rice paddies and poorly drained land, is so rife that some people are too anaemic and breathless to work. In 1980, there was an unprecedented epidemic of viral encephalitis, spread by a particular type of mosquito which flourishes in the water butts of the squatter settlements. The mortality rate was so high that leprosy control teams were moved to another district until the epidemic subsided (Pearson, forthcoming).

Migration may also alter the age-sex structure of the population as, for example, in the States of the Arabian Gulf where single male labour is imported from a wide area of the Middle East and Asia. Therefore health service planners must be alert and responsive to permanent, temporary and seasonal migrations which require flexible health service policies to accommodate the needs of the people involved. Leprosy control teams in Nepal regularly attend seasonal or religious festivals which attract people from a wide area. It is often easier for people to present anonymously for an examination whilst away from home, so that people from the family or the village need not know if the disease is confirmed (Pearson, 1982). Population movements not only alter the consumer population for which basic health services must be provided, but may in themselves affect the local epidemiology by introducing new diseases and facilitating the spread of epidemics. Disease control strategies which fail to incorporate the crucial dimension of migration and population movements cannot be effective. A striking example of this is the problems which large scale population movements have presented to malaria eradication programmes in Africa (Prothero, 1965). The diffusion of the cholera epidemic in West Africa in the early 1970's was strongly linked to population movements overland and between sea ports (Stock, 1976).

For an effective service delivery more detailed information is needed on the considerable variation in access to and communications within Third World countries, particularly in rural areas. A 'rural' area in Sri Lanka with roads and buses is vastly different from a remote part of the Himalayas in Nepal, where there are only 1000 miles of road in a national area of 50,000 square miles. Clearly, plans must be sensitive to the mode of transport and to seasonal variations in access such as the destruction of paths and roads by monsoon rains, if maximum access to services is to be achieved. Many villages in Far West Nepal are over a day's walk from a health post. In a subsistence economy, where the working day is long and profit margins are negligible, the time and effort needed to walk to a health post can rarely be afforded, particularly if paths have been washed away (Pearson, 1983). 10 per cent of respondents in community health surveys in Nepal were 'too busy' to use health posts, whilst another 30 per cent felt that their problem was too minor to warrant seeking advice from an official health post (Institute of Medicine, 1977 and 1979 a,b,c). If health services were physically more accessible and open for longer hours, people might be more able to use them, rather than relying on home remedies or taking no treatment at all. Since 70 per cent of ill people in Nepal receive no treatment at all, these are important considerations.

FORMULATION OF APPROPRIATE HEALTH POLICIES

Demographic structure, spatial distribution and health needs of the Third World are vastly different from those in developed countries. Infections and parasitic diseases are the major health problems and they could be tackled by public health measures to improve sanitation and drinking water, by simple chemotherapy for which paramedical training is adequate, and by a general improvement in living conditions which generally brings an improvement in health. Yet, despite the WHO policy of primary health care, the dominant ideology and approach to health problems in most countries of the Third World reflect the western medical model. Preventive care and the laying of water pipes and sewers are unglamorous as compared with the skilled specialist medical services, while their advocates lack professional power and status compared with the protagonists of intensive care units and other forms of curative hospital medicine. Moreover, the saving of the life of one child in hospital with typhoid or diphtheria is rather more identifiable and gratifying than less immediately visible attempts to improve public health measures.

An understanding of the ideology underlying the established health services which were exported to the Third World is necessary in order to grasp the fundamental nature of the radical policy shift in WHO strategy, and the enormous political task it faces in attaining its goal of health for all through primary health care.

The ideology of 'scientific' western medicine
Contemporary Western medicine is but one particular model and medical tradition, the methodology and concepts of which are rooted in the mechanistic view of life which won acceptance in the Western world in the nineteenth century. It originated in the Cartesian view of the body as dissociated from the soul, perceived as a mere set of component parts, each with discrete functions, whose workings could be explained on purely mechanical grounds. Deviation from normal processes resulted in disease, which can be precisely and objectively identified (Jewson, 1974 and 1976).

The emergence of the hospital as an institution for dealing with the problem of the ill and dying urban poor changed the entire framework of relations between the practitioner and the sick person (Waddington, 1973). The medical men were released from their dependence on the wealthy elite. The emphasis in medical practice changed from the art of subjective empathy and observation of the sick person to the science of objective examination of 'cases' of deviant organic matter, and the classification of specific diseases, according to pathology rather than symptoms. Medical practitioners, able to retreat behind an array of jargon, tests, procedures and equipment, often became detached from the sick person. The patient became increasingly alienated from the failing set of mechanisms which were yielded submissively to the medical mechanic for repair. Particularly in the treatment of poor sick people who were also often 'ignorant', the balance of power in the dialogue shifted radically towards the doctor.

The biomedical model, with its mechanistic view of disease and over-simplistic biological explanations, has several important implications. First, it paved the way for the depersonalisation of the experience of illness. In attributing the determinants of illness mainly to personal habits and hygiene and separating these from the socio-economic environment, the individual careless enough to become ill was often held morally responsible for their misdemeanour which could be avoided by healthy living.

A second implication of the mechanistic view for medical practice was that single causes of a biological nature were deemed to cause disease and that these demand simple specific solutions, such as pharmaceutical and scientific medical treatment. This became the preserve and jealously guarded domain of professionally trained doctors and drug companies, admission to whose ranks is rigidly controlled. Professional control of medicine has secured and maintained the hegemony of the biomedical model in the ideology of medicine and health care, despite well documented evidence of the strong association between the majority of illnesses and low socio-economic status. Glamour, status and finance for technocratic medicine and its 'disease palaces' (Mahler, 1974) have developed a powerful ideology which is in sharp opposition to the primary health care ethos of those who seek to deprofessionalise medicine (Newell, 1975).

Relevant and appropriate policies: public health and primary care

In working towards its goal of Health for All by the Year 2000 through a policy of primary health care, the WHO faces an enormous, almost impossible, task. Such a policy poses a major threat to the powerful interest groups which have benefited from the wholesale export of conventional highly expensive Western medical technology and ideology much of which is inappropriate to the basic health needs of the Third World.

Appropriate health policies must be based on a well informed analysis of the causes of the major health problems. Infections and parasitic diseases are a major reported cause of ill health, and dehydration during gastro-intestinal infections is a major cause of infant mortality in the Third World. The solutions to such health problems lie in good sanitation, a clean water supply and knowledge of simple health measures, not in expensive intravenous infusions and antibiotics. A more relevant and appropriate policy than centrally located, expensive and highly trained doctors would combine a major public health programme, the domain of engineers, with a primary health care programme staffed largely by paramedical workers of varied expertise and training. Locally trained village health workers who know the local area and problems and can promote health and health education which directly relate to people's life experience are a vital component of accessible primary health care. For example, primary health care workers who teach the population how to mix and administer rehydration fluid with the correct proportions of salt and sugar have been shown to be effective in treating gastro-intestinal cases. The same paramedical workers can also educate the population about the importance of breastfeeding and good nutrition and the dangers of bottle-feeding with unclean equipment (Pearson, 1983).

The primary health care approach may still preclude access to 'Health For All'. Perhaps one of the greatest contradictions is that it essentially remains the domain of professionals and 'experts'. Some of these may have less technological training than their colleagues in hospitals; nevertheless, there has been a trend to 'para-professionalise' Health for All. But the majority of ill people turn to the informal sources of health care: treating themselves on the basis of 'common knowledge' or 'old wives tales'; or turning to friends and relatives (Pearson, 1983). Many of the effective and simple treatments used widely in home remedies fall within the domain of women as housekeepers. It is they who give the yoghurt (dahi) to the child with a gastro-internal upset; it is the women who adjust the level of spices (piro) in the curry when a stomach complaint is diagnosed. Such 'old wives tales' are not all myth, and many are based on a body of knowledge developed with experience and observation (Pearson, 1984).

Neither are expensive drugs always the most appropriate treatment for disease, particularly in remote areas where supplies might be inadequate to ensure a full course of treatment for all patients. Many non-pharmaceutical treatments, such as saline or dextrose applications for infected wounds, are effective and cheap. Where curative treatment and simple drug therapy are appropriate a paramedical worker with two or three years' training can adequately cope with the task. High cost, technological care has its place in the Third World, but not as the major strategy for tackling the basic health needs. Moreover, such care is rendered futile if adequate follow-up and support services are not available.

The problem of drug resistance throughout the Third World is increasing due to suboptimal dosage as a result of inadequate supplies. This is particularly so in poorer areas where drugs have to be bought by the local population when health post supplies run out. As one health post assistant in Nepal put it: "we can diagnose, but we can't treat" (Pearson, 1983). All health posts have, at most, only 30 per cent of their annual medical and drug supply needs. The threat of drug resistance in foiling disease control strategies is such that expensive, oral therapy has been introduced to the tuberculosis and leprosy control programmes in many countries, including Nepal (Pearson, forthcoming). Where power supplies are inadequate, many drugs cannot be kept under the requisite cool temperature conditions. To focus largely on such technical care in the face of the prevailing epidemiology in the Third World is to provide the champagne for the few to which Mahler referred, and to preclude the chance of providing the daily bread for the many.

In essence, realistic policy formulation is the definition of feasible priorities. In the Third World, where finance, physical accessibility and the socio-economic infrastructure are major constraints, many of the basic health needs of the population can be met by accessible primary health care. To adopt and implement such a policy demands the political will to reverse a trend of thinking which has led to the adoption of the Western medical model with all its expense, alienation and spatial and social biases.

THE PROVISION OF ACCESSIBLE SERVICES

Policies and strategies designed to promote and implement primary health care to tackle the major causes of ill-health in the Third World must ensure that the basic health services will be accessible to the population. Apparently minor considerations such as opening hours are in fact of major importance for many people in rural communities where transport is difficult and the working day long and arduous. In many areas a day's journey may be necessary to attend a clinic and it is particularly in these areas that accessible and dispersed first line primary health care should take priority over more concentrated and technologically advanced services. Access is not just a matter of physical distance, though in remote areas with no transport this is a major factor. There are also several financial and social aspects to accessibility.

First, the services of paramedical staff are of little use if they are able to diagnose competently but unable to treat adequately because the patient cannot afford to pay the cost of a full course of drugs. Sadly this is an all too common occurrence in many parts of the Third World: as a result drug resistance has become a major problem. In Nepal, one vial of the most commonly available antibiotic, streptomycin, costs the equivalent of one day's average income in rural areas. In addition there is also the cost of foregoing perhaps a day's work to travel to the nearest health post. Secondly, it is imperative that paramedical workers do not seek to ape the social distance and acquired status of the medical profession, reinforcing the ideology that medical knowledge is a rare skill, available only to an elite few and alienating the patient. Well informed paramedical workers with a commitment to primary health care can command respect within the community without adopting such an attitude. Thirdly, local beliefs and customs should be respected and taken into consideration in formulating health policies.

160

Many women may prefer to be attended in childbirth by another woman or a local midwife, rather than by a male obstetrician or a formally trained nurse-midwife. Local midwives could be given basic training in hygiene which would enhance their practice, without denying their extensive acquired experience. Local herbalists and traditional practitioners should be respected and incorporated into health care plans where possible.

Varying constraints and aspects of access to health services highlight the need for flexible policies based on the principles of public health and primary health care, which can be sensitively varied in detail and practice to incorporate local beliefs, existing health services and physical conditions.

CONCLUSION

The provision of Health Care for All by the Year 2000 is an admirable goal, and is theoretically possible given the nature of the major health problems in the developing world outlined above. Population growth and demographic change in the Third World need not, in themselves, create insuperable obstacles to achieving that goal. The provision of more expensive physicians and hospital beds is less important than the spread of simple preventive and curative medicine at community level and the training and education of workers and people in ways that will help to bring this about. But this is the crux of the dilemma: the attainment of feasible goals is thwarted partly by the hegemony of a Western medical model which fails to tackle the fundamental causes of ill health because of its 'obsession with disease' and purely biological explanations of illness, partly because of ignorance and limited access to basic medical skills within the community. It is not more of the same established but over-thinly spread services that is needed. There is a need for a radical shift in policy and resources, backed by the political will necessary to achieve the provision of flexible and accessible primary health care for all which can anticipate and accommodate rapid demographic change.

REFERENCES

Basch, P. (1978) International health, OUP, New York
Blaikie, P., et al. (1980) Nepal in crisis, OUP, Delhi
Djukanovic, V., and E.P. Mach, (1975) Alternative approaches to meeting basic health needs in developing countries, WHO, Geneva
Institute of Medicine (1977) Rural health needs A study of Tanahu District, Institute of Medicine, Tribhuvan University, Kathmandu
Institute of Medicine (1979a) Rural health needs study no. 2. A study of Dhankuta District, Institute of Medicine, Tribhuvan University, Kathmandu

Institute of Medicine (1979b) Rural health needs study no. 3. A study of Nuwakot District, Institute of Medicine, Trihuvan University, Kathmandu

Institute of Medicine (1979c) Surkhet District community health survey. Institute of Medicine, Trihuvan University, Kathmandu

Jewson, N. (1974) 'Medical knowledge and the patronage system in eighteenth century England', Sociology. 8, 369-85

Jewson, N. (1976) 'The disappearance of the sick man from medical cosmology, 1770-1870', Sociology, 10, 225-44

McKeown, T., and C.R. Lowe (eds.) (1974) An introduction to social medicine, Blackwell, Oxford.

MacMahon, B., and T. Pugh (1970) Epidemiology: principles and methods, Little Brown, Boston

Mahler, H. (1974a) 'An international health conscience', WHO Chronicle, 28, 207-11

Mahler, H. (1974b) 'The health of the family' Keynote address to the International Health Conference of the National Council for International Health, Washington, D.C., October 16

Newell, K.W. (ed.) (1975) Health by the people, WHO, Geneva

Pearson, M.A. (1982) 'Social factors and leprosy in Lamjung, West Central Nepal: implications for disease control', Ecology of Disease, 4, 229-36

Pearson, M.A. (1983) 'Western medicine and the underdevelopment of health in Nepal', Proceedings of Primo Seminario Internationale di Geografica Medica, Perugia, 389-95

Pearson, M.A. (1984) 'Old wives or young midwives? Women in health and development: the case of Nepal', Paper presented to the Women and Geography Study Group, Institute of British Geographers, 1984

Pearson, M.A. (forthcoming) 'Leprosy and its control in West Nepal', University of Liverpool

Prothero, R.M. (1965) Migrants and malaria, Longmans, London

Soddy, K. (ed.) (1961) Cross cultural studies in mental health, Tavistock, London

Stock, R.F. (1976) Cholera in Africa: diffusion of the disease, 1970-75, International African Institute, London

Townsend, P., and N. Davidson (1982) Inequalities in health, Penguin, Harmondsworth

Waddington, I. (1973) 'The role of the hospital in the development of modern medicine: a sociological analysis', Sociology, 7 211-24

World Health Organization (WHO) (1974) 'Health trends and prospects 1950 - 2000', World Health Statistics Report, 27, 670-706

WHO-UNICEF (1978) Primary health care, A joint report by the Director-General of the World Health Organisation and the Executive Director of the United Nations Children's Fund, Geneva and New York

World Bank (1984) World Development Report, Washington, D.C.

Chapter Eight

EDUCATION PROVISION AND DEMOGRAPHIC CHANGE IN ENGLAND AND WALES

Eric Briault

THE DEMAND FOR EDUCATION

The provision needed for education has a very direct relationship to annual birth rates and the size of successive age-groups. After a quarter of a century of expansion in educational provision since the end of the Second World War, nearly all Western countries now find themselves in a period of contraction in demand for education as the trough of the wave-graph of age-groups passes through successive stages of the educational process. The annual numbers of births in England since 1960 and the corresponding numbers of pupils in schools since 1970 underline the marked decline of the 1970's and '80's, with the uncertainty of the trends in the early 1990's being reflected in the wide range of variants postulated (Fig.8.1).

A contracting industry displays three main features: overmanning, excess plant capacity and rising unit costs. Education is no exception, for with falling rolls it finds itself with too many teachers, too many schools and rising costs per pupil. The inescapable overhead costs of every empty school place - heating, cleaning, building maintenance - fall upon the cost-per-head of educating each remaining pupil. So the economists' response to contraction will be to try to reduce the teaching force pro-rata to the fall in pupil numbers, to close some schools and keep the remaining ones full, and to allow public expenditure to reap the benefits of falling rolls by keeping costs-per-head as nearly steady as possible. The enthusiast for education, not to say the trade unions concerned, take an opposing view: with no increase in total expenditure, schools may enjoy the advantages of a lower pupil/teacher ratio, by retaining all existing teachers; they will have sufficient rooms for smaller classes and space for new educational developments and will be able (so it is believed) to raise the quality of the product. In the long run better educated pupils will bring economic advantages in due course. With typical British compromise neither course has been pursued wholeheartedly, and those involved in planning have given themselves the satisfaction of being able to claim economies and improvements at one and the same time.

163

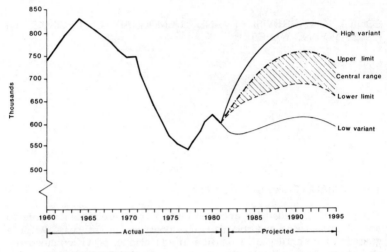

Fig. 8.1 (a) Births in England

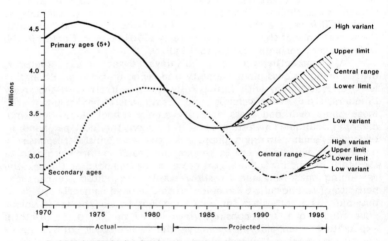

Fig. 8.1 (b) Actual and projected enrolment in maintained primary and secondary schools
in England
Source: D.E.S. report, May 1982.

164

Educational provision must be looked at in broader terms than provision for compulsory schooling between 5 and 16. There are in addition those groups for whom educational opportunities are provided in all Westernised countries but neither on a universal nor compulsory basis: pre-school provision; immediately post-statutory school-age education and training, in all its full- and part-time variety; higher or advanced education and training. Over and above all these, and much less susceptible to any firm calculations of numbers, lies the whole field of leisure-time education, from the youth service to classes for OAPs. The rise and fall of the birth rates in Western countries since the Second World War directly affect provision for all these needs except the last, but the distinction between compulsory schooling and the rest is very important since policy choices can be made in the non-compulsory sectors which do not exist in respect of provision for those of statutory school age. In relation to adult education, the rise in the numbers of the elderly add a growing and potentially significant group of people demanding more education provision as part of a fuller and more active retirement.

The changes in the number of live births per thousand women aged 15-44, since 1950 in selected Western countries show that changes in the United Kingdom are less dramatic than those in some of the countries. (see Figure 1.4). There are also important geographical variations in the demand for education which directly affect the application of broader policies, chiefly the following: the tendency in Western countries for the proportion of the population in urban areas to rise, reflected also in rural areas by the decline of smaller villages and the growth of a few larger villages and small towns; social, economic and population decline in the inner city; new town and suburban development, reflecting the modern dispersal of homes and jobs from cities and older industrial towns. Such variations can result in an overall fall in school rolls of 30-50 per cent in some areas, and an actual rise in the school population in others. One of the keys to the understanding of the management of a contracting education industry is the recognition that macro-level government level policies are necessarily applied to very varied circumstances at the micro-level, at which level political, social and economic considerations may differ widely from the overall national picture. One particular factor that greatly affects any international comparisons which may be made is the extent to which decision-making is centralised at government level or devolved to the local level. In the former case national policies can be universally applied whatever local circumstances. In the U.K., however, the balance of power between central and local government applies to the whole educational spectrum outside the universities; moreover needs of the different sectors can be considered in relation to one another. In such countries as Switzerland and Norway, on the other hand, different authorities control primary and secondary education and coordination of changing requirements is extremely difficult. In Norway, a village which can produce eight pupils is statutorily entitled to retain its primary school. In such federal states as the

165

United States and Switzerland, national planning of education is virtually non-existent, yet within the states of Australia, centralisation of decision-making is as complete as in France. Indeed, the distributed system of administration of education in the U.K. is a mystery to education officials in most other Western countries.

Alongside demographic and geographical variations, certain other factors affecting the management of education provision must be mentioned. The first of these is the expectation of the continuation of unemployment on a massive scale, including very high school-leaver unemployment (see Chapter 2). The latter has given rise in the U.K. to a new-found dichotomy between educational provision by the local education authorities and of training by the employment authorities. In general, unemployment promotes the need for and expectation of the retraining of adults, an extension of further education and training into the adult sector severely limited by constraints upon resources. Yet the need for such teaching is emphasised by a second factor, the growth of new technologies and the consequential change in the nature of work and in the numbers of workers required in both new and older styles of occupation. The ability to produce goods and services to sustain the growing demand for social services lies at the heart of national economic problems in the U.K. and should influence the provision of post-school education and training. This issue lies close to the possible role of the National Advisory Board for Higher Education. Thirdly, the growth of new information technology directly affects the possible styles and modes of teaching, as the success of the Open University demonstrates.

Such is the backcloth against which the management of educational provision must operate. In the issues facing management at the macro level, the first problem poses a choice: what balance is to be struck between economic efficiency and social benefit, between value for money and the educational advantage available through higher unit costs? What gain is to be expected from falling rolls, reduced expenditure or better provision? The assumption behind these alternatives is that the more you spend per head, the better the education you provide, but there are those who would not accept that that proposition is self-evident. While children in very large and overcrowded classes are almost certainly disadvantaged, there are many factors, in particular the skill and dedication of teachers, as well as the level of expenditure, which equally affect the quality of education. Better resources, well-managed and efficiently used, will produce better results than the same resources inefficiently used through ill-management. In either case management responsibility includes responsiblity for the quality of teaching.

A second issue is the balance between the objective of the broad education of the whole man and the specific preparation of the student for gainful occupation. True, the latter should be within the former, but the curriculum balance, especially at the upper secondary and further education level, can be tipped one way or the other. A third issue lies in the judgements to be made between priorities for public spending. With an ageing population, health care and financial and welfare provision for the elderly lay claims to increasing expenditure which arguably could be met, at least in part, by reduced expenditure on education made possible by falling school rolls and smaller school-age cohorts.

EDUCATIONAL PROVISION

Primary Education

The sharp fall in primary school rolls which have already taken place, accentuated in some areas by movements of population, have already given rise to the problems of the application of broad policies to individual schools. Most proposals for the closure of very small rural primary schools have met with opposition from parents, teachers and villagers. At some point, there would seem to be educational as well as financial advantages in a very small school. Are the children in a one-class primary school as well-off educationally as those in, say, a seven-class school for 5- to 11-year olds? What is the length of journey in time which can be tolerated to gain the expected advantage of a larger school, a richer curriculum, never mind a lower unit cost? But what are the consequences for a village when its school is closed, a circumstance quite different from that resulting from the closure of an inner urban primary school whose nearest neighbour is only a few hundred yards away?

There are two sorts of financial disadvantages in the retention of a small school whose roll has fallen. First, every empty place costs money, for much the same heating, lighting, cleaning and maintenance costs are incurred whether the school is full or one-third empty. The second factor raising unit costs is the diseconomy in staffing the small school, especially as its roll falls. An overall pupil/teacher ratio of 30:1 can be applied fairly even-handedly to schools over, say, 150 or 200. But in the small school consideration must be given to the minimum number of separate classes. Ninety children in three classes will merit three teachers at the standard ratio; but as the roll falls to 80 or even 75, it will be necessary to retain the three classes and their teachers; the unit cost will rise correspondingly. A school with no more than 40 children would almost certainly have to be allowed two teachers in addition to the headteacher.

The educational disadvantages of the small school also relate to two distinct factors. The first is the age range in each class. In a 5 to 11 school even three classes will mean there is a two-year span in each class and in the school of 40 pupils, each of two classes will have to cover a three-year span, although the classes will be small enough for a good deal of individual attention to be given. The second factor relates to the necessarily limited range of teacher skills. It is likely to be difficult to offer pupils, especially in the junior section (say 8 to 11 age-range), adequate teacher guidance in science, music, art, drama, as well as in the basic skills and historical and environmental studies. Three teachers, let alone two, are unlikely to be able to offer, in all those subjects, the kind of stimulus which would be available in a school of say 150 or 200.

There is no generally recognised minimum size for a primary school. In the end, management must decide on the preferred alternative of keeping open or closing a particular school in the light of all the factors, geographical, social, financial, educational. One thing is sure: the arguments are very different in rural areas from those applying to urban situations, where one primary school can usually be seen from the top window of the next.

Secondary education

As falling age-groups move through into the secondary schools, similar problems apply in principle, but several factors peculiar to the secondary schools affect their impact. Most teaching and staffing are by custom and practice specialist or semi-specialist; the curriculum is expected to allow for a fair measure of choice of specialist subjects by individual pupils from say 14+; the increasing gap in both attainment and educational need between the more able and the less able tends towards a teaching-group organisation based in part on ability; and the numbers remaining beyond the statutory school-leaving age become critical in relation to the ability of a school to meet the pupils' advanced educational needs. Smaller intakes at 11+ or 12+ began to enter the schools in the second half of the 1970's but for a while the effect on the total school roll was overshadowed by the larger age-groups ahead of them. Before the end of the decade, however, total rolls began to fall and the fall in the 16+ age groups, which began in the early '80's, will continue, well into the 1990's (Figure 8.2).

The effect of the overall fall in the birth-rate upon individual schools varies greatly from area to area and from school to school. Migration out of the inner city has affected most large urban areas: the city of Liverpool is an extreme example (Figure 8.3):

"The unprecedented and continuous decline in births recorded in Liverpool was particularly significant during the recent period from 1962 to 1977. The scale of this decline is underlined when expressed in round numbers: from a total of 16479 births in 1962 to only 6166 in 1977, a fall of 62.6%.

This fall can be explained in part by the large-scale migration out of the city that took place during this period. The loss of population had the effect of accentuating the impact of the concurrent fall in the birth rate, ... Had the population of the city remained constant at the 1960 level, the sets of plotted points would have continued to coincide. However, the decrease in the number of children born was much more pronounced than that displayed by the underlying birth rate trend, reflecting the significant movement of population out of

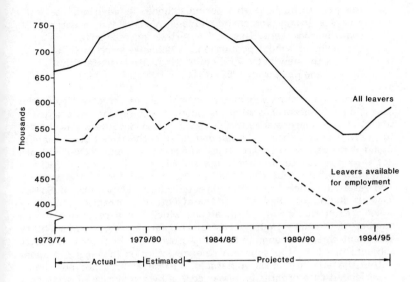

Fig. 8.2 Actual and projected pupils leaving school in England, 1973/74–1994/95
Source: D.E.S. report, May 1982

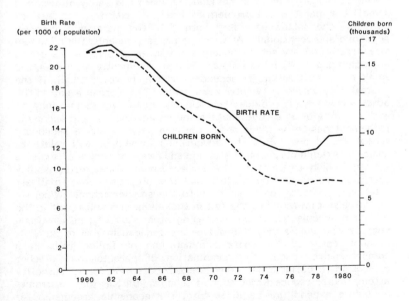

Fig. 8.3 Birth rate and number of children born to residents of Liverpool, 1960–80
Source: Brown and Ferguson, 1982

169

the city throughout this period. Since, in addition, the
city was losing women of childbearing age at a greater
than average rate, this had a further adverse effect on
the level of school population, as school-age children as
well as the new-born were emigrating with their families"
(Brown and Ferguson, 1982, p.177).

Variation from school to school arises chiefly from the
operation of parental choice as smaller age-groups entering the
schools leave spare places which can accommodate parental choices
for more popular schools. Urban education authorities have gradually
found it necessary to control these variations to some extent but are
not in a position to prevent some schools remaining comparatively
full while others bear the brunt of the contraction of the system.
The research which the writer directed at the University of Sussex
(Briault and Smith, 1980) showed the effects of contraction on twenty
schools each studied in detail, among which are a reduction in the
number of teaching-groups, constraints upon choices, a wider ability
and exam-objective range in teaching-groups. In time, some minority
subjects are lost: the separate sciences, foreign languages, choices
within the arts are most vulnerable. These effects are now being
experienced to a greater or lesser degree by a majority of secondary
schools.

Many authorities have reacted to contraction by the closure
through amalgamation of some schools, where geography allows, and
some have met the 16+ problem by creating sixth-form or tertiary
colleges, the latter providing both full and part-time courses,
academic and vocational. As with the primary schools, the minimum
size of a secondary school becomes a matter of critical discussion
and again geography plays its part. In a predominantly rural area, the
small town must retain its secondary school, however small, if the
nearest alternative is twenty miles away. In an urban area, on the
other hand, schools provided to meet the birth rate 'bulge' may be
within a mile or so of one another and an educational and economic
judgement has to be made about the size below which a secondary
school should not fall. The educational judgement will relate to
desired curriculum, specialist staffing and range of choice of subjects
- all tending to point to the larger school - and mixed ability
teaching, a common curriculum and the arguments for smallness
relating to pastoral care, pointing to the smaller school. Where a
selective system remains, the fall in the age-groups will result in the
selective schools taking an increasing proportion of the age-group
year by year unless they themselves are reduced in size or number.
In such cases or the more common one of falling rolls in a
comprehensive school, the combination of parental and teacher
opposition to closures has often proved too strong for an authority
attempting to reduce its number of schools. But, as the constraints
on public expenditure begin to bite, the economic arguments for
closing half-empty schools loom larger, whatever the educational
judgement.

170

The picture of further education or, more inclusively, 16 to 19 provision in England and Wales is a confused one, in which the effects of demographic factors are masked by two other major factors, namely youth-unemployment and economic constraint. Government has reacted in what many regard as contradictory fashion: restricting local authority expenditure so severely as to prevent any growth in further education expenditure to meet the larger age-groups and at the same time making large sums of money available to the Department of Employment and administered by the Manpower Services Commission to provide work-experience and training schemes for young people who would otherwise be unemployed.

Higher education

In the United Kingdom the demographic curve of those eligible to enter higher education reached its peak in 1982. In this country, as in many others - though not the United States - the size and cost of the higher education sector is largely controlled by central government. The discussion document, 'Higher Education into the 1990s' (DES, 1978), considered the policy options available to deal with a drop in the number of entrants to higher education from around 160,000 in 1978 to 110,000 by 1995 if the age-participation rate remained the same. This paper put forward five possible courses of action, not necessarily mutually exclusive, the first three of which assumed that the nature of the higher education provided would remain broadly as it is at present. Model A involved matching the volume of provision to the demographic curve, an option in part already rejected by the constraints recently imposed on higher education as the peak demand approached. Model B proposed anticipating the post-1982 decline in 18-year-olds by the deliberate reduction of provision and thus further restricting the opportunities for students at the time of the bulge to gain admission to higher education. In Model C, projected student numbers for the early 1980's would be catered for fully but more economically, particularly by avoiding capital expenditure on buildings which would later on no longer be required. Model D suggested altering the nature of educational provision in such a way as to keep numbers of entrants in line with demographic change by increasing the number of shorter and part-time courses - in a sense a special version of Model C. Model E by contrast in effect assumed that the fall in student numbers would be much shallower than the fall in the number of 18-year-olds suggested, because of a rise in demand due to an increase in participation rates and, especially, in the number of mature students. There is perhaps a further option, namely to keep up the number of admissions to courses but to expect an increase in the failure rate, especially in the first year of study, so that the total number of students would be kept in line with the places available: this would transfer the competition for places implied in Model B into the higher education institutions themselves.

A further report published in 1983 re-examined the factors upon which projections of the demand for higher education might be based (DES, 1983b). Figure 8.4 illustrates the overall trends in age-participation rates (left) and the participation rates of those qualified to enter higher education (right), and identified the relatively steady share of the unversities, the growth of non-university higher education and the dramatic fall in teacher training, reflecting the fall in school rolls discussed previously.

A discussion of the relevant factors led the DES to the conclusion summarised in Figure 8.5. The number of qualified leavers (qualified demand rate - QDR) is expected to fall less than the 18 year-old population projection, accounting for the level of expected

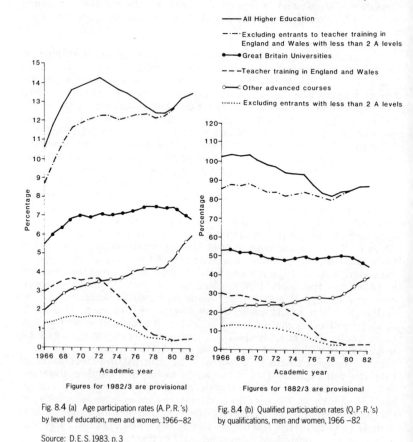

Fig. 8.4 (a) Age participation rates (A.P.R.'s) by level of education, men and women, 1966–82

Fig. 8.4 (b) Qualified participation rates (Q.P.R.'s) by qualifications, men and women, 1966 –82

Source: D.E.S. 1983, p. 3

demand being above the latest age-participation rate (APR). The report states that:

"During the period 1964 to 1977, when births overall fell by a third, the number occurring to families in social classes I and II (whose children are the most likely to stay on) rose slightly and thus such births formed an increasing proportion of total births in this period. As a result, the size of the sixth form population, and hence those obtaining qualifications for higher education, are projected to fall by less than the overall population decline. The projected fall of qualified leavers from the 1984/85 peak to 1995/96 is 25 per cent, compared with a fall of 31 per cent in the relevant age group" (DES, 1983b, p. 4).

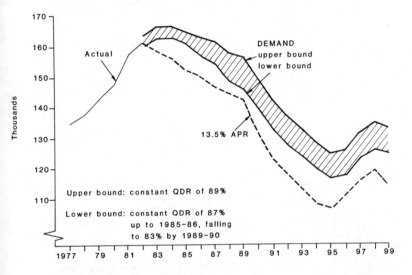

Fig. 8.5 Actual and projected home initial entrants in full-time and sandwich higher education in Great Britain
Source: D.E.S. 1983, p. 6

In 1983 a Royal Society paper prepared by Dr. P.M.D. Collins for its ad hoc Committee on University funding directed particular attention to the changing proportions of births in the different social classes and their relation to expected demand for University places (The Royal Society, 1983). These changes for England and Wales, 1960-80 (Figure 8.6) were applied to projections of the number of home candidates for U.K. Universities, 1983-1998, as follows:

"Knowing the size of the 18 year-old cohort for each social class year by year and the numbers in each cohort applying for university entrance, one can calculate the proportion of each cohort applying during the period 1977-81.
By applying the average proportions of candidates in each social class for the period 1977-81, to the 18 year-old

173

cohorts one can estimate numbers of candidates through to 1998. In doing this one needs to make some assumption about the behaviour of those who change social class between birth and age 18. Two sets of assumptions are tested here.

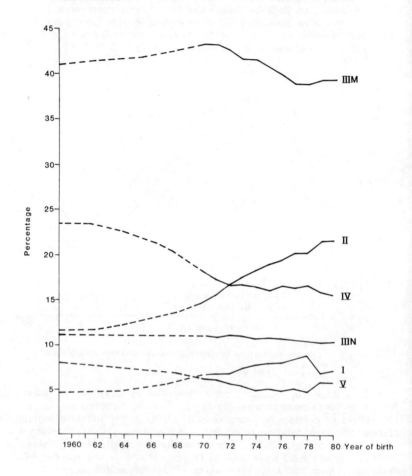

Fig. 8.6 Live births in each social class in England and Wales, 1959–80
Source: The Royal Society, 1983

(i) <u>Model A.</u> Those who move into social classes I or II between birth and 18 adopt the same attitudes towards applying for university entrance as those born into these groups.

174

(ii)   Model B. Those who move into social classes I or II between birth and 18 carry with them some of the attitudes typical of the social classes from which the came, i.e , they are less likely to apply for university entrance than those born into classes I or II. The quantification of 'less likely' allows, of course, a range of possible 'Model Bs' " (The Royal Society, 1983, p. 28).

The paper drew the following conclusions:

1.   The discussion document Higher Education into the 1990s (DES, 1978), in attempting to assess the future demand for higher education, concerned itself mainly with forward projections based on trends in the gross age participation rate since 1960. It did recognise that trends in birthrate and age participation rate differed markedly from one social class to another ('Model E'), but failed to elaborate this in detail. In the present paper attention has been focused solely on this problem because, of the many factors influencing demand for university entrance, the most important in a period during which large changes in the overall birthrate are occurring are the actual size and social composition of the 18 year-old age group, from which the great bulk of home candidates comes.

2.   The 35% drop in overall annual births in the UK between 1964 and 1977 (the years of maximum and minimum numbers of births, respectively) conceals a 9% rise in annual births in social classes I and II.

3.   Some 62% of home candidates for UK universities come from social classes I and II. Moreover, this proportion has been rising slowly but steadily in recent years.

4.   .. whatever assumptions one makes about the attitudes to university entrance of those who are upwardly socially mobile (e.g. models A or B), the future pattern of demand from home candidates for full-time undergraduate places at UK universities will be very different from the pattern of the overall UK birthrate 18 years earlier.

    (i)   During 1982-1989, while the overall size of the 18 year old age group falls by 11%, the number of candidates remains roughly constant (models A and B).

    (ii)   During 1989-1995, while the overall size of the 18 year old age group falls by 27%, the number of candidates falls by only 19% (model A) or 17.5% (model B)" (The Royal Society, 1983, p. 36).

In December 1983 the Council of the Royal Statistical Society set up a Working Party "to consider the various projections of student numbers in higher education into the 1990's and to establish and comment on the differences in the underlying assumptions". The report made a number of recommendations, one of which specifically endorsed the Royal Society Study:

> "That the methodology for taking into account the effects of social class employed by the Royal Society be adopted for projections of the numbers in the whole of HE" (Royal Statistical Society, 1984, p. 9).

The report was somewhat critical of the DES:

> "The only projections for HE as a whole are made by the DES. The DES methodology is based on a version of the flow model discussed in para 5. Since almost all candiates for HE have minimum qualifications the numbers of students in sixth form or further education sitting for 'A' levels or their equivalent is a leading indicator of the number of applications for HE. The DES calculate the QLR and from this use factors, currently 0.89 and 0.83, to provide upper and lower bounds for the QDR, which is then equated to the QPR. By using aggregate measures it is impossible to tell how these measures vary by age, sex and social class. As Table 1 shows the DES claim to take these factors into account but they do not provide either a methodology or a source of data for any of their claims. This makes it impossible to pass any sensible judgement on the DES projections. From a statistical point of view this is completely unsatisfactory and the working party recommend:
> That the DES provide full details of their method of projection and of the data upon which their projections are based.
> In defence of the DES, data on the age, sex and social class of entrants to the public sector or of students in sixth form or further education do not appear to be readily available. However, one could argue that it is just such data that the DES should be collecting so that satisfactory projections can be made. The working party recommend:
> That the DES collect data on the age, sex and social class of entrants to the public sector" (Ibid, p. 13).

The final conclusion of the report was as follows:

> "Taking into account the likely effects of both the major factors and the secondary factors the working party are of the opinion that relative to 1980/81 far

from being a decline there is likely to be an increase in the demand for HE throughout the remainder of this century" (Ibid, p. 16).

At the time of writing (in mid-1984) Government is adopting Model B of the 1978 report and, far from providing more places in higher education to meet the needs of the larger age-groups now entering upon it, has reduced the number of places below the previous maximum. The main reason is clearly that of financial constraint but one cannot help wondering whether there is a hidden element of belief in the minds of Ministers that too high a proportion of the age-group has been offered higher education places in the recent past, especially in the arts and social sciences.

Teacher training
The problems of the schools and of higher education resulting from demographic change come together in the teacher training sector. This presents an extreme example of massive expansion to meet the bulge in pupil numbers, followed by drastic reduction to avoid excessive supply of new teachers. The expansion was effected by a major building programme though some overcrowding was also involved and massive staff increases. The contraction was managed by heavy staff reductions helped by special compensation arrangements; by mergers or closures of whole institutions, the premises being sold or put to other uses; and by diversification of courses in those remaining, increasing the number of non-job-specific courses.

A DES report forecasting the need for teachers up to 1995 drew the main conclusions summarised in Figure 8.7 (DES, 1983a). The report makes two interesting assumptions which may or may not prove still valid in the 1990's. The first is that primary and secondary pupil/teacher ratios will be broadly maintained over the period of the report. There is however a good deal of experience to suggest that as rolls fall, the pupil/teacher ratio also falls. The Times reported:

"The number of teachers has fallen fast, as diminishing rolls and cuts have forced authorities to avoid filling vacancies caused by natural wastage and early retirement. England had 440,825 secondary and primary teachers in 1979; last year there were 414,621. Pupil/teacher ratios, however, have improved, from 18.9 in 1979 to 18.1 last year" (19th April, 1984).

The second relates to the reservoir of qualified teachers, mainly married women, who are not currently teaching. 'Married women returners' were a critical source of teacher supply when acute teacher shortages arose as the larger age groups came into the primary schools, before the teacher training colleges had expanded sufficiently to meet these needs. The DES report took the following line:

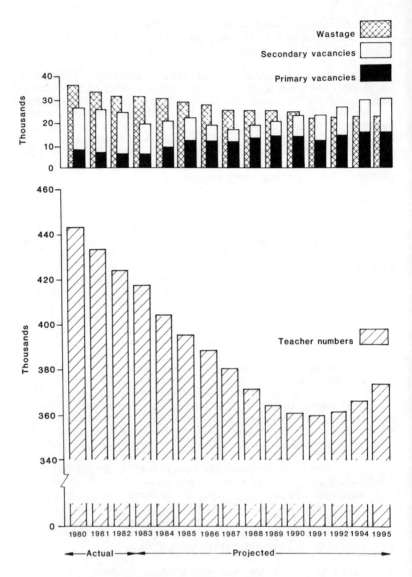

Fig. 8.7 Actual and projected teacher numbers, wastage and vacancies in England, 1980–94
Source: D.E.S. 1983, p.2

"For planning purposes it is necessary to make assumptions regarding the proportions of vacancies taken by new entrants and re-entrants both in primary and in secondary schools. These cannot be exact. This report assumes that in primary schools new entrants and reentrants will take up posts in approximately equal quantities (broadly in line with recent movements in actual proportions and reflecting the fact that women form the larger proportion of the total number of persons trained for primary teaching and are more likely than men to return to teaching). In secondary schools the majority of vacancies have been filled by new entrants - in recent years between 2/3 and 3/4 -and these are taken as indicators of the likely pattern in future" (DES, 1983a, p. 3).

The report concludes with a forecast of teaching's required share of qualified leavers. rising from some 8 per cent in 1983/84 to around 20 per cent in 1995. Those institutions with diversified courses including teacher training will be well placed to meet such a challenge and equally the universities will be in a position to expand post-graduate teacher training. However, while the projected vacancies for primary teachers rise steadily over the period, the secondary vacancies continue to fall to 1987-1989, rising only thereafter.

CHANGING ENROLMENTS AND INDIVIDUAL INSTITUTIONS

Changing population levels and trends pose problems and opportunities for management at the level of the individual institution, whether school, college, polytechnic or university. What are the principles of the effective management of change, especially of changing demand, in particular of falling numbers? The education industry has so long been accustomed to growth that it has shown itself ill-prepared for contraction. The first responsibility of management is the quality of education itself, to the customer, to the student. There is a dangerous tendency in some quarters to assume that it is to the staff, the employee, the teacher and to the institution, whether it be a small school or a college of higher education. Management will be the first to recognise that a contented staff and a flourishing institution are prerequisites of a successful product, an education of high quality. But it is also the role of leadership to seek to establish a consensus about objectives, which must be first and foremost concerned with the pupil, the student. Management - the use of resources - and objectives - the curriculum in the broadest sense - must be brought together. How may contracting resources be matched to a good curriculum? The wide-spread reaction to falling school rolls has been a strenuous effort to maintain existing curricula, within existing institutions whether school, college of education or other educational establishment; or, on the other hand, to reorganise institutions in the larger school, the sixth form college, the tertiary college, the Institute of Higher Education, to ensure that existing curricula can still be offered. Alongside such worthy efforts, ought there not to be a review of the whole curriculum, the whole range of learning and

179

social experiences, at least to identify priorities if there must be some loss, at best to think through again arrangements which in the past may have reflected as much the opportunities of an expanding staff as the real needs of students in a changing world?

Whatever the outcome of such a review, in a contracting situation management must seek the most effective and economical use of resources to achieve the desired end. This generally means two things: better use of staff and changed use of staff. The first involves a review of the 'class contact' (to use the jargon) load of individual teachers and the size of teaching groups. Too many small groups can no longer be afforded and so the organisation of subject choices must be arranged to avoid such a situation. The reduction of choice involved is an aspect of constraint upon the curriculum usually recognised only by the initiated. Secondly, the staffing of the desired curriculum in a contracting school or college will almost certainly involve some diversification of the teaching role of the individual teacher. When the amount of geography to be taught falls from a full-time load for two to no more than work for one and a half, one or both geographers must teach another subject as well. Such an over-simplified example points to a likely further need for staff re-training or refreshment. Management must make arrangements for such opportunities to be taken up. In the static staffing situation which tends to accompany contraction, career prospects for staff are much reduced. Management and planning at this micro-scale need to consider ways of distributing responsibility within the institution and also of changing duties to overcome frustration which may otherwise arise.

REFERENCES

Briault, E.W.H., and F. Smith (1980)   Falling rolls in secondary schools, Parts I and II, NFER, Slough

Brown, P.J.B., and S.S. Ferguson (1982) 'Schools and population change in Liverpool', in W.T.S. Gould, and A.G. Hodgkiss (eds.) The resources of Merseyside, Liverpool University Press, 177-90

DES and the Scottish Education Department   (1978)   Higher Education into the 1990s: a discussion document, HMSO

DES (1982) Report on Education, No. 97: Pupil numbers and school leavers: future numbers, HMSO

DES (1983a) Report on Education, No. 98: Teacher numbers -looking ahead to 1995, HMSO

DES (1983b) Report on Education, No. 99: Future demand for higher education in Great Britain, HMSO

OECD (1979) Demographic trends, 1950-1990

Royal Statistical Society (1984) Projections of student numbers in higher education, London

The Royal Society (1983) Demographic trends and future university candidates: a working paper, London

Chapter Nine

POPULATION ANALYSIS FOR THE PLANNING OF PRIMARY
SCHOOLS IN THE THIRD WORLD

W.T.S. Gould

INTRODUCTION

The quantitative expansion of primary school enrolments in each
country of the Third World in the last quarter century has been most
impressive by any standards, involving a great commitment of
financial and other resources by local communities, national
governments and the international community in general
(Fredricksen, 1981). This has occurred at a time of rapid growth of
the school-age cohorts in these areas, typically at a rate of between
two and three per cent per year. However, enrolment growth has
been more rapid than growth of the population at risk, and enrolment
ratios have risen substantially at all levels of the educational
pyramid: most sharply in the 1960's at the secondary and high levels,
but even more impressively in the 1970's in the primary school cycle.
This change in emphasis in the early ·1970's from secondary to
primary education may be attributed largely to more general shifts in
development strategies at that time towards the meeting of basic
needs, of which schooling is generally considered to be one of the
more important (World Bank, 1980).
    In terms of educational planning practice specifically, this shift
in emphasis has meant a reduced reliance on manpower planning or
cost-benefit approaches and greater emphasis on strategies that have
sought to ensure access to at least some schooling for all if not most
children. Such a shift is certainly politically attractive, and has been
justified in economic terms by the observed public and private rates
of returns to investments in primary education being much higher
than returns to secondary education (Psacharopoulos. 1982), and also
as a result of the methodologically more convincing comparative
studies of the relationship between primary schooling and rural
development. Christopher Colclough (1982) concluded that "primary
schooling increases productivity in both the urban and rural sectors"
(p.167), citing in particular the evidence of Lockheed et al. (1980) and
Jamison and Lau (1982) that "four years of schooling is capable of
enhancing the output of modernising farmers by as much as 10% per
year compared with uneducated farmers in the same area, keeping

land, capital and labour time constant" (p.177).

This chapter is premised on the strength of case for further quantitative expansion of primary school enrolments in the Third World, but considers rather the means by which that expansion may be most effectively planned. In particular it uses the contrasting cases of Kenya and Indonesia to examine aspects of the availability and use of population data on which much of the expansion is based, and concludes that major advances in collecting, presenting, analysing and using aggregate demographic data in educational planning have moved very far ahead of developments in collecting, presenting, analysing and using local demographic data. Since it is at the local scale that many of the most pressing planning problems are currently to be found, major attention now needs to be given to how local population structures and dynamics can be accounted for in planning the expansion of enrolments.

NATIONAL AND REGIONAL ANALYSIS

The school age population

The immediate impact of the demographic regime that is characteristic of Third World countries - of high fertility rates and falling mortality rates, particularly infant mortality rates - is abundantly clear. Each successive age cohort is growing and at rates higher than the overall rate of population growth. The population 'at risk' of being enrolled in school increases and in itself constitutes a major stimulus for enrolment expansion.

Rapid population growth means not only growing numbers, but has a major impact on age structures. Typically 40-45 per cent of the total population in countries with high current growth is aged less than 15 years, but this can rise to over 50 per cent as in Kenya currently (UNECA, 1982) (Figure 9.1). Age structures are very different from those currently found in low-growth countries, and even in the nineteenth century at the period of most rapid growth in the now-developed countries age structures were never as imbalanced as they are in most Third World countries at the present time. In England and Wales in 1841 only 23 per cent of the population was aged 5-14, the highest recorded in any English census, a proportion that fell consistently since that time. In Kenya the proportion recorded as aged 5-14 has been just below 30 per cent in the three censuses (1962, 1969 and 1979) for which age-specific data are available. Indonesia occupies a somewhat intermediate position, but, since fertility rates have fallen in recent years, the proportion aged 0-4 has fallen and that aged 5-14 has risen from 24.4 per cent in 1961 to 27.7 per cent in 1971 (Figure 9.2). The dramatic trend of age structures of England and Wales since 1821 is not yet apparent in the experience of Third World countries, but if fertility continues to fall in the Third World as a whole, then the proportion, if not the numbers, of school age will continue to fall.

182

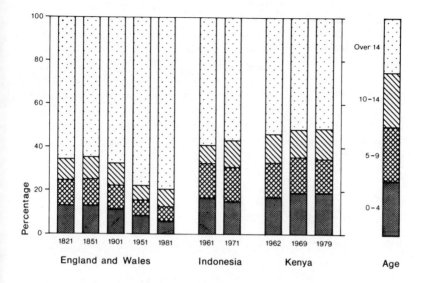

Fig. 9.1 England and Wales, Indonesia and Kenya : Age structures, selected years

Enrolments in the Third World, even at primary school level, are not universal and, since governments have sought, for political and economic reasons, to raise the enrolment rates, population growth alone does not account for all or even in many cases the greater component of enrolment expansion. Gross expansion must be considerable to cater for the growing cohort as well as the rising proportion of that cohort who can be provided with a school place. Rates of growth in enrolments of over 10 per cent per year have not been uncommon, especially in those African countries that started expansion in the 1960's from a low base. Governments have generally tried to establish national enrolment targets in policy documents such as National Plans, and have allocated resources to allow the targets to be reached. The targets themselves may be specified in absolute terms, in which case the real effects of population increase may be obscured, or in terms of raising enrolment rates which take account of population growth as well as improvements in the internal efficiency of the schools system by the reduction in numbers of dropouts or repeaters.

Some of the more general issues of the relationship between population change and primary school enrolments at the aggregate scale may be further developed by considering the sharply contrasting demographic and educational circumstances of Kenya and Indonesia.

183

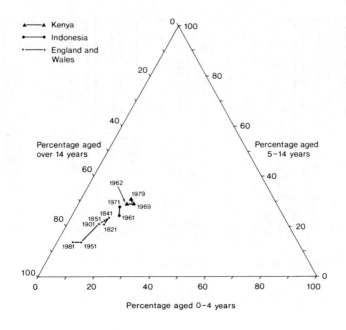

Legend:
- ▲——▲ Kenya
- ●——● Indonesia
- ·——· England and Wales

Percentage aged over 14 years

Percentage aged 5-14 years

Percentage aged 0-4 years

Fig. 9.2 England and Wales, Indonesia, Kenya : trends in age structures, selected years

Kenya

Kenya currently has one of the highest growth rates of any country in the world, estimated at 3.9 per cent p.a. by the Kenya Fertility Survey in the late 1970's, with a crude birth rate that rose from 50/1000 in 1969 to 54/1000 in 1977 (Mott and Mott, 1980). Total fertility rate is over 8 children per woman, an extremely high level that in the view of most commentators is likely to remain for some time (Dow and Werner, 1983; Kalule-Sabiti, 1984; UNECA, 1982, p.116). As a consequence there is an overwhelmingly youthful age structure that will produce slightly rising proportions in the school-age groups as the effects of rising fertility of the early 1970's proceed into the 1980's. Never-the-less in the years since 1962 primary school enrolments have risen rapidly and certainly much more rapidly than the size of the relevant cohorts (Figure 9.3). Expansion was from a low base and encouraged by political rhetoric and action (the massive increase evident for 1975 was due to the formal abolition of tuition fees in primary schools), as much as by a very strong demand by parents for schools for their children. Most Kenyan children now attend primary school for at least a few years, and while aggregate enrolments will be expected to expand as a result of fewer and later dropouts from school the major expansions in primary school enrolments in most parts of the country for the rest of this century will be largely a response to population growth.

The effect of these expansions on the educational status of the Kenyan population sharply differentiates age-specific education rates at different levels as identified by data on educational status in the 1979 Census, and these rates are further differentiated by sex and by region (Figure 9.4). Most people, boys and girls, aged less than 15 in

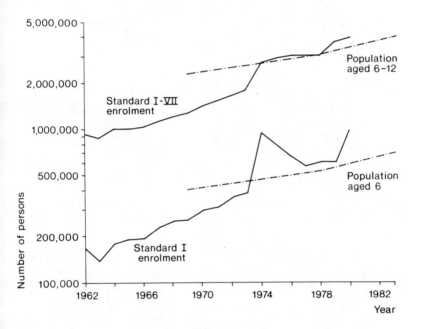

Fig. 9.3 Kenya : Primary school enrolment and population growth, 1962—83

1979 had some education but there is a regular decline in that proportion with age for males and an even steeper fall for females. Nationally less than 50 per cent of men and less than 20 per cent of women aged 50 in 1979 had any formal education. The recency of educational expansion is clearly illustrated by these declines, nowhere more so than in the very rapid expansion of secondary school enrolments in the 1960's such that the proportion of males aged 20-24 in 1979 (i e. who were in secondary school in the 1970 s) with some secondary education was more than double the proportion of those

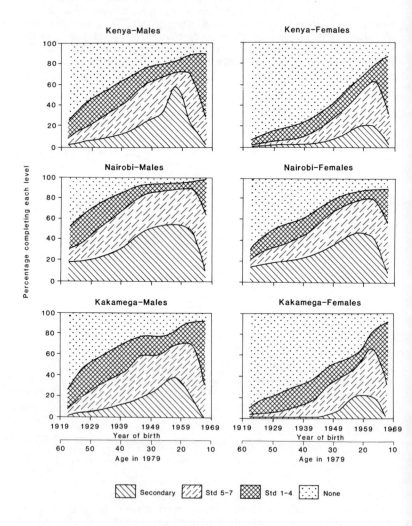

Fig. 9.4 Kenya : Educational status by age, 1979, selected areas

aged 35-39 (i.e. who were in secondary school in the late 1950's). Nairobi, the capital city, had considerably higher than average proportions of educated men and women at all ages, and particularly so for those with secondary education and above. Kakamega District, by contrast, has lower proportions than Nairobi, but an education structure of its population that is similar to the national picture. Nairobi is a major focus for migration and there has been a close relationship in Kenya, as elsewhere in the Third World, between education and migration. Districts such as Kakamega, despite enrolment rates that are and have been for several decades higher than the national average, lose many educated people to Nairobi, attracted by the disproportionate availability of jobs in the city for which educational qualifications are required. The national labour force survey of 1976-77 showed that 10.9 per cent of the rural labour force but 37.2 per cent of the urban labour force have some secondary education (Bigsten, 1984, p.34).

The implications of the current and projected impacts of continuing high rates of population growth on primary school enrolments in Kenya have been explored by Rushdi Henin (1981) using projections from 1969 census data. Under different projections, the dependency ratio will move adversely, and the primary school-age propulation, even at the lowest (and rather optimistic) rate of projection based on a total fertility rate of 8.1 in 1979 falling to 7.6 in 1989 and 7.1 in 1999, will rise from 3.480,000 in 1979 to 5,266,000 in 1989 and 7,630,000 by 1999, at an annual rate of increase of 4.5 per cent. 1979-89, and 4.3 per cent 1989-99. This brings massive recurrent cost implications, especially in Kenya for teachers' salaries if these children are to be provided with an education. Even by 1983, at the end of the 1979-83 plan period, an extra 11,000 primary school teachers at least would be required at prevailing pupil/teacher ratios with total costs much higher than those allocated in the National Plan for that period. Already 30 per cent of Kenya Government's expenditure is in the education sector, and Henin clearly points to the financial crisis implicit in the population projections if the educational status of the population is to continue to improve.

Indonesia

In Indonesia, on the other hand, enrolment expansion must be seen against the very different demographic background of lower overall growth rates than Kenya, and in particular a lower and declining fertility. McNicoll (1982) reports a fall in crude birthrate from 43/1000 for 1961-70 to 38/1000 for 1971-80, and a 17 per cent fall in total fertility rate from 5.6 for 1967-70 to 4.7 for 1976-79. However, as in Kenya, there was also a strong political motivation to increase enrolments at all levels, so that they more than kept up with population growth. During the 1970's there were major expansions in primary school (Sekolah Desar) provision, guided nationally by a special Presidential programme, that had brought near universalization of primary school enrolments by 1980, with a total enrolment of 23.9m. in 1981-82 compared with 13m. in 1972.

However, the picture into the 1990's looks distinctly more optimistic than it does in Kenya. In 1980 it was projected that there would be a need for 30m. places by 1990. However the fall in fertility, confirmed by the 1980 census, has meant a downward revision of projections of enrolment to 23.4m. in 1990 (assuming constant dropout rates), which is roughly the enrolment in 1982/83 (World Bank, 1983). This allows a very considerable reduction in pressure on resources in education that can be diverted to raising the quality of the education provided.

Advances and constraints for aggregate planning

The close but slightly lagged relationship between population change and primary school enrolments is now widely recognized by educational planners throughout the Third World. Demographic methods for measuring, monitoring and projecting change in actual and expected enrolments have, especially since the early 1970's, become a major feature of educational planning at the national and, to a lesser extent, regional scales. A major contribution to this integration was the work of the demographer Gavin Jones which, in various general and country specific studies sponsored mostly by the Population Council, illustrated the value of population analysis in planning and evaluating educational expansion programmes, especially in countries with currently high population growth (Jones, 1971; 1972; 1975). His work sought, with some success, to recognize and account for the two-way relationship between population growth and enrolments, that not only is there a direct impact of births on enrolment, but also that educational expansion will itself affect the number of births. However, the nature of that feedback remains a matter of considerable controversy and is certainly difficult to measure (Cochrane, 1979), and Jones' work more successfully addressed the technical issues of estimating and projecting educational enrolments and the incorporation of fertility projections into these estimates.

These studies were complemented by research and teaching activities in the International Institute for Educational Planning, Paris, associated particularly with Ta Ngoc Chau. This was concerned initially with the costs of providing for population growth in education (Chau, 1972) but was based on and further developed a set of demographic techniques that have been taught to successive classes of I.I.E.P. interns and in technical courses provided by I.I.E.P. in many countries (Chau, 1969). It was further supported by the work of the Division of Statistics on Education in the Office of Statistics of UNESCO which developed from the mid-1970's a series of technical manuals for educational planners applying demographic techniques to educational data, the most notable of which has been "Methods of projecting school enrolment in developing countries" (UNESCO, 1976) and which, as in the work of I I.E.P , have been directly used in the training of educational planners and in preparation of expansion programmes.

These contributions all provided valuable technical support for planning educational expansion, but of equal importance is that they also provided further pressure for the collection and publication of more appropriate population data. In their technical collaboration with demographers, educational planners were coming into direct contact with census planners who were then made aware of the value of collecting and tabulating data on educational status of the population, single year populations for the school age groups, and the development of national and regional fertility projections. Thus the analytical improvements fed back to improvements in the availability and appropriateness of the data that are collected.

Further technical developments at this aggregate scale have integrated general demographic methods with techniques specific to analysis of educational enrolments. In particular, cohort survival methods have been applied to patterns of survival and repetition within the schools system as part of the analysis of its internal efficiency (UNESCO, 1981a). Related techniques include the calculation of school life tables, incorporating a double decrement of mortality, as in standard life tables, and of survival in school (Kpedekpo, 1972). These are particularly important techniques where dropout and repetition are widespread, and enrolment projections are affected by the incidence and rate of survival in school.

The particular demographic and educational circumstances of Third World countries have been a great stimulus to valuable improvements in aggregate data and techniques for their analysis. Much has been achieved, but further developments are constrained by the general limitations of reliance on population projections. Fertility is generally falling, but the rate and timing of the fall are subject to great variation within and particularly between countries and techniques are not yet able to cope fully with the uncertainty of population change.

> "The freedom of the educational planner is governed by two sets of factors. The first consists of factors he can manipulate and control, the second of constraints which are given from outside and to which he has to adapt. Of the latter category by far the most fundamental are the size, structure and growth of population" (Preface, UNESCO, 1981b).

LOCAL ANALYSIS

Catchment areas and population distribution

Expansion of primary school enrolments in Third World countries has generally involved providing more schools rather than expanding existing schools, though both processes may occur simultaneously in any area. The increasing number of schools has meant a diffusion of facilities downwards in the urban hierarchy and outwards into previously unserved or underserved areas to create a convergence between the distribution of the school age population and the distribution of the schools themselves. This convergence is implicit in national objectives of meeting basic needs in education and improving access particularly for these unserved or underserved populations, but local planning must seek to make it explicit in its direct concern for the location of schools and the pattern of catchment areas.

In order to ascertain the distribution of the population 'at risk' it is therefore essential that small-area population distributions are known. Both census sources and, where available, registration sources of population data provide only aggregate totals for designated areas, however small. They do not directly describe the distribution of population within these areas. Yet these local distributions in patterns of settlement are clearly important for access, for the range of a primary school, which serves young children, is inevitably small. Empirical studies in various parts of the world suggest that a planning norm of about 4 km. is a realistic limit for initial access where most children are assumed to walk to school (Gould, 1978, Appendix B). Figure 9.5 illustrates the effects on access to schools of two distinctly different settlement patterns but in areas with the same overall population densities. In Map A, with a strongly nucleated settlement pattern, there is a highly peaked demand surface but no child lives beyond the 4 km. range. In Map B there is a dispersed settlement pattern and an evenly distributed demand surface such that many children live beyond the range of the schools. As argued at length elsewhere, school planning needs to be aware of local population circumstances and to organize its delivery system to take local settlement patterns into account (Gould, 1982). This will require more, but smaller, schools where the principal objective is to maximize access rather than minimize internal costs. This is an objective in social provision which has been more widely recognized in the planning of health care than it has in education (see Chapter 7), but it is clear that considerable flexibility in sizes and norms for individual schools is needed to meet local circumstances. It may require, inter alia, more multi-grade rather than single grade classes at lower pupil/teacher ratios and with appropriate teacher-training, with financial implications that are necessary and often inevitable costs of pursuing equity. It will also require specific management structures to ensure better support for and supervision of smaller schools (Lyons, 1981, p.16).

Planners must also be sensitive to the risks of dealing with population distributions in purely geometrical terms, and of defining catchments solely in terms of distance minimizing 'rationality'. Experience in all countries illustrates how the size and shape of catchment areas of individual schools are affected not only by population distribution, but also by features of the physical landscape (mountain and stream barriers), the economic context (communications network, availability of transport) and the social context (social class, religious or denominational affiliation, sex, tribe or language). Even more important are the quality of physical facilities and instruction in the school itself, for these can vary very considerably within any small area. A survey of primary school catchment areas in two contiguous densely populated sub-locations of Western Kenya has shown that not only are there considerable overlaps in the catchment areas of sampled schools in Northern Bumbo (Figure 9.6a) and in the three primary schools of Bulokhoba (Figure 9.6b), but that the extent of overlap is systematically related to differences in school quality. Pupils attending schools whose

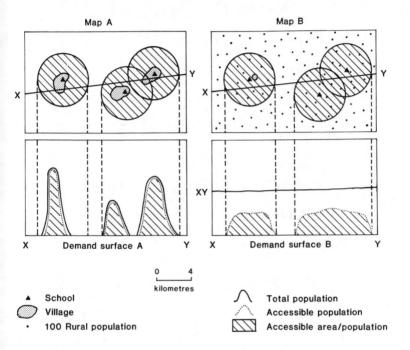

Fig. 9.5 Local population distribution and access to primary schools

pupils performed best on public examinations have longest mean home/school distance, and these pupils in these 'better' schools were disproportionately from wealthy homes (Gould, 1983, pp.18-32).

Sensitive planning must be aware of such local circumstances as these for they reflect matters of major concern to the consumers of the service provided. Catchment areas that do not absolutely conform to a spatially efficient geometry cannot be dismissed as mere irrationalities, and therefore ignored. This does not preclude the use of distance-minimizing criteria as a starting point for local planning, but it does preclude 'off-the-shelf' solutions that cannot adjust to each set of local circumstances of social and economic

(a) BUMBO

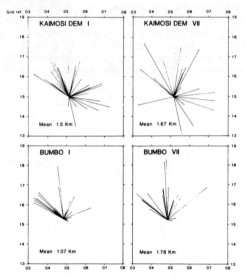

(b) BULOKHOBA

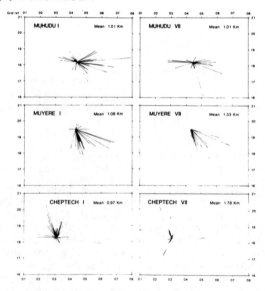

Fig. 9.6 Western Kenya : primary school catchments

relationships and their related mobility patterns.

Expansion and contraction
The ways in which enrolments can expand or contract is an important
issue for local educational planning. Expansion, as noted above, has
in the past generally been hierarchical, downwards and outwards to
rural areas. Primary schools are initially small, but once established
grow in size of both the cohort admitted to each grade and also in the
number of grades offered at the school. Schools that were once
feeder or branch schools for more established centres become
independent, and in their turn may generate feeder schools. Since
independence Kenya has experienced both the expansion of the
number of schools and also in overall enrolments under the combined
pressure of growth of the relevant cohorts and proportions of those
cohorts enrolled. That expansion has been disproportionately
concentrated at the upper grades of the primary school cycle. The
missions, especially in the 1940's, had developed an administrative
system of central and out-schools from which pupils went to central
schools, often as weekly boarders, for the upper years of the primary
cycle, if home-school travel distances were long. Most of the mission
out-schools have now become fully independent primary schools, and
have in their turn seen their own foundations of the early 1960's
expand to their own full cycle, supported by community involvement
in building classrooms and providing other facilities to cope with the
expansion. By the mid-1970's the number of schools was expanding
much more slowly than enrolments. Mean school size was growing,
rising from 251 in 1972 to 267 in 1973 and to 384 in 1980 (Kenya
Government, 1981). New schools were still being created in the arid
and semi-arid margins of the more densely settled areas, but most
expansion of enrolment is now in existing schools that are being
upgraded to the full primary cycle as well as expanded in each grade.
This trend is likely to continue as fertility rates are likely to remain
at their current high level. Were fertility rates to fall, it is likely
that there would be a larger percentage fall in enrolments than in the
number of schools, as the current distribution of schools would be
maintained and class size reduced. Henin's (1981) aggregate
estimates (cited above) of teacher requirements to meet the needs of
an expanding cohort may, conversely, underestimate the local effect
of enrolment increases being absorbed in existing classes with the
existing complement of staff.

The potential local effects of population decline are also a
matter of direct current interest in Indonesia. The special INPRES
programme for primary schools (Sekolah Desar) was particularly
important in the 1970's in extending primary schooling to remoter
areas (Heneveld, 1978), but the INPRES schools tended to be small,
with average enrolment of 149 in 1978 compared with 226 for other
primary schools (Indonesian Government, 1979, Table 1). Most
additional enrolments were, therefore, in existing schools. Since the
birth rate had been falling substantially in the 1970's primary school-
age cohorts are now getting smaller, but enrolment decline will not

193

be matched by equivalent decline in the number of schools. Once a school is established, especially in a special Presidential programme, local political pressures can prevent closure even though national norms for school or class size may be infringed. Geographical and political criteria of access and the strength of the community/school relationship will win out over financial criteria of cost-reduction. As in Liverpool (Brown and Ferguson, 1982; see also Chapter 8), so in Indonesia.

Small area population data
Data on and concerned with distributional aspects of population and population change are important at the local scale for identifying the size of current and future age groups in particular schools. But the problems of identifying and using available distributional data are further complicated by difficulties of ensuring these data are adequately differentiated by appropriate age groups. Ideally age data should be available by single years for at least the first 15 years for the smallest area of census management, even though they are subject to the same problems of settlement nucleation and dispersion discussed above. In practice, availability of appropriate age data varies very considerably from country to country. Better than average is the case of Uganda, 1969, where data were published by 5-year age groups only for gombololas, with a mean population of about 2000 people (Masser and Gould, 1975). The census of Kenya, 1969, provided 5-year age data for only each Province, and the population of the smallest census unit, the sub-location, was differentiated in published tables only by sex and two age groups - 15 and below, 16 and above (Kenya Government, 1970). The situation with the full publication of the 1979 census is likely to be no better. Even less valuable is the case of the census of Burundi, 1975, where 5-year age and sex estimates are available for only each arrondissement, and the populations of the lower census divisions, the commune and the colline, are given only by sex, a situation that requires very considerable assumptions in formulating demand estimates in educational planning (Carron, 1983). In Uganda, Kenya and Burundi most rural settlement is highly dispersed, and area-based census data would need in any case to be complemented by map and other settlement evidence. In Pakistan, however, where rural settlement is highly nucleated, the census of 1972 provided data for five-year age groups for each sub-tehsil (sub-district), but for each village, separately identified in the Census reports, population is differentiated only by sex.

There are two major causes of the inadequacy of small-area age data, both of which are related to the reliance on the census source and the biases implicit in its methodology. The first concerns the general unreliability of age reporting in societies where there is neither formal registration of births nor a document of baptism. Demographers have been greatly concerned to develop techniques for identifying and eliminating errors in age reporting but, while these techniques may be applicable for aggregates, they cannot normally be applied to small populations (Ntozi, 1981). The second cause of the problem arises because age data are often gathered from only a sample of the population, usually a cluster sample, such that the data can be aggregated only to the larger population from which the sampling frame is constructed, and generalization to sub-populations involves large sampling errors.

Census authorities must therefore ensure that age data are not sampled and that tabulations of age and sex structures are made available for small areas which are similar to those covered by other data sources, including previous censuses. Registration methods are clearly preferable for collecting small-area data and using them to identify patterns of population change, but registration systems have been poorly developed in the Third World. Where civil registration has been attempted it has not been at all successful, except where associated with security or taxation purposes, and in these cases children are often omitted from consideration. Most direct, school-specific registration systems with appropriate sanctions (e.g. registration of birth within one year of birth as a precondition of admission to school) would probably prove unworkable in most countries.

Local decision making.
However, the problems of educational planning at the local scale in Third World countries are not only those of data collection and availability, but also of how and by whom data which are available are to be used. Education and schooling are such politicized issues, even in countries where formal party political activity is banned, that decisions over allocations of new or additional scarce investments require a political and not merely a technical rationale. National policies of enhancing equality may be satisfied by a reduction of inter-regional inequalities, and these aggregate trends are normally found where enrolments are expanding, as they have been in Kenya and Indonesia since the 1970's, but national policies may be interpreted in different ways by local decision makers. In some cases they may be ignored or even undermined by differential local allocations that maintain or exacerbate existing inequalities within each area of administration, and are made for reasons other than criteria of need based on the analysis of available population and enrolment data.

Typically in the countries with which this chapter is concerned, the local managers of the education system - i.e. District Education Officers, Area Superintendents or their equivalent - are not well trained in educational planning and administration, including data collection and management. They are usually former headmasters or school teachers whose formal training for their present post may be limited to a course lasting a few weeks or even less. If they have acquired any new skills as a result these are most likely to be in financial management. Technical weakness, coupled often with a political weakness in the local power hierarchy, makes them highly susceptible to political pressure from within and beyond the education service. They may take or implement decisions without direct recourse to technical criteria or whatever data may be available to them.

A major contribution can be made to local planning by enhancing the skills of these local officials, especially in the use of population and enrolment data, to construct basic diagnostic indices, including enrolment rates, dropout and repeater rates, and the rudiments of cohort analysis for individual schools and communities or sub-areas within their general area of responsibility. The essence of these indices is that they are easily calculated with data, however imperfect, that are normally available. Armed with these simple indices and an appreciation of their significance for planning purposes, technical personnel can take the initiative in identifying quantitative and qualitative inadequacies that might be remedied, and thus provide a case against which politically-motivated interest groups will need to react more postively. Many current projects for expansion have large amounts of resources allocated to training courses for local and regional officials to include elementary population analysis e.g. in Indonesia (Gould, 1985). Enhancing the skills of the technician cannot in itself be sufficient to undermine the strength of established interest groups, but it can temper their influence and in the longer term lead to a greater willingness to use data-based solutions to planning problems.

A further related issue concerns the sophistication of the analytical techniques that may be appropriate at the local scale. While sophisticated, computer-based techniques have been shown to be valuable for national and regional analyses, where large data sets are available and more officials are technically skilled, much less complex techniques are more appropriate for local analysis, however much data are available. Indices that can be calculated locally and appreciated by the public at large in local communities are to be preferred. Community involvement in the planning process will only become a reality when the planning techniques are seen not to be a 'black-box' whose secrets are available only to the initiated, but can be developed and used within that community with the advice of officials. This is certainly a danger in the application, even with modification, of the elaborate administrative procedure used in France for annually formulating school admissions and the type of classes offered in each school - 'la carte scolaire' (Hallak, 1977). I.I.E.P. has used the French model in its teaching of 'school mapping' (a much used but thoroughly misleading translation from the French) and, though it has certainly sought to grossly simplify for the particular circumstances of Third World countries, it has still been promoted as a technical 'in-house' exercise with minimal community involvement.

The skills of geographers and others can be usefully used in the future to provide training programmes for local officials, ensuring that data are more readily available and that simple analytical techniques are used and more generally appreciated. This 'low-level' activity would seem to demand higher priority than further development of, for example, technically elaborate techniques for defining school catchment areas or making detailed projections of local population change.

CONCLUSION

This chapter has considered the demand for and methods of collecting, tabulating, analysing and using population data at different scales in the particular context of educational planning in the Third World. Within all countries taken as a whole and at a regional scale in most of them, there have been major developments at each of these four stages of data management in the last two decades to the extent that use of general techniques of population analysis is now standard practice, and they are likely to become even more important as (if?) fertility rates continue to fall and that fall spreads to a wider range of countries, particularly in Africa. Since the first direct effects of fertility decline will be felt by Governments in falling demand for primary school places, the measurement and prediction of fertility and the financial impact of any change for hard-pressed government finances give an importance to population analysis in educational planning that extends beyond the education sector.

However, neither the demand for population data nor progress in its management at the aggregate scale have been matched by developments at the local scale. Problems of shortage of data and the technical weaknesses of many local education officials have allowed local interest groups, both community or individually based, to maintain the local management and planning of educational provision as a matter for <u>ad hoc</u> power broking in such issues as decisions for locations of new schools or teachers or allocations of additional resources. Yet the need for systematic population analysis at this scale is strongly linked to equity objectives in education, and locally derived measures of population distribution and population change can be important tools in the effort to achieve these objectives within sub-regional units and individual communities. The involvement of local political interests in decision-making will continue, but a better availability of data and diagnostic indices will heighten their awareness of broader issues. Technical sophistication would seem in this particular context to be less important than ensuring greater accessibility by the actors in the decision-making process to a simple diagnosis of current population change and to the planning assumptions on which developments in education may be based.

REFERENCES

Bigsten, A., (1984) Education and income determination in Kenya Gower Aldershot

Brown, P.J.B., and S.S. Ferguson (1982) 'Schools and population change in Liverpool', in W.T.S. Gould and A.G. Hodgkiss (eds.), The resources of Merseyside Liverpool U.P., 177-90

Carron, G. (ed.) (1983) Cours intensif de formation sur la méthodologie de la carte scolaire, Burundi, 22 novembre-3 decembre 1982 : Rapport, I I.E.P., Paris

Chau, Ta Ngoc (1969) Demographic aspects of educational planning, I I.E.P., Paris: Fundamentals of Educational Planning, no. 9

Chau, Ta Ngoc (1972) Population growth and costs of education in developing countries, I I.E.P , Paris

Cochrane, S.H. (1979) Fertility and education. What do we really know?, Johns Hopkins U.P., Baltimore: World Bank Staff Occasional Papers, no. 26

Colclough, C. (1982) 'The impact of primary schooling on economic development: a review of the evidence', World Development, 10, 167-85

Dow, T.E., and L.H. Werner (1983) 'Prospects for fertility decline in rural Kenya', Population and Development Review, 9, 77-97

Fredricksen, B. (1981) 'Progress towards regional targets for universal primary education : a statistical review', International Journal for Educational Development, 1, 1-16

Gould, W.T.S. (1978) Guidelines for school location planning, The World Bank, Washington, D.C. : Staff Working Paper, No. 308

Gould, W.T.S. (1982) 'Provision of primary schools and population redistribution', in J I. Clarke and L.A. Kosinski (eds) Redistribution of population in Africa Heinemann, 44-49

Gould, W.T.S. (1983) 'The school/area controversy in migration of school leavers : evidence from Western Kenya', Liverpool Papers in Human Geography, no. 14

Gould, W.T.S. (1985) 'Some spatial issues in secondary education', in J. Maas (ed) Papers on educational planning in Indonesia, The World Bank, Washington D.C., Staff Working Paper

Hallak, J. (1977) Planning the location of schools: an instrument of educational policy, I.I.E.P., Paris

Heneveld, W. (1978) 'The distribution of development funds : new school building in East Java', Bulletin of Indonesian Economic Studies. 14 (1), 63-79

Henin, R.A. (1981) 'Characteristics and development implications of a fast-growing population', in T. Killick (ed.) Papers on the Kenyan economy : performance, problems, policies (Heinemann), 193-207

Indonesian Government (1979) Statistik Persekolahan, 1978, Department of Education, Jakarta, Statistical Yearbook

Jamison, D.T., and L.J. Lau (1982) Farmer education and farm efficiency Johns Hopkins U.P., Baltimore

Jones, G.W. (1971) 'Effects of population change on the attainment of educational goals in developing countries', in National Academy of Sciences, Rapid population growth: consequences and policy implications (Johns Hopkins U.P , Baltimore), 315-67

Jones, G.W. (1972) 'Educational goals in tropical Africa', in S.H. Ominde and C.N. Ejiogu (eds.) Population growth and economic development in Africa, Heinemann, 291-303

Jones, G.W. (1975) Population growth and educational planning in developing nations, Halstead Press for Population Council, New York

Kalule-Sabiti, I. (1984) 'Bongaarts' proximate determinants of fertility applied to group data from the Kenya Fertility Survey', 1977/78 , Journal of Biosocial Science, 16, 205-78

Kenya Government (1970) Kenya population census, 1969. Volume 1, Statistics Division, Ministry of Finance and Economic Planning, Nairobi

Kenya Government (1981) Statistical Abstract, 1981 ,Central Bureau of Statistics, Ministry of Economic Planning and Development, Nairobi

Kpedekpo, G.M.K.(1972) 'Tables of school life for Ghana (1960)', in S.H. Ominde and C.N. Ejiogu (eds.) Population growth and economic development in Africa Heinemann, 336-40

Lockheed, M.E , D.T. Jamison and L.J. Lau, (1980) 'Farmer education and farm efficiency : a survey', Economic Development and Cultural Change, 29, 37-76

Lyons, R.F. (ed.) (1981) The organisation of education in remote rural areas, I.I.E.P , Paris

McNicoll, G. (1982) 'Recent demographic trends in Indonesia', Population and Development Review, 8, 811-19

Masser, I., and W.T.S. Gould (1975) Inter regional migration in tropical Africa Institute of British Geographers, Special Publication, no. 8

Mott, F.L., and S.H. Mott (1980) 'Kenya's record population growth : a dilemma of development'. Population Bulletin, 35. 1-42

Ntozi, J.P.M. (1981) 'Age-heaping in African demographic enquiries', Jimlar Mutane. Jnl. of the Population Association of Africa, 2, 20-42

Psacharopoulos, G. (1982) 'Education, employment and inequality in LDCs', World Development, 10, 37-54

United Nations Economic Commission for Africa (UNECA) (1982) Demographic and related socio-economic data for ECA member states, Population Division, E.C.A., Addis Ababa

UNESCO (1976) Methods of projecting school enrolment in developing countries, Division of Statistics on Education, Office of Statistics, Paris

UNESCO (1981a) Statistical methods for improving the estimation of repetition and dropout : two methodological studies, Division of Statistics on Education, Office of Statistics, Paris

UNESCO (1981b) World school-age population until year 2000 : some implications for the Education Sector, Division of Statistics on Education, Office of Statistics, Paris

World Bank (1980) Education: Sector Policy paper, Washington, D.C

World Bank (1983) Indonesia : secondary education : issues and programs for action, Unpublished discussion paper, East Asia and Pacific Education Division, Washington, D.C.

CONCLUSION

The Editors

CONVERGENCE AND DIVERGENCE IN POPULATION BEHAVIOUR

Since the papers which led to the writing of this book were delivered, events have served only to confirm the need for the broad view of population planning that is advanced in all of them. At global level, a stagnant world economy with weak commodity markets, together with continuing rapid growth of their mainly youthful population, have continued to place pressure on the poorest nations of the earth. China's success in reducing its natural increase through a stringent policy of family limitation, a success shared with other Chinese societies of East and South East Asia, has brought the prospect of zero growth by the early twenty-first century. Yet that experience, however large its impact in numerical terms on world population, may be quite exceptional, for elsewhere in Southern Asia, notably India, Pakistan, Bangladesh and Indonesia, population growth continues despite a deceleration in the explosive growth of the 1960's and the slow spread of fertility control. A similar situation prevails in most Latin American countries. Even where, as in Mexico's Campaign launched in 1973, the state is giving full support to family planning, declines in rates of population growth have not generally been spectacular.

In the poorest nations, particularly those of tropical Africa, the rapid growth of population continues and in some cases is accelerating. In too many areas this combines with environmental mismanagement and woefully inadequate resources for development - not least from external sources- leading to famine as a distressing symptom of economic and demographic collapse. In such circumstances the plight of the people, especially of the old and young, shows only too clearly that the spectre of Malthus is not yet exorcised.

Yet these symptoms are clearly not caused by population growth alone; nor does a dismally static conceptualization of the relationships between population and resources contribute significantly to any analysis of the problems. It is where there is political instability, inadequate use of available resources (including human resources), limited opportunities for people to share in the benefits of national development and for nations to participate on fair terms in international trade and aid that the most devastating consequences of population growth are to be found, part of a wider context, both locally and at the global scale, of environmental, economic and social stress.

As the experience of several newly industrialized countries has shown, progress can be made by some Third World countries in the international economic system, but many of those that have become successfully involved in manufactures and trade - Korea, Hong Kong, Taiwan and Singapore, for example - are small and, more importantly, have a coherent social structure that seems to be responsive to the economic and social imperatives of rapid change. All seem responsive also to political pressures to control their population growth. Indeed, the demographic response to development of the ethnic Chinese and other East Asian peoples suggests that of all the varied and complex forces shaping marital behaviour, family planning and responses to a changing lifestyle, cultural attitudes may be one of the strongest. In attempting to influence these attitudes worldwide, the powerful, persistent and often strident voice of the international family planning lobby has yet to prove that it is the most effective or the cheapest way of bringing population and resources into better balance in many parts of the Third World.

The problem of the population:resources relationship is, as we have shown, not simply one of population size and rates of growth. In the developed world, where without - sometimes despite -government prompting people respond to long- and short-term changes in economic and social circumstances by adjusting the size of their families, fertility behaviour seems to be primarily conditioned by a social climate in which education, access to information and services, and perceived societal norms and economic expectations combine to produce an increasingly uniform, largely secular view, of marital behaviour and family patterns. Certainly the general decline in fertility in higher income countries and, in particular, among more educated and higher income groups, within both developing and developed countries, adds credibility to this view.

However, there are signs, such as growing illegitimacy rates, that in a time of growing economic uncertainty and rising unemployment, the generation born in the relative prosperity of the 1960's and reaching adult years in the chillier economic climate of the 1980's are, even in a world of collapsing family relationships, reacting against the trends of the last decade. This current generation of workers is all too aware of the demands placed on it in terms of the cost of pension funds and of the health and social services by growing numbers of the elderly. The need of the comfort and security of children and grandchildren are concerns which are felt not only in the ageing populations of Europe, where such trends have been evident from the early twentieth century, but in more recently modernized countries such as Japan, and, especially, those newly industrialized areas of East Asia where government pressures and economic change have combined to compress the transition from high to low fertility into a single generation.

Relatively rapid changes in the size of cohorts, combined with economic fluctuations and shifting social attitudes, produce population problems which call for shifts in emphasis on the part of governments: from fear of over rapid growth to concern over stagnation of population; from provision for the young to concern over jobs for those in the economically active age groups and stress on social and health services for the elderly. Frequently that concern is not translated sufficiently early into policy, as governments react to the issue of the moment rather than the foreseeable consequences of past events. After an era in which in most parts of the developed world, it has been increasingly assumed that the state will provide, there may well have to be a greater emphasis in future on the need for society to provide both within the family and the community. This may well draw population behaviour into a more convergent set of norms even between societies with very different social values.

It is difficult to envisage a situation in which cultural contrasts in marriage patterns, fertility, family structure and the like take on a more universal character, but in one particular respect, education, there may be a certain tendency for that convergence. Education seems everywhere to promote certain common characteristics which affect demographic behaviour : for example promoting higher age of marriage, greater inclination to use contraceptives and to have smaller families; a stress on the nuclear rather than the extended family. Similarly the transfer of growing numbers of people into non-traditional (mainly non-rural) environments may well - as in the European world of a century ago - induce more rapid adoption of new norms of population behaviour such as longer child-spacing and regular birth control measures. Moreover. in many sectors of these societies rising expectations and access to improving personal and public health facilities extend life expectancy and are a further inducement to fertility control.

Such an optimistic scenario may seem at odds with the turmoil of societies in the painful transition to 'modern' society, but it may eventually produce a world in which people will be in better balance with their resources. What are the approaches that might promote such a progress towards the creation of more stable populations and that will be a recipe for coherent and practicable population policy ?

THE NATURE OF POPULATION POLICY

Some of the contributors to this volume are more optimistic than others over policies to solve the problems on which they write. All are agreed on the need for long-term planning strategies which stress the promotion of the social and economic well-being of people - as individuals, families, communities and nations. Such matters require continuing, indeed greater, emphasis on those themes to which the international community has sought to address itself in the post-war years: for example, Population and Development was the theme of the UN Population Decade culminating in the 1974 World Population Conference; the status of women - a key factor in social and demographic policy - was highlighted in 1975 in International Women's Year as a prelude to a drive in the UN Decade for Women (1976-85) for the status and rights of women; a new emphasis on provision for life and work of the rapidly growing number of young adults in both developed and developing countries form part of the concerns of 1985's Year of Youth: the WHO campaign for 'Health for all by the year 2000'. All those have been pursued in the spirit of the great humanitarian aims of the international community, most clearly manifest in the four freedoms of the Atlantic Charter - freedom from want, from fear, freedom of speech and to worship- which helped promote and were themselves made attainable by the remarkable post-1945 growth in the international economy. The international institutions that were created at that time, in particular the United Nations and its family of specialised agencies and the Bretton Woods institutions of the International Monetary Fund and the International Bank for Reconstruction and Development (The World Bank) have helped sustain, albeit imperfectly, a doubling of the world's population over the last 40 years.

The scale and complexity of such global and fundamental objectives makes planning for people a daunting task. Most often national planners have sought to meet these by formulating policies addressed to specific areas of provision for changing demands over limited time periods and at a variety of spatial scales. Too often, however, this is directed to meet a particular issue as the need arises: maternity services, then schools, then jobs or further training, then retirement. At one extreme such an approach becomes little more than crisis management, with a series of crises to which short-term solutions are applied. What is needed, however, is a more integrated approach that takes account of the implications of past population events and is aware of the nature of changes in society and their likely impact on future needs. Where there are specialized agencies charged with population planning they have all-too-often taken the narrow view and targetted their activities towards fertility control, with other aspects of planning for people as the responsibility of a wide spread of other agencies of government at various tiers of the administrative hierarchy.

Population Planning must cater in an integrated way for both quantitative and qualitative aspects of human existence. Central to such a perspective is the recognition of different life-systems that are dependent not only on physical resources but also the ability to harness human skills. Concepts of 'productive' activity have undergone a radical transformation in the past generation in all parts of the world. Work, as it has commonly been understood in the capitalist world, will surely change as existing manufacturing techniques give way to high-productivity methods providing more time for leisure, home and family and a variety of informal social. economic and educational activities. Such changes will affect the structure of the work force, the age and intensity of activity, the location of work and its relationship to other activities. In the Third World traditional skills will no doubt continue to co-exist with 'advanced' systems which both draw labour from and supply it to the international economy. Policies will need to be directed to ways of integrating traditional and 'informal' sectors with the formal part of the economy if the supply of food, goods and services is to cope with growing demand, and if the enormously increased potential workforce is to be able to contribute to meeting such demands.

Indeed one of the major problems posed by population trends in all parts of the world is the ability to balance the demand:supply equation and to do so in other than the purely economic terms. Planners must also take account of environmental, social and cultural needs. Most of our authors recognise this broad, integrative approach as an essential part of 'planning for people': welfare, educational and recreational services and those who provide them can be seen as productive' just as is the provision of food and basic necessities, and goods. In the Third World many of the basic services should come from within- including traditional methods, for example of health care and craft training - but will also benefit from access to new ideas and methods developed elsewhere.

The contribution of different sub-groups of the population to supply and demand is also changing in both developed and developing societies. On the one hand dependency of the aged at the expense of the young raises again the question of retirement, the utilisation of the skills and experience of older people in the home and the community as well as in the workforce. We are too often obsessed with the implications of their demand for welfare services and the narrow monetary implications of their support. Everywhere the role of women in society is experiencing rapid change. As their place in the workforce increases, so their role in the home and in public life must undergo a transformation. Such a change can be nothing but beneficial for the population as a whole if it gives rise to better overall educational provision and more open enhanced economic opportunities.

LOCATION-SPECIFIC PLANNING

New activities will also involve changed locations. The very broad view of the world's population problem as one of universal pressure on resources is far removed from the complex pattern of changing population:resource relationships in which pressure in some aspects and areas of activity are found alongside diseconomies and mismatches in provision due to underuse of resources. While underuse is more evident in stagnant or declining areas of the developed world than in the more populous Third World countries, it is nevertheless found everywhere in under-utilised and under-provided countrysides and areas of heavy out-migration. A direct concern for spatial allocation is therefore critical in all aspects of planning for people. This also provides some of the most difficult policy alternatives. On the one hand the mobile, footloose but global economy of the later twentieth and early twenty first centuries has generated an international elite of 'experts' who move from country to country within the developed world and between it and the Third World on behalf of national governments and international agencies or as employees of multi-national corporations. At the other extreme many people are locked into declining areas in the peripheral areas of the world (at global and regional level) and even within the urban system. Such areas of economic stagnation are also usually areas of social and demographic stagnation. The gulf between these and the areas which attract capital, growth, jobs and people, engendering great pressures and frequently involving unbalanced population growth, is enormous.

Location specific policies in the economic sphere directly and indirectly impinge upon policies for spatial population change and population mobility at various scales, from daily commuting to work, school or for health care within an urban area, to interregional and international migrations. It is this aspect of population change that is most directly affected by policies and specific planning decisions. In countries of the Third World, as in most socialist states, governments have sought to formulate policies to achieve a given distribution of population that may necessitate regional and or rural/urban migrations. Whether in major long distance population transfers, as in Indonesia's transmigration programmes from overcrowded Java and Bali mainly to the outer islands of Sumatra, Kalimantan and West Irian, or in the development of new capital cities such as Brasilia (Brazil), Islamabad (Pakistan), Lilongwe (Malawi), Dodoma (Tanzania) and Abuja (Nigeria), planning for population change has been strongly integrated with other aspects of national and sectoral planning in its specifically geographical aspects. The integrated view of population planning is most evident in planning for migration, but needs to be extended to other aspects.

WHO PROVIDES WHAT, WHERE AND FOR WHOM?

A major challenge for any government or society is to be able to achieve better provision of goods and services for its people. Growth and stagnation both impose costs. The ability to recognize needs and to finance and determine the disposition of scarce resources to meet those needs is focal to all planning. This involves political decisions that reflect the consent and involvement of society. For example, should the future economic 'good' of a people transcend all other factors and require stringent - even repressive -measures of fertility control, or, as the recent apparent holding back from the extremes of such planning even in China and Singapore suggest, should more gradual measures prevail? Do the pressing needs of people in decaying inner cities or overcrowded shanty towns have precedence over services for declining and often very poor, remote and underprovided rural areas? Such questions involve integrated structural and spatial planning of a high order. Moreover, they raise the question of who pays and for what? While private finance might be expected to take care of profitable ventures there are many areas where without public provision many people, especially in the more vulnerable and poorly rewarded sectors of society, would be in want. There are few simple and general solutions to such questions, especially in much of the Third World where the scale of need is so enormous and the resources so limited. Here there is need to mobilize international support, but this in itself may affect the political process and introduce an exogenous factor into planning criteria. Nowhere is this more apparent than in current policies of the U.S. Government towards population policies and its withdrawal of financial and technical support in many countries for some population programmes that condone abortion. Who decides the planning criteria and whose interests or requirements determine them?

A further question is the ability to balance the distribution of resources between advantaged and disadvantaged cohorts within any population. In traditional societies, families have learned to support their own, but, as the generations increasingly go their own way, the often conflicting coincidences of population and economic trends call for different approaches involving public policies. Dependency is a complex demographic concept involving the relationship between different generations within a society or different groups (social, ethnic, cultural) within a community. 'To each according to his need' is an attractive doctrine, but one which is difficult both to determine and implement. In doing so both society and governments are often the prisoners of their own perceptions and prejudices. Governments find it easier to be negative rather than positive in population policy. Individuals are often myopic and sometimes selfish in their evaluation of their responsibilities towards others. Yet humanitarian issues have probably never been so much before the world or, as in the response to recent African famine and disaster, received such positive reactions. It is through such positive responses that the world as a whole might yet learn to cope with its population dilemmas and to plan in a wider and more coordinated way for its people.

More generally, however, the parameters of population change, both of demographic structure and population distribution, are matters about which much is already known in specific contexts, and that knowledge needs to be used to enhance the integrated view of population planning towards which this book has been a contribution. The stronger integration of population research into sectoral and spatial planning must be a major priority of all agencies, official and unofficial, global, national or local. Otherwise there is a danger of seeing population change either merely as a threat to stability or as a residual that simply complicates the already difficult task of planning. The realisation of that danger has been all-too-apparent in many areas of planning, and can only be minimized by placing the

opportunities created by population change at the forefront of policy
objectives and then designing and implementing policies to address
these opportunities.

INDEX

abortion 2, 18, 20, 27, 90, 91,
    128, 207
Africa 5, 6, 77, 116, 156, 183,
    East 121
    North 17
    South of the Sahara 15, 17,
    18-20, 79, 119, 201
    Southern 121
    West 124, 156
age structure 7, 11, 22, 24-28,
    30, 34, 39, 44, 65, 88, 111
    132, 154, 163, 176, 182,
    184, 194, 195, 201, 207
ageing population 2, 25, 27,
    28, 89, 93, 94, 166, 202
Algeria 69
Arab World 79, 156
Argentina 78
Asia 5, 15, 19
    East 6, 16, 69, 70, 201,
    202,
    South 6, 155
    South-East 70, 201,
Austria 89, 92
Australasia 27, 89
Australia 79, 116

Bangladesh 24, 201
Barcelona 96
basic needs 120, 129, 147, 148,
190, 205
Belgium 42-49, 51, 89,
    100
Black Report 133, 134,
    139-42
Blackburn 142
Bogota 125

Bolivia 76
Bombay 6
Boserup, Ester 1
Botswana 79-84, 122
brain drain 76, 79
Brandt Report 4, 16
Brazil 24, 66, 70, 73, 117, 124,
    206
bubonic plague 10
Bulgaria 26
Burkina Faso (Upper Volta) 76
Burundi 194

Caldwell, Jack 118
Cameroun 76
Canada 26, 79, 98
Caribbean 51, 71, 119
census data 14, 25, 33, 44, 80,
    82, 84, 100, 103, 104, 115
    135, 190, 194
children 116-18
    economic value 10, 92, 117
    education 3, 5, 73, 83, 163-
    80, 181-97
    health care 115, 116
    in labour force 83 117
    migration 44, 78
Chile 74
China 5, 6, 17, 20, 23, 64, 70-
    72, 115, 126, 127, 147, 201,
    206
cholera 10, 15, 152, 156
Club of Rome 4
cohort analysis 5, 6, 11, 14,
    23, 30, 35, 53, 91, 163, 170,
    181, 189, 196, 207
Colombia 74, 78, 124